LATER LIFE, SEX AND INTIMACY IN THE MAJORITY WORLD

Sex and Intimacy in Later Life

Series Editors: **Paul Simpson**, University of Manchester, **Paul Reynolds**, International Network for Sexual Ethics and Politics and The Open University and **Trish Hafford-Letchfield**, University of Strathclyde

---

This internationally focused series builds on, extends and deepens knowledge of sexual practice amongst older people. Compiling work by established and emerging scholars across a range of disciplines, it covers the experiential, empirical and theoretical landscapes of sex and ageing.

Scan the code below to discover new and forthcoming titles in the series, or visit:

policy.bristoluniversitypress.co.uk/
sex-and-intimacy-in-later-life

LATER LIFE, SEX AND INTIMACY IN THE MAJORITY WORLD

Edited by
Krystal Nandini Ghisyawan, Debra A. Harley,
Shanon Shah and Paul Simpson

With a foreword by
Gayatri Reddy

First published in Great Britain in 2026 by

Policy Press, an imprint of
Bristol University Press
University of Bristol
1–9 Old Park Hill
Bristol
BS2 8BB
UK
t: +44 (0)117 374 6645
e: bup-info@bristol.ac.uk

Details of international sales and distribution partners are available at
policy.bristoluniversitypress.co.uk

© Bristol University Press 2026

British Library Cataloguing in Publication Data
A catalogue record for this book is available from the British Library

ISBN 978-1-4473-6841-0 hardcover
ISBN 978-1-4473-6842-7 paperback
ISBN 978-1-4473-6843-4 ePub
ISBN 978-1-4473-6844-1 ePdf

The right of Krystal Nandini Ghisyawan, Debra A. Harley, Shanon Shah and Paul Simpson to be identified as editors of this work has been asserted by them in accordance with the Copyright, Designs and Patents Act 1988.

All rights reserved: no part of this publication may be reproduced, stored in a retrieval system, or transmitted in any form or by any means, electronic, mechanical, photocopying, recording, or otherwise without the prior permission of Bristol University Press.

Every reasonable effort has been made to obtain permission to reproduce copyrighted material. If, however, anyone knows of an oversight, please contact the publisher.

The statements and opinions contained within this publication are solely those of the editors and contributors and not of the University of Bristol or Bristol University Press. The University of Bristol and Bristol University Press disclaim responsibility for any injury to persons or property resulting from any material published in this publication.

Bristol University Press and Policy Press work to counter discrimination on
grounds of gender, race, disability, age and sexuality.

Cover design: Robin Hawes
Front cover image: Getty/4FR

Bristol University Press' authorised representative in the European Union is:
Easy Access System Europe, Mustamäe tee 50, 10621 Tallinn, Estonia,
Email: gpsr.requests@easproject.com

Thanks and acknowledgements

We would especially like to thank the contributors whose critical scholarship, hard work and conviviality have made this volume possible. Specifically, Krystal Nandini Ghisyawan would like to thank her parents, Celia and Haimchan Ghisyawan, for their unfaltering support, her husband Shivanan and her son Ishaan, who keeps her busy. Debra A. Harley would like to thank her parents, Thelma and Morise Harley, for their ability to respect all people and teaching her the same. Shanon Shah would like to thank his partner, Giles Goddard, for being there in love and faith. Paul Simpson would like to thank his late parents, John and Barbara Simpson, and his husband, Gordon Blows, for being there. Finally, thanks go to the anonymous reviewer for their detailed, supportive and constructive feedback.

Contents

Notes on editors and contributors		ix
Series editors' introduction		xv
Paul Reynolds, Paul Simpson and Trish Hafford-Letchfield		
Foreword by Gayatri Reddy		xxv

1	Introduction to the volume: themes, issues and chapter synopses Paul Simpson, Krystal Nandini Ghisyawan, Debra A. Harley and Shanon Shah	1

PART I In/visibility and ambivalence

2	Under the *orhni*: intimacy and near-invisibility among older Indo-Trinidadian queer men Krystal Nandini Ghisyawan and Marcus Kissoon	21
3	Older *kinnars*, ageism and sexuality during the COVID-19 pandemic Anushkaa Arora अनुषूका अरोड़ा.	38
4	Doing complex intimacy in the later life of Chinese gay men in Hong Kong Barry Lee 李文偉 and Travis S. K. Kong 江紹祺	54

PART II Women questioning age/ing intergenerationally and intragenerationally

5	Deep within the eye of the beheld: exploring hidden accounts of intimacy in the lives of older Indian women in urban Malaysia Sally Anne Param	75
6	From age of despair to window of opportunity? Reframing women's sexuality in later life in the Middle East and North Africa Shereen El Feki and Selma Hajri	93
7	Lost voices of Partition: carrying gender, nation and femininity across the life course Nafhesa Ali	115

PART III Agency through fantasy, erotic tales and pleasure

8	Sexual fantasies and older, Indigenous Purépecha women: sociocultural constraints and possibilities Cuauhtémoc Sanchez Vega	139
9	Indigenous elders as sexual agents through storytelling as a queer and decolonial practice in 'Canada' Madeline Burns	157

| 10 | Sex, intimacy and older life in Muslim contexts
Shanon Shah | 174 |
| 11 | Reflections: themes and issues emerging from the volume
Debra A. Harley, Krystal Nandini Ghisyawan, Shanon Shah and Paul Simpson | 192 |

Index 209

Notes on editors and contributors

Editors

Krystal Nandini Ghisyawan was born and raised in Trinidad and is an Indo-Trinidadian queer scholar, activist, educator and artist. Her research and writing have documented Indo-Trinidadian cultural forms, such as Pachraat folk songs; critiqued cultural practices such as ritual purity, specifically the religious purdah of menstruating women; and detailed the identity politics, personal resilience and collective space-making practices of Trinidadian same-sex loving women. Her monograph *Erotic Cartographies: Decolonization and the Queer Caribbean Imagination* (2022) highlights the ways in which same-sex loving women embody their sexual identities to challenge normative (colonial) notions of Caribbean femininity, space, culture and family as defined through colonial discourse and enactments of power. *Erotic Cartographies* refers to the processes of mapping territories of self-knowing and self-expression, both cognitively in the imagination and on paper during a subjective mapping exercise, exploring how meaning is given to space, and how it is transformed. Also, Dr Ghisyawan is Director of Research at the Silver Lining Foundation in Trinidad and Tobago. The group's pioneering nationwide school climate study gathered data on bullying in secondary schools across Trinidad and Tobago. She is the primary author of the Foundation's survey reports, as well as guides and manuals for its teacher training programme, focusing on conflict resolution and managing diverse classrooms. She also runs a successful consultancy as a content editor and personal tutor, based in Lawrenceville, Georgia, USA.

Debra A. Harley PhD, CRC, LPC, is a Provost Distinguished Service Professor in the Department of Early Childhood, Special Education and Counsellor Education at the University of Kentucky. She is coordinator of the doctoral programme in Counsellor Education and former department chair, past coordinator of the Rehabilitation Counselling programme, and past director of the Gender and Women's Studies programme. Her research interests include disability, cultural diversity, substance abuse, gender, LGBTQ issues and ethics. She has published books entitled *Cultural Diversity in Mental Health and Disability Counselling for Marginalized Groups* (2019); *Disability and Vocational Rehabilitation in Rural Settings* (2017); *Handbook of LGBT Elders: An Interdisciplinary Approach to Principles, Practices, and Policies* (2016); and *Contemporary Mental Health Issues among African Americans* (2004). She works collaboratively with Counsellor Education programmes and Rehabilitation Counselling programmes at South Carolina State University, North Carolina State Agricultural and Technical University, and Langston University, US.

Shanon Shah was awarded his PhD in the sociology of religion from King's College, London in 2015, where he is currently Visiting Research Fellow. He has lectured in religious studies there and currently teaches religious studies at the University of London's Divinity Programme. He is the author of the monograph, *The Making of a Gay Muslim: Religion, Sexuality and Identity in Malaysia and Britain* (2018). Shanon is currently the Director of Faith for the Climate, a London-based network of faith-inspired climate justice activists, and also conducts research on minority religions and alternative spiritualities at the Information Network on Religious Movements (Inform), a research charity based at King's College London. His research and teaching interests include the ethnographic study of religion, contemporary Islam and Christianity, new religious movements, gender and sexuality, popular culture and social movements. Before moving to the UK, Shanon was an award-winning singer-songwriter, playwright and journalist in his native Malaysia.

Paul Simpson was awarded a PhD in Sociology in 2011. He lectures and researches in Sociology at the University of Manchester. He has published extensively on gay male ageing (including a monograph, *Gay Men, Ageing and Ageism: Over the Rainbow?*), on socio-economically disadvantaged men and health, and on sexuality and intimacy in later life. Since 2012, he has co-edited four volumes in this book series, published 12 book chapters and had published 24 journal articles variously on ageing sexualities and on forms of masculinity rendered disadvantaged. He has published in quality journals such as *Ageing & Society*, *The British Journal of Sociology*, *Men and Masculinities*, *Journal of Sex Research*, *Qualitative Research in Psychology*, *Sociological Research Online*, *Sociological Review* and *Sociology of Health and Illness*.

Contributors

Nafhesa Ali has a PhD in Sociology and is Assistant Professor in Criminology and Sociology at Northumbria University. She is an interdisciplinary Sociologist with expertise in the everyday lives of racialised and minority communities. Nafhesa's research interests include ageing, migration, Muslim sexualities and life histories. Her recently published book is titled *Older South Asian Women's Experiences of Ageing in the UK: Intersectional Feminist Perspectives* (2023). Her previous publications include a co-authored book *Storying Relationships* (2021) and an edited collection titled, *A Match Made in Heaven: British Muslim Women Write about Love and Desire* (2020). She has also published in academic journals *Sexualities*, *Ethnicities*, *Ethnic and Racial Studies* and *Cultural Geographies*. Nafhesa's other roles include co-lead for the Power and Intersecting Identities (PII) Research Cluster at Northumbria University, Honorary Fellow of the Sustainability Consumption Institute at the University of Manchester, and Reference Group Member for The British Academy's Net Zero programme.

Anushkaa Arora अनुष्काअरोड़ा is the Principal and founder of a leading Indian law firm, headquartered in Delhi. She is the appointed Senior Panel Counsel of the Central Government of India, for Central Government Litigation, the Jail Visiting Advocate, appointed by the Delhi High Court and Senior/ Retainer Counsel for private leading clients/companies of India. Anushkaa also heads the firm's Criminal, Commercial and Civil Litigation practice. She has more than five years' experience in legal practice nationally and internationally, including in Singapore, and a decade of experience in pro bono legal work. Anushkaa has a Master's degree in Intellectual Property Laws from the National University of Singapore, and graduated from Guru Gobind Singh IP University, University School of Law and Legal Studies (USLLS), New Delhi. She has written various research papers in leading national and international journals and curriculum law books for leading universities in India.

Madeline Burns (she/they) is a Red River Métis and Scottish guest on lək̓ʷəŋən and W̱SÁNEĆ territory ('Victoria, BC Canada'). They are a young academic and recent graduate of the University of Victoria, with a double major in Gender Studies and Political Science. As an Indigenous young person, Madeline works as an Indigenous Youth Support Worker within the Friendship Centre Movement and frequently directs their attention towards events, supports and programming for 2SLGBTQIA+ (Two-Spirit, Lesbian, Gay, Bisexual, Transgender, Queer and/or Questioning, Intersex, Asexual plus many affirmative ways that people choose to self-identify) Indigenous youth. Campaigning for and promoting Indigenous wellness across so-called Canada, Madeline also serves on two Indigenous Youth Councils (provincially and nationally) within the Friendship Centre Movement. Madeline has published a peer-reviewed journal article in *The Arbutus Review*, on reclaiming Indigenous sexual being as a decolonial and sovereign practice. In their academic, personal and professional life, Madeline frequently focuses on Indigenous sovereignty, community wellness, sexual being and safety, decolonization and queer theory.

Shereen El Feki is the author of *Sex and the Citadel: Intimate Life in a Changing Arab World* (2014), a groundbreaking study of sexuality and its intersection with politics, religion and culture across the Middle East and North Africa (MENA). Most recently, she served as Regional Director for the Middle East and North Africa (MENA) at UNAIDS. Previously, Shereen was a Regional Director with Equimundo (formerly Promundo), where she led the International Men and Gender Equality Survey Middle East and

North Africa (IMAGES MENA), a pioneering study of men, masculinities and gender roles across seven countries in the region. Shereen has also served as Vice-Chair of the UN's Global Commission on HIV and as a board member for Advocates for Youth, a leading international non-governmental organization (INGO) on young people's sexual health and rights. Shereen currently sits on the Chatham House Commission on Universal Health, as well as serving as a member of the Sexual Justice Initiative of World Association for Sexual Health. Shereen started her career as a healthcare correspondent with *The Economist* and presenter with *Al Jazeera*, and is a regular commentator on sexual and reproductive health and rights in both mainstream media and academic fora. Shereen is an immunologist by training, with a BSc from the University of Toronto and an MPhil and PhD in molecular immunology from the University of Cambridge.

Selma Hajri is a Tunisian physician, reproductive health researcher and women's rights advocate. Specialising in reproductive endocrinology, she has more than 25 years of clinical, research and teaching experience on hormonal contraception and medical abortion in Tunisia, across the Middle East, north and sub-Saharan Africa. Since 1997, Selma has worked with Gynuity Health Project, the National Family Planning Office of Tunisia, as well as IPAS, UNFPA and Marie Stopes among others, to advance safe contraception, medical abortion and values clarification and attitude transformation (VCAT). She is also a leading expert on menopause, publishing extensively on her research and clinical experience in the Tunisian context. In 2012, Selma founded Groupe Tawhida Ben Cheikh, a Tunisian feminist NGO, and in 2019, she established RAWSA, a MENA regional network to advocate for the right to safe abortion.

Marcus Kissoon is a Trinibagoian activist who has worked alongside the women's movement for over a decade. His areas of interest are sexual assault, domestic violence, HIV, migration and child sexual abuse and exploitation, safeguarding and children's policies. His research centres on Caribbean masculinities, Indianness and their implications for disclosing and seeking help among male survivors of child abuse. He holds an MSc in Gender and Development Studies from the University of the West Indies and MA in Woman and Child Abuse Studies from London Metropolitan University.

Travis S.K. Kong 江紹祺 is Associate Professor and Programme Director of Media, Culture and Creative Cities in the Department of Sociology at the University of Hong Kong. He mainly teaches gender, sexuality, media and cultural studies. His research specialises in Chinese homosexuality and masculinity, prostitution in Hong Kong and China, social impacts of HIV/AIDS, and transnational Chinese sexuality. Travis is the co-editor of

Sexualities: Studies in Culture and Society and the sole author of *Chinese Male Homosexualities: Memba, Tongzhi and Golden Boy* (2011), *Oral Histories of Older Gay Men in Hong Kong: Unspoken but Unforgotten* (2019), and *Sexuality and the Rise of China: The Post-90s Young Gay Generation in Hong Kong, Taiwan and Mainland China* (2023). He has published numerous articles in such journals as *The British Journal of Sociology, Urban Studies, The Sociological Review, The British Journal of Criminology, Qualitative Research, Men and Masculinities, Journal of Homosexuality, AIDS Care* and *The Lancet*.

Barry Lee 李文偉 is a guest lecturer with the Department of Special Education and Counselling at the Education University of Hong Kong. His primary area of interest and research encompasses masculinities, sexual health, sexual minorities and sexuality. Prior to joining academia, he was a senior social worker with the Hong Kong AIDS Foundation for over 14 years, working with people living with HIV/AIDS. He has also been a committee member for Grey and Pride (a charitable organisation for older LGBTQ in Hong Kong) since 2014, advocating and promoting social inclusion for the older LGBTQ community.

Sally Anne Param was awarded her PhD in 2016 from the University of Malaya and is currently a lecturer at Sunway University, Malaysia. A sociologist by training, Sally Anne is passionate about the study of identity politics, where her research focus is that of 'othered' or marginalised identities. While gender and ethnicity are identity markers that feature strongly in Sally Anne's work, her recent research looks at how age and generations enable intergenerational identity to be understood. Sally Anne's work addresses how older and younger people in Malaysian society are generally othered, given primacy placed on the in-between adult phase in terms of status and decision-making power. Her recent work, therefore, aims to give voice to both the older and younger groups in society, as their views are usually politicised as unimportant, eclipsed behind popular 'adultist' narratives. Her most recent joint publication on the lives of the elderly can be found in *Educational Gerontology* (2021), and her latest publication on young people's mobilities is a book chapter in *Aspirations of Young Adults in Urban Asia* (2021). Sally Anne is currently a research team member on Future Cities, a funded collaborative research project between her university and the University of Lancaster, UK. When not working, Sally Anne enjoys a literal walk in the park, together with a cup of *teh tarik*.

Cuauhtémoc Sanchez Vega is a psychologist with a Master's degree in Sexuality and Gender Equity. Over 24 years, he has specialised in sexuality, HIV and AIDS, HIV pre- and post-test counselling, follow-up counselling training for people with HIV, thanatology (how people deal with death), and group work and life skills. In the last 20 years, Cuauhtémoc has specialised in ageing and old-age issues in relation to sexuality, gender, violence against older women and empowerment in ageing and later life. Since 2000, Cuauhtémoc has collaborated as a consultant and external teacher at: the National Autonomous University of Mexico (UNAM): Continuing Education Center of the National School of Social Work; Faculty of Higher Studies of the University of Zaragoza, Division of Postgraduate Studies of the Faculty of Medicine (now the Coordination of the Open University, Educational Innovation and Distance Education, CCADET); Open and Distance University of Mexico (UnADM). Cuauhtémoc also serves as academic coordinator and teacher on the Diploma of Sexology and Sexuality in the Twenty-first Century and as academic coordinator and teacher of the Master's programmes, 'Sexuality and Gender Equity' and 'Comprehensive Gerontological Care' at the Mexican University of Postgraduate Studies. He has published extensively on later life, sexuality and gender violence. His publications include: *Scale of Attitudes and Beliefs around Aged Women's and Men's Sexuality* (2019); *Accumulation of Gender-based Violence in Aging Women's Lifetimes* (2019); *Sexual Potentialities: A Theoretical Framework for Sexuality* (2018); *Human Development and the Capacities of Older Adult Women* (2015); and *Health Promotion for Women Carers* (2015).

Series editors' introduction

Paul Reynolds, Paul Simpson and Trish Hafford-Letchfield

This *Sex and Intimacy in Later Life* book series will explore, interrogate and enlighten upon the sensual, sexual and intimate lives of older people. The motivation for launching this series was a concern with the relative lack of attention in public, professional and academic/intellectual spheres to sex and intimacy in later life (indicatively, Hafford-Letchfield, 2008; Simpson et al, 2018a, 2018b). The series is intended to contribute to and enrich the development of the field of studies in the intersections of age, sex, sexuality and intimacy as a critical and important area of scholarship. It is only beginning to be recognised as an important social, cultural and political issue within and beyond the 'Western' academy, from which it has emerged. Its earliest contributions, of which this volume are a part, are motivated by a desire to recognise and reject the pathologies and prejudices that have infused this intersection – what Simpson has termed 'ageist erotophobia' (Simpson et al, 2018b: p 1479) – and fuels the failure to acknowledge older people as sexual agents. This is both an intellectual and a political agenda, to question and evaluate the impact of real rather than assumed losses of cognitive, physical, social and sexual capacity, and to recuperate older people as sexual agents from dismissal, ridicule and trivialisation.

If the latter half of the twentieth century was characterised by challenges to the pathologies of social identities – particularly gender, ethnicity and race, disability, sexuality – and struggles for recognition, rights and liberties, more intersectional struggles and recognitions characterise the twenty-first century (on intersectionality, see indicatively Hancock, 2016; Hill Collins and Bilge, 2016). Significant among these has been the re-evaluation of what it is to age and to be an older agent in contemporary societies. Older people have historically experienced both veneration and respect and neglect and pathology, largely based on differing cultural stereotypes of the value of age (Ylanne, 2012). The most common characterisation is that older people are not sexual, past being sexual or represent a problematic sexuality – or their sexuality is a superficial concern and secondary to concerns of health, care, life course and support by public services and engagement and pensions/resources. Such concerns are those mainly of 'Western' cultures and reflected in the Western influence across the globe in respect of state intervention and provision, but elsewhere they have been subsumed and often rendered invisible into family and kinship structures.

Older people's intimate and sexual lives and experiences have transformed in the last 40 years, as a consequence of a number of significant social changes: new technologies – digital, mechanical and pharmaceutical – and their interventions; the recognition of older people as exploitable markets for consumption; healthier lifestyles, changes and extensions to life course and life expectancy; the erosion of social and sexual pathologies around age and recognitions of different intersections and their importance (LGBTQI older people, older people of different ethnicities, older disabled/neurodiverse and 'able-bodied/minded' people; older men and women).[1] These transformations demonstrate evidence of increase in the sexual relations and intimacies of older people and their impacts, such as increased rates of STD transmission, or implications for healthy sex lives for older people in care institutions (indicatively, Drench and Losee, 1996; Lindau et al, 2007; Bodley-Tickell et al, 2008; Chao et al, 2011; Simpson, 2015; Age UK, 2019). The scholarship exploring these developments has only recently begun to catch up. A small but growing literature has focused on age and sexuality (represented in the sources authors draw from in this series), with a principal focus on the erosion of easy pathologies and stereotypes of older people's heteronormativity and heterosexuality.

Particularly as the 'baby boomers' of the 1950s and 1960s move into old age, changed sexual attitudes, wants and needs require changed political, cultural and institutional responses. The older generation of baby boomers in the late 1940s and 1950s may have remembered Vera Lynn (an iconic British wartime singer singing patriotic songs during World War 2) and post-war society – retaining traditional stereotypes of older people. However, their horizons will have been formed and broadened more by influences from the 1960s' pop and rock culture (notably with such artists as the Beatles, Rolling Stones and Janis Joplin), women's and LGBT liberation struggles, the proliferation of accessible public representations of sex and the 'pornification' of society in the digital age.

Ageing and becoming 'older', intimacy, sexual identity, relations and practices, and sexual pleasure are all contested concepts and subject categories. They are understood as being constituted by different demarcations, distinctions and understandings arising from different intellectual disciplines, conceptual approaches, cultures, geographical contexts and historical contexts. While it is neither desirable nor credible to preclude critical and constructive debate on the meanings and demarcations of these intersections, it is necessary to draw some broad conceptual boundaries rather than hard-and-fast definitions.

'Ageing' and 'older' are broad categories that are attached to people considered in their 'third age' or 'later life' – in more affluent countries/regions of the mainly Global North, the threshold is often seen as the age of 50+. This reflects common practice in the literatures of social gerontology, psychology and the sociology of ageing (see Zaninotto et al, 2009; Cronin and King, 2010; Stenner et al, 2011). It is after that, and into their sixth decade, that older people experience a process of de-eroticisation that could be called 'compulsory non-sexuality' (taking our cue from feminist theorist Adrienne Rich (1981), who articulated pressures on women's sexuality towards 'compulsory heterosexuality').

Ageing and being older can be understood mainly in two ways. First, the terms describe ageing as a chronological and physiological process involving key changes, which become particularly marked (and can be stigmatised) in the later stages of the life course. This raises questions around the differential impact of life course experience and physiological change – which may include loss and/or reduction of physical and mental capacities for some people at different stages in the life course. It is structured both by physiological change and by the (often imperceptible) internalisation and normalisation of orthodoxies describing ageing and being older in cultural and social discourse, and everyday practice and experience of how older people are perceived and how older people see themselves – often as lacking – and in relation to younger people (Foucault, 1977, 1978). Such is the means by which older people (as much as younger people or social and cultural institutions) both produce and accept the discursive limits to ageing. Second, ageing and being older could be described as an attribution constituted by ideology and discourse, structural-hierarchical and cultural-discursive influences and material contexts, such as the structure of organisations, public spaces, cultural representations and spaces of connection (for example, labour markets). Ageing is usefully regarded as a product of intersections between the symbolic/discursive and structural/material dimensions of existence. The attribution of a particular age – young, mature or older – is an ideological construct suffused by power relations and composed of cultural attributions, instantiated in material processes and practices. These structural factors impose all manner of constraints on older people's sexual agency (though these can be questioned, challenged and resisted). Put simply, age is a social, cultural and political construct and how older people are perceived and valued – whether prejudicially or with respect – is constituted in the wider character of social values and dominant discourses. While age is an experienced and embodied phenomenon, its meaning is socially, culturally and politically mediated.

'Sex' and 'sexuality' are often distinguished by the former being focused on practices and behaviour, and the latter being focused on identities, relations and orientations. The terms are nevertheless porous and intertwined (Weeks, 2010). Sexuality describes the processes of being sexual (or not) in the world and through self-recognition, expressing (or not) sexual choices and preferences and enjoying (or not) sexual pleasures. It involves the expression of emotions, desires, beliefs, self-presentation and how we relate to others. It most commonly relates to sexual identity – for example hetero, lesbian, gay, bisexual, queer, asexual (Rahman and Jackson, 2010). Sexuality is multidimensional, being co-constituted by the biological (for example bodily sensations interpreted as 'sexual'), the psychological (for example emotions and reasoning) and cultural and socio-economic influences such as dressing up and flirting and so on (Doll, 2012). It is often understood narrowly as genitocentric, itself tied to the heteronormative relationship between genital sex and reproduction. Yet it encapsulates a range of practices that bring sensual pleasure and fulfil wants and desires, such as the agglomeration of practices that are subsumed under the umbrella term BDSM (indicatively Weiss, 2011; Ortmann and Sprott, 2013). 'Intimacy' refers to involvement in close and interpersonal relations. It can be a feature of diverse relationships, from those that are sexual, or with strong close personal friendship bonds, or characterised by physical and emotional closeness, to those where a particular relation or facet of life is shared closely, such as close work relationships. It encompasses a spectrum of emotions, needs and activities ranging from feelings of caring, closeness and affection (that can go with long-term companionship) through to 'romance', where an individual 'idealises' a person(s) (Ehrenfeld et al, 1997). Intimacy is to a degree conceived in gendered terms: if men tend to define it more in physical terms, women usually emphasise more its emotional content (O'Brien et al, 2012). It is often conceived as two people sharing intimacy rather than a larger number and is constituted subjectively as a value that is owned or shared with others, although equally it is sometimes seen as an arena that reinforces oppressive conventions of private– public divides and 'compulsory monogamy' (Bersani and Phillips, 2008; Heckert, 2010; Musial, 2013).

These three conceptualisations – age/older, sex/sexuality and intimacies – intersect in complex ways. For example, the prevailing assumption that sexual relationships involve shared intimacy fails to recognise 'fuck buddies' or so-called casual relationships for mutual sexual gratification (though intimacy is sometimes used to describe a particular event without relationship – 'they were intimate' (Wentland and Reissing, 2014). Likewise, sex and age often enmesh in complex ways, though these linkages too often involve mutually reinforcing negative representations. Decline in sexual capacity – often reduced to coital/genital function – is associated with ageing and later life as a standard correlation as opposed to a graduated contingency. Drawing in other intersections, the relationship between sexual capacity and potency is a significant feature of masculinity and therefore sexual capacity is considered more challenging for men, given fears of loss of status and greater reluctance than women to seek help concerning sexual and relationship problems (O'Brien et al, 2012). This reflects gendered assumptions that male sexuality is more active and women's more passive that is rooted in classical sexology (indicatively Davidson and Layder, 1994; Bland and Doan, 1998). Nevertheless, the sexuality of older women could be constrained by biological changes, understood through cultural pathology as decline and loss of attractiveness. As female sexuality tends to be more associated with youth-coded beauty, older women become excluded from the sexual imaginary (Doll, 2012). In addition, women face the moral constraints of being a good wife/mother/grandmother, where being non-sexual is seen as a virtue and not a deficiency, whereby older women face moral censure for transgressing an approved ageing femininity when not acting their age (Lai and Hynie, 2011). As such, the narrative of decline is perpetuated. Since the 1970s, however, women now over 50 will have encountered the countervailing influences of feminism and challenge such culturally constituted assumptions (Bassnett, 2012; Westwood, 2016).

Even where the idea of older sexual agents meets with approval because of its contribution to well-being and self-esteem, their sexuality has been subject to a medicalised, book-keeping approach that disregards emotions and pleasures and focuses on who is still 'doing it' (Gott, 2004), in the context of declining physical capacity for genitocentric penetrative sex (see Trudel, Turgeon and Piché, 2000, as an example). However, more encouragingly, we perceive the beginnings of challenge to these negative discourses in European, Australian and US contexts and writing, which attempt to recuperate older people, including the oldest citizens (commonly care home residents) and across the spectrum of genders and sexualities, as legitimate sexual/intimate citizens (see Gott, 2004; Hafford-Letchfield, 2008; Bauer et al, 2012; Doll, 2012; Simpson et al, 2016, 2017; Villar et al, 2014). The purpose of elaborating these brief examples is to underline that a focus on sex and intimacy in later life involves the recognition of intersections both within and beyond the conceptual constituents of the series focus. Lives are not lived in sexual, intimate or aged based singularities, but in complex differentiated yet overlapping and intertwined experiences with myriad intersections, such as class, race/ethnicity, gender, disability, embodiment and affect (Simpson, 2015).

It is this rich patina of experience and knowledge creation that this series seeks to elucidate, working outward from a critical focus on the core concerns of sex/sexuality, intimacy and ageing, and providing the space for innovative and high-quality scholarship that can inform institutions, policy, professional practice, current and future research and older people experiencing this focus as lived experience and not simply subject of inquiry. The vision behind the series is summarised in the following eight points.

- It will put the sex back into sexuality (and into ageing). This arises from the observation that while sexuality studies has progressed considerably over the last 40 years (Fischer and Seidman, 2016), its development as an intellectual field of enquiry has to some extent dampened the subversive character of a focus on the 'messy physicality' of sexual pleasure. Put simply, there is lots of scholarship about sexuality, but less focus on the pleasures of sex. There is an aspiration that this series might be one avenue by which that can in a small way be corrected. Putting the 'sex' back into 'sexuality' is part of an agenda to recuperate older people to continue to be recognised as sexual citizens (or more specifically to have the choice to be sexual agents or not). As such, this series can support the vanguard of an intellectual project that will establish sex in later life as a serious yet neglected political issue and thus stimulate and advance debate. If what is at stake in understanding current experience is the impediments and constraints to choice and pleasure, embodied sensual practice and agency must constitute part of the site of scholarship.

- It will promote and offer an avenue for critically engaged work on the subject matter, whether it is empirical and theoretical-philosophical, from across the social sciences, humanities and cultural studies, incorporating scientific and aesthetic insights. An essential part of the project is that assumptions, claims and received knowledge about sex and intimacy in later life are always questioned, challenged and subject to critical review. This is the means by which both extant knowledge is tested, refined and strengthened or rejected, and new knowledge is produced. A critical frame also offers the opportunity to move beyond traditional academic frames – insofar as a book series allows – in presenting new ideas, evidence and conjectures.
- It will emphasise the value of multidisciplinary and interdisciplinary approaches to sex and intimacy in late life. Though the series is open to critical research studies from specific disciplinary positions, such as sociology, psychology or gerontology, it recognises the value of multi-disciplinary studies that draw on more than one discipline or field, and interdisciplinary studies that cut across and suture together different disciplines, perspectives and approaches in understanding the complexity of older people and their sexual and intimate lives. This extends to recognising the value of the interweaving of social science, aesthetic and critical approaches across paradigm and disciplinary boundaries.
- It will recognise the value of different approaches that foreground the experiential and/or empirical and/or theoretical landscapes of sex and intimacy in later life, whether they form layered responses to a question or are presented as discrete levels of analysis.
- It will have an international focus, recognising global differences, inequalities; there is value in both the specificity and depth afforded regional, national and locally based studies but there should be acknowledgement of supranational, international and global contexts to phenomena, trends and developments and political, cultural and social responses. It should be acknowledged that the emergent knowledge on sex, intimacy and later life has been generated mostly within academies of the Global North, but it does not follow that this necessarily implies

progress in comparison to other parts of the globe. It also recognises that there are inherent difficulties of resourcing, organisation and common conceptualisation in the development of international projects with a global, reach, and these difficulties are unevenly distributed across the globe. In some parts of the globe, researching this focus is not simply difficult but inherently risky to those who might be researched or researched with intolerance, hostility and lack of recognition. Genuine attempts at a global research agenda require properly distributed and balanced strategies for collaboration to meet relevant constraints and challenges. There should be both attention to the seeds of emergent scholarship in the Global South, and sensitivity to the tendency of Western scholarship to reflect a bias towards a 'colonial' approach to knowledge production. Notwithstanding the tendency for scholarship to focus on the Global North and particularly North America, Europe and Australasia, the series seeks – in a small way – to promote international understandings. This is achieved through the conviction that cross-cultural and spatial perspectives, drawing from insight and evidence across the globe, can contribute to better understandings of experience and avenues for research, policy and practice and reflection.

- It will allow for language, labels and categories that emerge from partial geographical and cultural contexts in the development of scholarship to be questioned, adapted, resisted and brought into relief with alternatives and oppositions in how age, sex, sexuality and intimacy are conceived.
- It will recognise and explore the constraints on and complications involved in expression of sexual/intimate citizenship as an older person and across a spectrum of sexual and gender identities, interrogating and challenging stereotypes of older people as prudish or sex-negative and post-sexual. Equally, the series seeks to explore, examine and advocate sex-positive approaches to sex and intimacy in later life that can help empower, enable and support older people's sexual and intimate relations.
- Finally, it will be accessible to readers in order to inform public understanding, academic study, intellectual debate, professional practice and policy development. This is an ambitious agenda to set for any enterprise, and the series hopes only to make modest contributions to it. Nevertheless, the series has been born of a conviction that unless this sort of agenda is adopted, the experience everyone shares of growing old will always be unnecessarily impoverishing and incapacitating. At the core of this series, and what it should exemplify, is the flourishing that arises from older sexual agents making choices, giving and enjoying pleasure and recognising options and experiences that are open to them as they age.

The Series Editors
March 2021

Note

[1] The long full version of what has been called the 'alphabet soup' of sexual identities LGBTIQAPGNGFNBA ('Lesbian', 'Gay', 'Bisexual', 'Trans', 'Intersex', 'Questioning', 'Curious', 'Asexual', 'Pansexual', 'Gender Non-conforming', 'Gender-Fluid', 'Non-Binary' and 'Androgynous'). This list is neither exhaustive nor does it take on non-Western sexual identities and cultures that should not be assumed to be equivalent in their conception.

References

Age UK. (2019). *As STIs in Older People Continue to Rise, Age UK Calls to End the Stigma about Sex and Intimacy in Later Life*: Available from: https://www.ageuk.org.uk/latest-press/articles/2019/october/as-stis-in-older-people-continue-to-rise-ageuk-calls-to-end-the-stigma-about-sex-and-intimacy-in-later-life/.

Bassnett, S. (2012). *Feminist Experiences: the Women's Movement in Four Cultures*. London: Routledge.

Bauer, M., Fetherstonhaugh, D., Tarzia, L., Nay, R., Wellman, D. and Beattie, E. (2012). 'I Always Look Under the Bed for a Man': Needs and Barriers to the Expression of Sexuality in Residential Aged Care—the Views of Residents with and without Dementia. *Psychology and Sexuality,* 4(3): 296–309.

Bersani, L. and Phillips, A. (2008). *Intimacies*. Chicago, IL: Chicago University Press.

Bland, L. and Doan, L. (1998). *Sexology in Culture: Labelling Bodies and Desires*. Cambridge: Polity Press.

Bodley-Tickell, A.T., Olowokure, B., Bhaduri, S., White, D.J., Ward, D., Ross, J.D.C., Smith, G., Duggal, H.V., and Gould, P. (2008). Trends in Sexually Transmitted Infections (other than HIV) in Older People: Analysis of Data from an Enhanced Surveillance System. *Sexually Transmitted Infections,* 84: 312–17.

Chao, J.-K., Lin, Y.-C., Ma, M.-C., Lai, C.-J., Ku, Y.-C., Kuo, W.-H., and Chao, I.-C. (2011). Relationship among Sexual Desire: Sexual Satisfaction and Quality of Life in Middle-aged and Older Adults. *Journal of Sex and Marital Therapy,* 37(5): 386–403.

Cronin, A. and King, A. (2010). Power, Inequality and Identification: Exploring Diversity and Intersectionality amongst Older LGB Adults. *Sociology,* 44(5): 876–92.

Davidson, J.O. and Layder, D. (1994). *Methods, Sex, Madness*. London: Routledge.

Doll, G.A. (2012). *Sexuality and Long-term Care: Understanding and Supporting the Needs of Older Adults*. Baltimore, MD: Health Professions Press.

Drench, M.E. and Losee, R.H. (1996). Sexuality and the Sexual Capabilities of Elderly People. *Rehabilitation Nursing,* 21(3): 118–23.

Ehrenfeld, M., Tabak, N., Bronner, G., and Bergman, R. (1997). Ethical Dilemmas Concerning the Sexuality of Elderly Patients Suffering from Dementia. *International Journal of Nursing Practice,* 3(4): 255–59.

Fischer, N.L. and Seidman, S. (eds). (2016). *Introducing the New Sexuality Studies* (3rd edition). London: Routledge.

Foucault, M. (1977). *Discipline and Punish: The Birth of the Prison.* London: Penguin.

Foucault, M. (1978). *The History of Sexuality, Volume 1: an Introduction.* London: Penguin.

Gott, M. (2004). *Sexuality, Sexual Health and Ageing.* London: McGraw-Hill Education.

Hafford-Letchfield, P. (2008). 'What's Love Got to Do with It?': Developing Supportive Practices for the Expression of Sexuality, Sexual Identity and the Intimacy Needs of Older People. *Journal of Care Services Management,* 2(4): 389–405.

Heckert, J. (2010). *Love without Borders? Intimacy, Identity and the State of Compulsory Monogamy* Available from: http://theanarchistlibrary.org/library/jamieheckert-love-without-borders-intimacy-identity-and-the-state-of-compulsory-monogamy.

Hill Collins, P. and Bilge, S. (2016). *Intersectionality.* Cambridge: Polity Press.

Hancock, A.-M. (2016). *Intersectionality: an Intellectual History.* Oxford: Oxford University Press.

Lai, Y. and Hynie, M. (2011). A Tale of Two Standards: an Examination of Young Adults' Endorsement of Gendered and Ageist Sexual Double Standards. *Sex Roles,* 64(5–6): 360–71.

Lindau, S.T., Schumm, P., Laumann, E.O., Levinson, W., O'Muircheartaigh, C.A., and Waite, L.J. (2007). A Study of Sexuality and Health among Older Adults in the United States. *New England Journal of Medicine,* 357: 762–74.

Musial, M. (2013). Richard Sennett and Eva Illouz on the Tyranny of Intimacy: Intimacy Tyrannised and Intimacy as a Tyrant. *Lingua Ac Communitas,* 23: 119–33.

O'Brien, K., Roe, B., Low, C., Deyn, L., and Rogers, S. (2012). An Exploration of the Perceived Changes in Intimacy of Patients' Relationships Following Head and Neck Cancer. *Journal of Clinical Nursing,* 21(17–18): 2499–508.

Ortmann, D. and Sprott, R. (2013). *Sexual Outsiders: Understanding BDSM Sexualities and Communities.* London: Rowman and Littlefield.

Rahman, M. and Jackson, S. (2010). *Gender and Sexuality: Sociological Approaches.* Cambridge: Polity Press.

Rich, A. (1981). *Compulsory Heterosexuality and Lesbian Experience.* London: Onlywomen Press.

Simpson, P. (2015). *Middle-aged Gay Men, Ageing and Ageism: Over the Rainbow?* Basingstoke: Palgrave Macmillan.

Simpson, P., Brown Wilson, C., Brown, L., Dickinson, T., and Horne, M. (2016). The Challenges of and Opportunities Involved in Researching Intimacy and Sexuality in Care Homes Accommodating Older People: A Feasibility Study. *Journal of Advanced Nursing,* 73(1): 127–37.

Simpson, P., Horne, M., Brown, L.J.E., Dickinson, T. and Torkington, K. (2017). Older Care Home Residents, Intimacy and Sexuality. *Ageing and Society,* 37(2): 243–65. DOI:10.1017/S0144686X15001105.

Simpson, P., Almack, K., and Walthery, P. (2018a). 'We Treat Them All the Same': The Attitudes, Knowledge and Practices of Staff Concerning Older Lesbian, Gay, Bisexual and Trans Residents in Care Homes. *Ageing & Society,* 38(5): 869–99.

Simpson, P., Wilson, C.B., Brown, L.J., Dickinson, T., and Horne, M. (2018b). 'We've Had Our Sex Life Way Back': Older Care Home Residents, Sexuality and Intimacy. *Ageing & Society,* 38(7): 1478–1501.

Stenner, P., McFarquhar, T., and Bowling, A. (2011). Older People and 'Active Ageing': Subjective Aspects of Ageing Actively'. *Journal of Health Psychology,* 16(3): 467–77.

Trudel, G., Turgeon, L., and Piché, L. (2000). Marital and Sexual Aspects of Old Age. *Sexual and Relationship Therapy,* 15(4): 381–406.

Villar, F., Celdrán, M., Fabà, J., and Serrat, R. (2014). Barriers to Sexual Expression in Residential Aged Care Facilities (RACFs): Comparison of Staff and Residents' Views. *Journal of Advanced Nursing,* 70(11): 2518–27.

Weeks, J. (2010). *Sexuality* (3rd edition). London: Routledge.

Weiss, M. (2011). *Techniques of Pleasure: BDSM and the Circuits of Sexuality.* Durham, NC: Duke University Press.

Wentland, J.J. and Reissing, E. (2014). Casual Sexual Relationships: Identifying Definitions for One-night Stands, Booty Calls, Fuck Buddies and Friends with Benefits. *The Canadian Journal of Human Sexuality,* 23(3): 167–77.

Westwood, S. (2016). *Ageing, Gender and Sexuality: Equality in Later Life.* London: Routledge.

Ylanne, V. (ed.) (2012). *Representing Aging: Images and Identities.* Houndsmill: Palgrave Macmillan.

Zaninotto, P., Falaschetti, E., and Sacker, A. (2009). Age Trajectories of Quality of Life among Older Adults: Results from the English Longitudinal Study of Ageing. *Quality of Life Research,* 18(10): 1301–9.

Foreword

Gayatri Reddy
Gender and Women's Studies, Anthropology,
University of Illinois, Chicago

The fourth in this important series, *Sex and Intimacy in Later Life*, this volume, edited by Krystal Nandini Ghisyawan, Debra A. Harley, Shanon Shah and Paul Simpson, adds another important set of interventions in this newly emergent field of ageing and sexuality studies. Not only does this volume extend the important and critical framework calling into question the conceptualisation of ageing as decrepitude, lack, inherently asexual and non-pleasurable, but also, importantly, it does so by privileging frameworks and voices from the global South and East and from minoritised communities here and in the global North. In this process, it makes (at least) three important interventions into the burgeoning literature on ageing, sexuality and intimacy.

First, as mentioned, it complicates and fractures universalising narratives of ageing in relation to sexuality and intimacy by intentionally focusing on epistemologies, experiences and framings from the global South and East, and from Indigenous and migrant communities in the global North. Too often, research on sexuality and intimacy in relation to ageing has emerged from privileged, largely white communities, in the global North, implicitly privileging the lenses and logics of Western liberal modernity and its epistemological frameworks. Such logics stem, in part, from problematic colonial framings that mapped morality onto geography, differentiating and hierarchising analytic categories and 'illiberal' communities in the global South in its wake. These analytic framings sometimes live on today, manifesting as neocolonial, Orientalist dichotomies between ostensibly ahistoric and 'queerphobic' post-colonies versus modern, progressive and sexually liberated metropoles; in bounded understandings of self and sex, unmoored by familial and social milieus, in conceptualisations of relationality and intimacy; in the privileging of positivist epistemologies and methodologies of visibility and certainty, for example, as the primary modes of being and relating in the world. This volume intentionally problematises these framings and the analytic privileging of such Western epistemologies, dichotomies and 'proper' objects of modernity – focusing on sex, desire, intimacy and pleasure among those ageing to do so. It attempts to draw on multiple perspectives from the global South and East and from marginalised and minoritised communities in the global North to tease out, complicate and speak back to these partial and culturally and temporally myopic framings.

As such, it not only fractures these universal narratives and highlights less-seen modes of relating, but it also speaks to the necessary connections across geo-political boundaries in the contemporary globalising world. To use just one example, the first three chapters of the volume engage with *invisibility and ambivalence* in how ageing Indo-Trinidadian queer men, Indian *kinnars* and Chinese gay men in Hong Kong *negotiate and navigate* the long afterlives of colonialism, ongoing constraints of state and capital, and culturally specific normative discourses of gender, class and race (and their intersections), in articulating and enacting intimate lives. The thematic connections as much as the political-economic structural affinities and resonances across geographic boundaries speak to the value of a volume such as this.

Second and relatedly, through the framing described, this volume highlights ageing *as a process*, as a complex series of acts of *becoming*, not only in terms of a gradient of embodied change over time, but also in terms of contesting simplistic and Manichean binaries in the conceptualisation and analysis of ageing in relation to sexuality and intimacy. As such, it speaks to the necessity of relativising the understanding (and value) of ageing and 'later life' globally, given the varying culturally inflected thresholds and meanings of this concept outside privileged spaces of the global North. In this context, the chapters in the volume that speak to conceptualisations of ageing and sexuality among Indigenous women in present-day Canada, as well as unpacking agentive spaces to manoeuvre *within* the confines of patriarchy, whether in the Middle East and North Africa region, among older Indigenous Purépecha women, older migrant women in Britain who experienced the Partition of India, or through an intergenerational dialogue about sex and intimacy in Malaysia, are particularly germane. Collectively, this volume also allows for a more nuanced, *processual* understanding of the often-dichotomous analytic categories deployed in earlier research, such as young versus old, sexual agency of youth versus asexual passivity of older people, progressive sexual modernity in the global North versus regressive, conservative attitudes towards sex and intimacy in the global South.

Third, this volume not only critiques the limited representation of ageing as decrepitude but, importantly, it also highlights this process and the intimacies it engenders as fundamentally agentive and pleasurable, whether in pre-modern Islamic sex manuals, or contemporary post-colonies, within Indigenous spaces or migrant communities in the global North. Capturing what Saidiya Hartman (2019: 30) refers to, in a very different register, as the 'secondary rhythms' of life, the multidisciplinary and intersectional research gathered here speaks to abundance, not paucity; polyvocality, not uniformity; intimate joy, not lack of desire or pleasure.

Ultimately, what emerges from this collaborative and collective labour is an embodied text that pushes the emergent field of sexuality and ageing in new and productive ways. *Later Life, Sex and Intimacy* allows us to frame and experience the mutually imbricated logics of geography, ageing and sexual agency differently, reorienting epistemological frameworks, histories and referents in the process. In so doing, it not only enlivens our understanding of sexuality, intimacy and ageing in the global South and East, but also engenders agency and animates the process and value of *becoming* in global world-making.

Reference

Hartman, S. (2019). *Wayward Lives, Beautiful Experiments: Intimate Histories of Riotous Black Girls, Troublesome Women, and Queer Radicals*. New York: W.W. Norton and Co.

1

Introduction to the volume: themes, issues and chapter synopses

Paul Simpson, Krystal Nandini Ghisyawan, Debra A. Harley and Shanon Shah

Key issues and themes

The book series, *Sex and Intimacy in Later Life*, was created to develop and add to the under-researched but emerging field of knowledge concerning sexual practices, pleasures and relations in later life. The relative paucity of research on this subject reflects how sexual and intimate relations among older people, largely in post-industrial Western or global North regions, have traditionally been framed within various pathologies, which, in turn, reflect prejudices and stereotypes of desexualised status (Simpson et al, 2018). The kind of thinking just referred to is predicated upon presumptions of ageing as decrepitude and typically associated with lack of sexual appetite and allure (Simpson, 2021).

Given the greater economic resources and prestige of Western/Northern academies in terms of recognition and ability to publish and marginalisation of global South scholars and their work (Go, 2017), it is no surprise that extant studies of ageing sexualities have emerged largely from the former. Two of the first three edited volumes in this book series reflect this phenomenon and address, respectively, diversity and inequality in relation to sexual citizenship and desexualisation in later life. These two themes and that of resexualisation motifs are present in this volume, albeit reflecting diverse local conditions.

However, it was envisaged from inception that the series would look beyond (self-)obsession with Western/global North accounts of experience of sexuality in later life. (The terms 'later' life and 'sexuality', and their intersection, are defined in the series editors' introduction). The third volume in this book series, *HIV, Sex and Sexuality in Later Life* (Henricksen et al, 2022), in featuring work from and/or about diverse countries such as Bangladesh, Hong Kong, India, Kenya and Ukraine, was the first important step towards wider, global coverage. The intention of this book series and this present volume all-along was to develop and bring to light critical work by scholars from and/or knowledgeable about cultures in the global South and East. Accounts of experience of ageing sexualities and sexual expression from these regions are obscured by global economic, political and cultural inequalities that privilege Western/Northern theorisations and thus maintain the latter's intellectual hegemony. We would like to note, in the spirit of contesting traditional, individualistic, intellectual hierarchies, that we have consciously attempted to edit this book in the most egalitarian way possible, which is consonant with our decision to share equal billing in ordering our names in alphabetical order on the book's cover.

By way of context, the global South and East represent the majority world in terms of land mass and population. Based on a world population of 8.05 billion in 2023, just over 1.17 billion people live in Europe, North America and Oceania (mainly Australasia) taken together, compared with 4.54 billion people living on the continent of Asia (59 per cent of the world's population), 1.34 billion people in Africa and 654 million people in South America. The global South and East contain 6.63 billion people or 85 per cent of the global population (Worldometer, 2023). Of course, we do not wish to homogenise these two (humanly invented) world regions, which contain economically developed, post-industrial and culturally and politically diverse nations such as Argentina, Australia, Japan, Singapore and South Korea. However, the global South and East contain most of the less affluent nations where income and wealth are much more unevenly distributed, and which are linked with higher morbidity and mortality and lower healthy longevity rates. (As seen in the chapter on older *kinnar* in India by Anushkaa Arora, the latter is fundamental for sex in later life.) In more recent years, life expectancy at birth in North America has been reported as 79.2 years, which contrasts with 59.4 years on average on the continent of Africa and averaging 62.2 years in less developed countries generally (United Nations, 2017). In such contexts, the mid-thirties or early forties onwards might constitute the threshold of later life. See also the later discussion and the chapters acknowledging the relativisation of later life.

Crucially, there is much to learn about ageing sexualities in cultures that think and 'do' sex and intimacy in later life differently. Indeed, we must also consider, as apparent in the chapter by Madeline Burns, that such cultures actually exist within the global West and North, given the long-standing subjection of Indigenous communities in North America to capitalist, white-settler colonialism. The links between capitalism and colonialism and their combined effects upon ageing, gendered, raced and classed sexualities are a key presence in most if not all chapters (and have been well documented by decolonial and postcolonial feminists, respectively, such as Lugones (2007) and McClintock (2013)). Further, the thinking expressed in Madeline Burns' chapter has also been taken up in the decolonial theorising of Driskill (2010), which seeks to reinstantiate the (gendered, sexual and age-related) understandings of Indigenous North Americans that have been obscured by ongoing, neocolonial capitalist dominance.

Interestingly, we gain from 30 years ago some early intimations of alternative understandings of ageing sexuality in work by British anthropologists, Hockey and James (1993), which briefly drew attention to how some sub-Saharan African cultures value older women as sexual beings, if not sexual agents. Such positive representations of older women that normalise their sexual citizenship, are a far-cry from what we see in contemporary consumer capitalist cultures where older women's socio-sexual status is routinely denied (Hafford-Letchfield, 2021; Pryzbylo, 2021) and coexists with pressures to maintain youthful appearance. In the North/West of the globe, ageing and later life are to be postponed, if not avoided (through neoliberal lifestyle and consumption efforts) where we witness devaluation of older women's body-selves routinely subjected to harsh (and often class-inflected) scrutiny (Åberg et al, 2020).

The contrast just outlined between an African culture and Western cultures, (much more organised around consumerism, which problematises ageing and promotes cures for it), seriously challenges, if not disrupts the telos characteristic of Western notions of linear time inevitably evolving towards (liberal-individualistic) attitudinal and societal progress. Such thinking, as reflected in the respective chapters by Madeline Burns and Shanon Shah, unsettle the entrenched narrative developed in/by 'the West' as sexually progressive and liberal and 'the rest' stereotyped as the opposite. The contrast, therefore, offers a refreshing and enlightening counterpoint to the ideas of global South and East cultures/societies, which are grossly misunderstood and stereotyped in the global North/West as sexually conservative if not 'backward', oppressive and intrinsically LGBTQ-phobic (Puar, 2018). This Orientalist discourse has been used to position global South and East cultures and their subjects as representative of inferior civilisations arrested in time and forever mired in 'tradition' (Saïd, 1978). It has also been used to justify neo-imperial invasion and war and bodily and symbolic violence, and, hypocritically, torture, to force such societies and their subjects into line with Western standards of progressive 'civilisation' (Butler, 2008).

Taking into account the urgent sexual, cultural, political and socio-economic considerations just mentioned, this volume brings together current research in relatively new areas of exploration. It aims to do so while remaining grounded in a strong theoretical, conceptual and empirical base largely premised on ideas and forms of theorising familiar within sociological, social anthropological, postcolonial and decolonial perspectives applied by scholars from and/or with links to the majority world of the global South and East. While this is not a book premised squarely on decolonising knowledge of (ageing) gender and sexuality (see the edited volume of Oyewumi (2011)), it draws on a plethora of theory that includes decolonial, poststructuralist/queer, phenomenological and feminist theory, as well as structuralist (Marxist-feminist) theory. As an intellectual project, the volume contributes from the particular, under-researched angle of obscured ageing sexualities, to a rich and extensive literature on intersectionality that regards individual and collective forms of self-expression as strongly influenced by the enmeshments of age/later life with sexuality, ethnicity, gender, class and so forth.

More innovatively, the volume involves questioning of the rigidity of Western binaries (of progressive and regressive) and temporalities of age/ageing, as well as sex and intimacy themselves. In effect, the volume encompasses scholarship that is critical of, complicates or is dialogic and, at times, consonant with accounts of experience of later life sexuality within the Western academy. The two latter instances could be said to reflect the long shadow of neocolonial capitalist relations.

The volume also contributes to a broader literature (see the forthcoming edited volume in this series on *Resexualisation* (expected 2025)), which seeks to acknowledge ageing and later life as dynamic, processual and historically and culturally contingent and that involves a constant becoming. This is evident in Madeline Burns' chapter on Indigenous sexuality where elders are understood as keepers of knowledge and hope (rather than repositories of despair). We are all becoming elders as we live, but the reverence for the bodily autonomy, erotic subjectivity and knowledge of elders holds a different place in this particular society. Furthermore, becomings involve not just self-reclamation (or emancipation from male sexual demands in patriarchal cultures), but also perceived deterioration (most commonly), or else it can occur in more ambivalent ways in-between these two poles.

While the comparisons and contrasts just described are central to our enquiry, we have attempted to curate a volume that avoids (mis-)representing and reifying the global North or West as the benchmark by which other sexual and intimate cultures and practices are (mis-)understood or to be evaluated. Indeed, the contributions in this volume speak back, in various ways, to the dominant North and West and address particularities of the cultures they are concerned with that are affected by enmeshed, internal-local and external-global influences.

Because of its challenge to neocolonial thinking, the collection variously indicates how ageing body-selves, sexual categories and practices have been transformed by legal-political, economic-material and cultural-ideological impositions that were integral to capitalist colonial encounters and subsequent relations of domination and subordination. The volume also, at times, calls attention to persistent socio-economic and cultural inequalities within formerly colonised societies and which can accrete often around an age-inflected politics of respectability and value, which can contribute to and impact harshly on 'muted' subjectivities, as exemplified in Sally Anne Param's chapter on Malaysian women's intergenerational narratives. Recognising the enmeshed character of multiple differences and inequalities (intersectionality), and recalling Audre Lorde's (2017) conceptualisation of multiple selves, we have tried to avoid reproducing accounts of experience of the more economically and culturally privileged within the various local cultures being examined.

As will be seen, this volume is transdisciplinary in drawing from Sociology, Anthropology, the Psychology of Ageing, Gender Studies, Cultural Studies, Religious Studies and Legal and Policy Studies. It draws on insights from a mix of established and emerging scholars from a range of international locations and including activists and policy advocates working outside academe. Like previous volumes in the book series, this one includes a mix of the empirical, theoretical and experiential in exploring limitations on expression of sexualities, as well as creative sexual pleasures, practices and relations and much ambivalence between the two poles of constraint and agency.

However, two caveats are required. First, and as intimated in the series editors' introduction, 'ageing', 'older' and 'later life' are broad and discursive categories, grounded in everyday interaction and practice, which become attached, if not habitual, to subjects. In more affluent countries/regions, the common threshold of later life within social gerontological studies appears to be 50 plus when people report more significant change in experience and how they are regarded (Simpson et al, 2021). This traditional and regulatory 'chrononormative' assumption (Freeman, 2010) does not serve well the less economically developed parts of the global South and East, handicapped from creating and maintaining welfare systems sufficient to enable improvements in longevity across their populations. For this political-material reason, which ramifies discursively, in some cultures, countries or regions, later life may be thought to occur at a much earlier point. What those in the West might regard as midlife would mark in some areas the onset of later life. We have, then, become aware, particularly in the chapters addressing later life sex and intimacy intergenerationally, of the necessity of relativising later life (see the chapters by Sally Anne Param, by Shereen El Feki and Selma Hajri, and that by Nafhesa Ali). These intellectual projects are very much part of a questioning of Western and global North conceptualisations of ageing, later life and temporality more broadly.

The second caveat concerns the potential criticism that the volume is lacking contributions from/about a particular culture or global region. Although we consider that most key regions are covered in this volume, inevitably there are limits on what we can include. That said, we did make considerable efforts to include scholars from, and/or able to write about, an aspect of ageing sexuality within cultures or countries south of the Sahara but we were unable, within the constraints of time, to secure participation from anyone with expertise to write about sexuality in later life. Indeed, from the outset, our editorial strategy has been more concerned with cultural than regional constructions of ageing sexuality, which entails a conscious decision to avoid the tokenism, homogenising and stereotyping that comes with assuming that any culture is representative of how sex and intimacy are practised in a particular geo-political region. Experiences of later life sex and intimacy in Hong Kong are not representative of thought and practice in East Asia. Besides, Westerners would be rather upset if thought and practice in Britain, France, Sweden or the US was made to stand for the whole of Western/global North thought and practice on any issue.

Themes, chapters and synopses: in/visibility and ambivalence; women questioning age/later life generationally; and fantasy, erotic tales and pleasure

With an overview of all contributions to this volume, three main themes emerged. First, and perhaps more immediate were concerns about in/visibility of older people as (il)legimate sexual beings. The chapter on older men who have sex with men, by Barry Lee and Travis S.K. Kong, contains significant elements of ambivalence as a key part of their argumentation. Second, we were struck by how three chapters bore a family resemblance in addressing women's intergenerational and intragenerational stories of sex and intimacy, which question Western notions of ageing and age categories as universal. Two of these chapters, by Sally Anne Param (with an intergenerational focus) and Nafhesa Ali (with a largely intragenerational focus) concern migrant South Asian women (in Malaysia and Britain, respectively), which address ageing sexuality in different diasporic contexts. In-between these chapters is a chapter by Shereen El Feki and Selma Hajri, which contains elements of mainly intragenerational dialogues over ageing sexuality in Middle Eastern and North African contexts. Third, while the previous contributions tended to emphasise constraint and/or negotiation with capitalist colonial legacies and/or their own internal proscriptions, we noticed that several contributions placed significant emphasis on sexual agency or at least its potential via fantasy, erotic storytelling and invocation of sexual pleasures with distinct decolonial overtones and much debunking of racialised myths and stereotypes. We thought it would be strategically better and a reward for the reader to finish the volume on more of an upbeat. Of course, each chapter may well contain elements of each major theme, but we had to place the emphasis somewhere in order to group the contributions in a meaningful way. We hope that readers will appreciate the logic of how we have divided up the intellectual 'cake' to make it more digestible.

Having introduced our organising themes, we now provide an exegesis of each chapter (in numerical order). We consider how each chapter relates to the relevant theme under which it is grouped, the over-arching theme of sex in later life beyond Western/global North normativity, and its contribution to knowledge.

In/visibility and ambivalence
Older Indo-Trinidadian queer men

In the first chapter, 'Under the *orhni*' (an Indian head-covering now symbolising tradition and mystery), Krystal Nandini Ghisyawan and Marcus Kissoon use in-depth analysis of the stories of four men to explore the 'near-invisibility' of older, Indo-Trinidadian queer men (who have sex with men) and the meanings they attach to intimacy. The analysis invokes the point made earlier about constraints of the colonial encounter and legacy and how subjects are required to negotiate them, as well as the contradictory demands of local culture and Western 'modernity'. The authors' examination is predicated on a racialised gender system installed by capitalist colonialism that has positioned white and European as the benchmark of civilisation and modernity that 'people of colour' must try to embody to approximate 'respectability' and thus avoid infra-human status. However, the racialised gender order also divides people of colour and has contributed to contradictory understandings of Indo-Trinidadian men that comprise feminisation and desexualisation (in contrast to Afro-Caribbean or Afro-Trinidadian men associated with hyper-virility), and hence exclusion from a valued masculinity. This process coexists with stereotypes of absolute, patriarchal control over women. Such stereotyping (bordering on scapegoating) is exacerbated by pressures internal to Indo-Trinidadian cultural traditions that require distance from signs of anti-normative queerness. This scenario provides the historical and cultural conditions that explain why Indo-Trinidadian men, and especially older ones, are obliged to deploy 'silence and secrecy' as necessary survival strategies, given severe penalties attached to being visible.

Despite a quasi-mandatory secrecy and considerable constraints on expression of an older sexual and intimate self, dominance and erasure are rarely complete. In effect, the authors provide evidence of creation of a (spatialised and class-inflected) queer community in which older, Indo-Trinidadian men have a hand, such as Pride and drag events and community support organisations in the more affluent North of the island. In such in-between cultural-political spaces, collectively carved out between public and private or visible and invisible (or less visible), the authors' analysis of such events complicates the clear binary politics of in/visibility historically central to individualistic, lesbian and gay politics in the West and global North. (See Stella (2012) for an account of less visible queer scenes in sexually conservative parts of post-Communist Eastern Europe.) Further, the chapter opens out understanding of these events as involving decolonising body projects that could involve recuperation from the alienating effects of symbolic colonial violence. Just as noteworthy is the relative absence in Indo-Trinidadian queer culture of the harsh ageism characteristic of the more visible, largely white, European and Anglo-American gay commercial 'scenes' (Simpson, 2015: chapter 7).

Older kinnars

This chapter is deliberately placed between chapters on older gay men and has been positioned early in the volume, as work addressing trans people tends to appear in edited collections and other works after cisgender identities, and thus reinforces a hierarchy of value and minoritisation. The acronym 'LGBT' itself indicates such a hierarchy.

Addressing the under-researched issue of ageing *kinnar* ('third sex') in India during the COVID-19 pandemic, we see, in the chapter by Anushkaa Arora, the terrifying, exclusionary consequences of being visible as individuals thought to represent non-normative identities on the intersecting grounds of gender mixed with age and sexuality. Like the previous chapter, we get a glimpse of the long shadow of the British colonial legacy. In effect, *kinnars* had been positively valued for centuries until the colonial encounter (and imposition of Western sexology), which led to their pathologisation and criminalisation, and the former remains despite recent decriminalisation. Such thinking indicates that cisgenderism constitutes a colonial importation or imposition. However, we also witness the challenges of capitalist postcolonialism and pressures internal to India that a social group rendered highly vulnerable has to contend with and try to negotiate within a country currently ruled by a sexually, socially, culturally, politically and economically conservative government. Here, there is much less scope to develop collective support and agency.

Deploying a phenomenological lens (Colaizzi, 1978), and based on interviews with 20 *kinnars* aged between 23 and 68, the chapter explores age-related, gendered and sexual stigmatisation and its impacts on older *kinnars'* accounts of sexuality and survival. Although it is highly moot to suggest that ageism is solely an effect of colonial occupation and dominance, the author's exploration of the specific desexualising ageism narrated by *kinnars* (in three age groups – younger, middle and older study participants) would resonate with older women and gay men in the West. Besides, the internalisation of ageism in *kinnar* culture, and its association with anxieties of loss and decline, and loss of tradeable beauty (sexual capital), have particular material consequences for *kinnars* who rely heavily on sex-work for subsistence.

This situation has been exacerbated by pandemic-related social and health protection measures. Such factors impact upon the mental and physical health of older individuals whose recounted experience is largely of ostracism, rejection as sexual partners (by paying customers and otherwise), as well as histories of physical violence from and desertion by male partners. Indeed, the two oldest study participants could only speak of a socio-sexual status that had been erased if not rendered abject and constituting a form of social death (Gilleard and Higgs, 2015). Nevertheless, the chapter indicates the relativisation of age, ageing and later life, albeit in negative mode, but the author concludes the chapter with positive recommendations for legal and policy reforms that would make life palatable for *kinnars* and represent key steps towards social inclusion. As with many other chapters in this volume, implicit within it lies Butler and Scott's (1992) theoretical and political exhortation that we attempt to broaden discourse to make intelligible and thus legitimise a wider range of (age-inflected) gendered, sexual identities.

The complex intimacies of older Chinese gay men in Hong Kong

In the chapter by Barry Lee and Travis S.K. Kong, based on in-depth interviews with nine Chinese men in Hong Kong aged 60 and over who have sex with men, we gain a clear sense of ambivalence in conditions of relative invisibility, concurrent with diverse, complex relationships. Again, the dialectic between the legacy of British colonialism (which saw male homosexuality criminalised from 1842 until 1990) and concerns internal to local Hong Kong Chinese culture, actually come into view. We also see how patriarchy can constrain *men*, albeit a subordinated group (though it can constrain all men, including those most interested in perpetuating it). The theme of necessary secrecy and circumspection here resonates with the earlier chapter by Krystal Nandini Ghisyawan and Marcus Kissoon. In this instance, the men's diverse sexual relationships represent a necessary, careful negotiation with or creative responses to the tension between Confucian traditionalism that demands 'filiality' and thus reproduction and heteronormativity, which together, constitute 'familial heteronormativity'. While there are some clear parallels with some gay men's accounts of experience in the West/global North, specifically, the authors explore how 'intimate lives are primarily affected by heteronormative culture intersecting with homonormativity and ageism embedded in a Confucian cultural context'.

The older men's stories, invoking 'non-confrontational' strategies, again, provide a counterpoint to the (humanist-individualist) Western/global North politics of visibility ('coming out') deployed by LGBTQ movements. Such a politics has coexisted with dyadic, egalitarian, 'pure relationships' (Giddens, 1992) and the constructed 'friendship families' of lesbian, gay and bisexual people, which form part of 'newer experiments' in living, loving and relating (Weeks et al, 2001). In contrast, such experiments are less available to the men in this study. Instead, we see in their stories, the influence of the more relational Confucian self 'embedded in a socially reciprocal relationship network in family-centred Chinese culture'. Nonetheless, we can observe some diversity and creative adaptations to circumstances in the relationships that men forge, aided by a strongly homosocial society, to satisfy familial-traditional requirements and their own sexual needs. Indeed, the chapter invites reckoning with an elaborate typology of relationships, involving sub-types, which, variously, involve monogamy and polyamory, and some of them some suggesting distinct local 'experiments' in sex and intimacy. All relationship types described in this chapter involve some negotiation with the discourse of monogamy, peculiar to both Western and local culture.

Women questioning age intergenerationally and intragenerationally
The hidden accounts of intimacy of older, migrant Indian women in Malaysia

Shifting the focus onto relativising age and later life, the chapter by Sally Anne Param shines light on the hidden and ambivalent accounts of sex and intimacy of older Indian women who migrated to Malaysia for employment opportunities when younger. (Both India and Malaysia have been subjected to British colonialist capitalism and its legacies of classed, gendered, sexualised and racialised regulation.) Given the taboo around sex talk that applies to this social group (which is also prone to prejudice, discrimination and cultural and socio-economic marginalisation), the author, of necessity, accesses older women's accounts through in-depth interviews with eight daughters aged 30–57 (some of whom would count as older) of eight mothers aged 60–84. We get a sense of historicity, given that the younger women felt more licensed to talk about sexual matters (albeit within the context of a carefully considered, reflexively informed research design). While this might be considered a mere proxy measure, it amounted to a 'blessing in disguise', as this pragmatic strategy 'opened up an intergenerational conversation about stories of sex and intimacy', and their avoidance, which affords simultaneous exploration of 'Indian female lives in Malaysia … and familial relationality'.

Using Marxist-feminist-inspired Muted Group Theory of anthropologist Ardener (1975, 1993), the author examines how patriarchal ideology, related to socio-economic structure, contributes to the silencing of older women and normalises their subordination in this context. These related theories prove useful in accounting for how macro-level structures and their concomitant ideologies impact upon discussions of intimacy at the everyday micro-level. As intimated earlier, muted subjectivities is a major structuring theme of this volume. Besides, this theoretical approach marks a refreshing return of structuralist analysis to an intellectual field dominated since the 1990s by poststructuralism. This chapter is, then, significant for using a strand of Western anti-capitalist, feminist thought to draw attention to the covert, subtle connections between age-inflected, gendered sexuality and a capitalist work ethic, (based on sacrifice and individualised success). Such an ideology is mobilised strategically, mainly by mothers from middle-class families to maintain class position, and displaces familial dialogue on sex and intimacy. Nevertheless, and challenging Western stereotypes of the passive, male-dominated, South Asian woman (Mohanty, 2003), the author highlights ways in which women's intergenerational kin relationships negotiate with and empower older women to subvert patriarchy at the domestic level.

Reframing the sexuality of older women in the Middle East and North Africa (MENA)

Staying with the broad theme of women's questioning (or 'reframing') of older, gendered, raced and classed sexuality, and as the title of the chapter by Shereen El Feki and Selma Hajri indicates, we get a view of ageing sexuality, articulated especially around the menopause, as a situated, dynamic and intragenerational process that is within a life course. Basing their analysis on literature addressing older women in a region that has been affected by French and British colonial occupations, the authors recognise the deeply historically rooted, patriarchal constraints on women's sexuality within the region and, simultaneously, how (some) women have begun, in the last decade or so especially, to speak out, in the newer in-between spaces of social media, on a range of related and 'controversial' issues connected with gender and sexuality. However, in a region where youth predominates, there remains a general silence and relative invisibility (and ambivalence) concerning older women's sexuality, something which has elicited tentative but important signs of challenge. Debunking imperialist myths about Islamic societies (like the chapter by Shanon Shah), the authors link this phenomenon to long-standing traditions in Islamic writing that have mediated between 'faith and flesh', and which have contradictorily both celebrated and expressed fears about female desire (and thus women's sexual autonomy).

The authors find a range of responses to menopause among differently situated (older) women, mainly along lines of class and education (and the intensity of local, religious patriarchal discourse), from those reflecting wider traditional framings of loss (of fertility, attractiveness and desire) to those expressing liberation from fear of conception (or even unsatisfying sex). The latter are indicative of local feminist articulations of women's pleasure. Even in the former narrative, sexual loss can be compensated by increased value and authority accorded older women in MENA, who are thus spared the harsh bodily scrutiny commonly accorded to their peers in the West and global North. Indeed, the authors' main message appears that while conservative, authoritarian patriarchy remains embedded, there have been important political shifts in the region in the last decade or so that have increased scope for older women (menopausal or otherwise) to articulate their need for sexual and companionate enjoyment. In doing so, menopausal women in some MENA societies are questioning why this life transition should be understood as an 'age of despair' when it can facilitate freedom from male pressure for sex, enhanced status in family life and other opportunities for autonomy. Sadly, health services, mired in reductionist ideas of menopause as dysfunction, have not kept pace with such thinking and largely remain poorly equipped to support older (menopausal) women's sexual and emotional needs, which would also involve support for male partners. Nevertheless, the authors highlight significant cultural shifts often missed by Western optics and which challenge stereotypes of the passivity of Eastern women (Mohanty, 2003).

Carrying gender, nation and femininity across the life course

Also referencing more intragenerational interrogation of ageing sexuality, Nafhesa Ali draws substantially on interviews with 20 South Asian women, aged 60–80, to explore the subtle 'interconnections of how socio-historic events', that is the nationalist violence implicated in the Partition of India, 'magnified the sexualisation of the female body'. Such an analytic strategy is used to understand how the process described earlier and formative experiences resonate much later in the life course and continue to shape age-inflected, gendered, ethno-religious and *transnational* forms of intimate self-expression that can encompass older, South Asian, female migrants to Britain positively claiming desexualised status. Specifically, the author draws on tools and insights from decolonial analysis and Black Feminism to consider: how 'patriarchal positioning of the nation and its protection of "vulnerable" sexualities locate women's bodies as sites of *izzat* (honour/shame/respect)'; and how older migrant women 'carry honour … into later life, where the desexualisation of the ageing body and bodily desires create space for … autonomy'. While moving into a 'more revered elder position' has enabled (some) older women to reclaim their body-selves, such a transition also symbolises a challenge to the hegemonic Western idea that desexualisation in later life, especially for women, represents a loss of attractiveness and value and, more generally, a downward slide towards decrepitude and mortality (Simpson et al, 2018).

Agency through fantasy, erotic tales and pleasure
Sexual fantasies and older, Indigenous Purépecha women

Turning to the final theme, which aims to strike a more agentic note, the chapter by Cuauhtémoc Sanchez Vega is keenly aware of deeply historically rooted constraints on sexual expression, but also imparts a clear sense of the sexual agency that can be mobilised by Indigenous Purépecha women (situated in the north-west of Mexico). This is particularly important given that rare studies of Purépecha communities have tended to focus on youth, early fertility and sexual function, involving a great deal of pathology, thus neglecting considerations of pleasure and later life sexualities, and by a particularly oppressed social group. Like the previous chapter, the author takes the long view to consider how pre-Hispanic, pre-Imperial and hetero-patriarchal Purépecha culture, where women were a means of exchange, has resonated through history and later inter-articulated with (equally patriarchal) Spanish settler colonialism to reinforce regulation of (older) women's sexuality in ways that continue to deny them pleasure and autonomy. More recently, in postcolonial (or neocolonial) times, women's sexual and wider oppression have been cemented by modernist, monogamous romantic love that reinforces ideas of women as property. Such thinking recalls McClintock's (2013) observation concerning how women in the global South have had to reckon with colonialism and heteronormative patriarchy of colonised men and their colonial oppressors. Lugones (2007) has made a similar observation in relation to South American neocolonialism, which is implicated in gender and sexuality oppression.

Drawing largely on interviews (n = 5) and a workshop discussion (n = 15), involving in total 20 women aged 50–82, this chapter appreciates the value of Western critical feminist analysis in asserting women's sexual autonomy. Simultaneously, it is suggestive of a decolonial sensibility in highlighting the value of Indigenous, older women's sexual knowledges via fantasies, 'suggesting new ethics of pleasure … pointing towards a more convivial model of sexual morality' and capable of transcending patriarchy. Such thinking resonates with analysis that envisions productive and potentially emancipatory dialogues between Western and Indigenous or global South epistemologies (Mohanty, 2013; Bhambra, 2014).

Indigenous older sexual agents via storytelling as queer, decolonial practice

Also addressing Indigenous 'elders' (a term of respect) and, indexing another structuring theme concerning the dynamism of age and the value of becoming and *growing* older, Madeline Burns continues the theme of socio-sexual agency through storytelling within her/their culture in 'so-called Canada'. Her/their analysis is more squarely aligned to a decolonial epistemology. Involving a consciously self-reflexive positioning, Madeline describes her/their self as, 'a Métis community member displaced from Red River homelands on my mother's side, and as a person with Scottish roots. … Indigenous, sexually fluid, femme-presenting, white-bodied, middle-class, able-bodied, younger person'. There are various ways in which the author embodies and mobilises a productive diasporic 'double consciousness' first identified by Du Bois (1903) and more recently developed by Gilroy (1993), between coloniality and indigeneity.

Moreover, and contrary to Western assumptions, the author recognises Indigenous elders as guardians of intimate and sexual (hi)stories and sexual agents, whose storytelling involves more-than-human-beings, incorporating 'lands, waters, elements, spiritual beings, tricksters [disruptors of boundaries], plant and animal'. These 'multi-species relations' occur within a culture that values and has normalised sexual and gender diversity. They transcend the hubris of the human as the-be-all-and-end-all and recognise human beings as fluidly enmeshed within ecology and the spiritual (and not separate from, exceptional to or in control of them). These relations constitute an 'eco-erotics' that disrupts heteronormative, patriarchal settler-colonial ideas of age, time and 'acceptable' sexual (and other) forms of relating. As the author argues, in the Indigenous cosmology, such stories and the relations they envision, form part of an urgent and necessary resistance to the colonial 'logic of elimination'.

Later life sex and intimacy in Muslim contexts

The final substantive chapter, by Shanon Shah, addresses imperialist Western/global North assumptions of Islam as inherently conservative and thus opposed to gender equality and LGBTQ+ identities and relationships. Questioning the putative civilisational clash, whereby the West others the East as regressive or forever fixed in tradition, this chapter acknowledges an emerging body of scholarship, including that delivered by Islamic feminist and/or queer-identified Muslims, which challenges this simplistic binary and thus questions Orientalist, Eurocentric conceptions of gender, sexuality and LGBTQ rights.

Indicating the nuances of historicity, this recuperative project recognises the diverse ways in which (age-inflected) gendered sexualities have been conceptualised and experienced in different eras and up to contemporary Islam. Acknowledging the current paucity of analysis on sexual intimacy in later life within extant scholarship on Islam and sexuality, the author begins to address this knowledge gap by applying the combined lens of sex, intimacy and age to a close reading of two pre-modern Islamic sex manuals – *The Perfumed Garden* (from the fifteenth century AD) and *The Delight of Hearts* (from the thirteenth century AD). These texts were selected due to their prominent reception – and often sensationalist reproductions – by Western, Orientalist writers, as well as their historical and contemporary influence on other genres of Islamic writing. This chapter, therefore, adds to the nascent study of Islamic sex manuals as a specific genre. Such an approach expands and enhances understanding of how gendered and sexual relationships were expressed, sometimes in subversive ways, and regulated in Muslim societies, and the implications of all of this for contemporary studies of ageing, gendered sexualities within Islam.

Further themes and issues

We have briefly drawn attention to common and inter-related themes of value and respectability, muted subjectivities and ageing/later life as becomings, which will be taken up in the concluding chapter. These themes indicate unique contributions to knowledge, which deploy later life and ageing as analytical categories that show how these overlapping forms of politics work.

In addition to the three organising motifs, several other themes emerge within this collection. First, and most distinctly, we espy the effects of the tension or dialectic between neocolonial capitalist and Indigenous influences shaping ageing sexualities. These enmeshments reflect a complex, unpredictable politics where global and local patriarchies meet and are particularly apparent in the chapters on Trinbagoian queers, Hong Kong gay men, Malaysian women, Indian women, older Purépecha women and women in the Middle East and North Africa. Indeed, these political influences are often so historically embedded that they can be hard to separate and especially where colonialist, patriarchal capitalism meshes with local patriarchal capitalism. Such concerns suggest a long-term, rich and fruitful terrain of research for critical historians of imperialism.

Whatever the case, these interarticulations can result in constraints on, and contradictions (sometimes confusing, sometimes thought-provoking) concerning expressions of ageing sexualities across the diverse majority world. We must also acknowledge that all contributions have drawn on, at least to some extent (including those deploying a decolonial lens or sensibility), Western thought (be it Marxist-feminism, phenomenology or poststructuralist queer theory) in their analysis of a particular culture. Moreover, the chapter on older *kinnar* by Anushkaa Arora, that on Indian migrant women's intergenerational stories by Sally Anne Param and that by Cuauhtémoc Sanchez Vega on older Purépecha women are clear about how aspects of Western thought could be adapted for purposes of emancipation in local contexts. Their ideas resonate with Mohanty's (2013) postcolonial thinking about productive transnational feminist dialogues.

Second, and as a corollary of the point just made, there are multiple iterations in this volume of the constraints, ambivalences and opportunities for intimate and sexual expression described by older subjects in the global North/West. However, these accounts of experience from the South and East ramify in very different ways, especially when we consider the ontological threats faced by Indigenous North Americans plus the actual physical threats to *kinnars* in India: both communities are forced to reckon with the prospect of annihilation. Narratives from the South/East have also brought into view a diversity of experience of ageing, gendered sexualities that would be difficult to appreciate through Euro- or Anglo-centric lenses. In so doing, they have roundly questioned the Western binary that sees itself as (sexually) progressive and 'the rest', the majority world, as bearers of regressive sexual mores. All of the chapters in the volume invoke colonial history, but the more historically focused contributions, in particular, help destabilise the progressive–regressive nexus.

Third, and although it may now seem like an old adage, we are struck by how many chapters indicate that older subjects' accounts of sex and intimacy are imbricated in many other issues and fields of existence (Plummer, 1995). As shown in various chapters, it can be hard to separate sex and intimacy from neocolonialist capitalism, whether evident in an everyday politics of social class, value/respectability, belonging and survival in economically impoverished areas or traumatic events such as Partition and migration. Finally, and as intimated in the chapter by Cuauhtémoc Sanchez Vega, we are hopeful that readers will see in this volume possibilities across the globe for greater epistemological justice (Bhambra, 2014). This project would involve, as per Madeline Burns' chapter, the emergence of more convivial, egalitarian modes of intimate and sexual self-expression for older people that associate them with growth and that normalise their inclusion in sexual citizenship.

References

Åberg, E., Kukkonen, I. and Sarpila, O. (2020) 'From Double to Triple Standards of Ageing: Perceptions of Physical Appearance at the Intersections of Age, Gender and Class', *Journal of Aging Studies*, 55. Doi.org/10.1016/j.jaging.2020.100876

Ardener, S. (1975) *Perceiving Women*, London: Malaby Press.

Ardener, S. (1993) 'Introduction: The Nature of Women in Society', in Ardener, S. (ed), *'Defining Females, the Nature of Women in Society'*, Routledge: London, pp 1–16.

Bhambra, G. (2014) *Connected Sociologies*, London: Bloomsbury.

Butler, J. (2008) 'Sexual Politics, Torture and Secular Time', *British Journal of Sociology*, 59(1): pp 1–23. Doi.org/10.1111/j.1468-4446.2007.00176.x

Butler, J. and Scott, J. (eds) (1992) *Feminists Theorise the Political*, New York: Routledge.

Colaizzi, P. (1978) 'Psychological Research as a Phenomenologist Views It', in Valle, R.S. and King, M., *Existential Phenomenological Alternatives for Psychology*, New York: Open University Press, pp 48–71.

Driskill, Q.L. (2010) 'Doubleweaving Two-spirit Critiques: Building Alliances between Native and Queer Studies', *GLQ: A Journal of Lesbian and Gay Studies*, 16(1–2): pp 69–92.

Du Bois, W.E.B. (1903) *The Souls of Black Folk: Essays and Sketches*, New York: Bantam Classic.

Freeman, E. (2010) *Time Binds: Queer Temporalities, Queer Histories*, Durham, NC: Duke University Press.

Giddens, A. (1992) *The Transformation of Intimacy: Sexuality, Love and Eroticism in Modern Societies*, Cambridge: Polity Press.

Gilleard, C. and Higgs, P. (2015) 'Social Death and the Moral Identity of the Fourth Age', *Contemporary Social Science*, 10(3): pp 262–71. Doi: 10.1080/21582041.2015.1075328

Gilroy, P. (1993) *The Black Atlantic: Modernity and Double Consciousness*, Cambridge, MA: Harvard University Press.

Go, J. (2017) 'Decolonizing Sociology: Epistemic Inequality and Sociological Thought', *Social Problems*, 64(2): pp 194–9.

Hafford-Letchfield, T. (2021) 'Heterosexual Sex, Love and Intimacy in Later Life: What Have Older Women Got to Say?', in Hafford-Letchfield, T., Simpson, P. and Reynolds, P. (eds), *Sex and Diversity in Later Life: Critical Perspectives*, Bristol: Policy Press, pp 57–78.

Henrickson, M., Charles, C., Ganesh, S., Giwa, S., Kwok, K.D. and Semigina, T. (eds) (2022) *HIV, Sex and Sexuality in Later Life*, Bristol: Policy Press.

Hockey, J.L. and James, A. (1993) *Growing Up and Growing Old: Ageing and Dependency in the Life Course*, London: Sage.

Lorde, A. (2017) *A Burst of Light: And Other Essays*, North Chelmsford, MA: Courier Dover Publications.

Lugones, M. (2007) 'Heterosexualism and the Colonial/Modern Gender System', *Hypatia*, 22(1): pp 186–219.

McClintock, A. (2013) *Imperial Leather: Race, Gender and Sexuality in the Colonial Context*, New York: Routledge.

Mohanty, C.T. (2003) '"Under Western Eyes" Revisited: Feminist Solidarity through Anti-capitalist Struggles', *Signs: Journal of Women in Culture and Society*, 28(2): pp 499–535.

Mohanty, C.T. (2013) 'Transnational Feminist Crossings: On Neoliberalism and Radical Critique', *Signs: Journal of Women in Culture and Society*, 38(4): pp 967–91.

Oyewumi, O. (ed) (2011) *Gender Epistemologies in Africa: Gendering Traditions, Spaces, Social Institutions and Identities*, New York: Palgrave Macmillan.

Plummer, K. (1995) *Telling Sexual Stories: Power, Intimacy and Social Worlds*, London: Routledge.

Pryzbylo, E. (2021) 'Ageing Asexually: Exploring Desexualisation and Ageing', in Hafford-Letchfield, T., Simpson, P. and Reynolds, P. (eds), *Sex and Diversity in Later Life: Critical Perspectives*, Bristol: Policy Press, pp 181–98.

Puar, J.K. (2018) *Terrorist Assemblages: Homonationalism in Queer Times*, Durham, NC: Duke University Press.

Reynolds, P., Hafford-Letchfield, T. and Simpson, P. (eds) (2024) *Resexualising Later Life*, Bristol: Policy Press.

Saïd, E.W. (1978) *Orientalism*, New York: Pantheon Books.

Simpson, P. (2015) *Middle-aged Gay Men, Ageing and Ageism: Over the Rainbow?* Basingstoke: Palgrave Macmillan.

Simpson, P. (2021) 'At Your Age???!!! The Constraints of Ageist Erotophobia on the Sexual/Intimate Relationships of Older People', in Simpson, P., Reynolds, P. and Hafford-Letchfield, T. (eds), *Desexualisation in Later Life: the Limits of Sex and Intimacy*, Bristol: Policy Press, pp 35–51.

Simpson, P., Brown Wilson, C., Brown, L., Dickinson, T. and Horne, M. (2018) '"We've Had Our Sex Life Way Back": Older Care Home Residents, Sexuality and Intimacy', *Ageing and Society*, 38(7): pp 1478–501.

Simpson, P., Reynolds, P. and Hafford-Letchfield, T. (2021) 'Introduction to Volume Two: Themes, Issues and Chapter Synposes', in Simpson, P., Reynolds, P. and Hafford-Letchfield, T. (eds), *Desexualisation in Later Life: The Limits of Sex and Intimacy*, Bristol: Policy Press, pp 1–16.

Stella, F. (2012) 'The Politics of In/visibility: Carving out Queer Space in Ul'yanovsk', *Europe-Asia Studies*, 64(10): pp 1822–46.

United Nations (2017) *World Mortality Report: Highlights*, New York: United Nations.

Weeks, J., Heaphy, B. and Donovan, C. (2001) *Same Sex Intimacies: Families of Choice and Other Life Experiments*, London: Routledge.

Worldometer (2023) *Regions in the World Population (2023)*, www.worldometers.info/world-population/population-by-region/ [accessed 15 February 2023].

PART I

In/visibility and ambivalence

2

Under the *orhni*: intimacy and near-invisibility among older Indo-Trinidadian queer men

Krystal Nandini Ghisyawan and Marcus Kissoon

Introduction: queer erasure on the (post)colonial plantation

Indo-Caribbean people are not culturally 'Indian' but represent a distinct diasporic culture that combines traditional Indian cultures with modern African-Caribbean ones (Sampath, 1993, Raghunandan, 2012). The hyphenated identity 'Indo-Caribbean' establishes the existence of Indianness that is rooted in the Caribbean space, its legacies of indentured labour and slavery, and its past and contemporary socio-economic and cultural relations. The figures of Indian masculinity and femininity, as well as Indo-Caribbean masculinity and femininity, were constructed in different ways over time and space, and from different perspectives, to fit various narratives of citizenship and belonging. Old photographs and postcards from the days of Indian indenture on Caribbean sugarcane plantations, themselves symbols of antiquity and empire, were invested in representing the exotic and 'othered' coolies (Bahadur, 2015). The women were depicted with ornate jewellery, in either traditional saris or Western dresses, their heads covered with a head scarf, the *orhni*, a symbol of Indian femininity; young women's purity, married women's modesty, and older women's piety are represented by the veil covering the head and sometimes the face. Men too wore head-coverings, such as the turban or *pagri*. Although these garments are today mainly used during ceremony and rituals, the *orhni* symbolises tradition, privacy, secrecy and mystery, tropes that are also associated with Indian gender and sexuality, which Tejaswini Niranjana contends is a deliberate creation of nationalist moralities, with 'appropriate "Indian" modes of sociosexual behaviour, the parameters for the state's regulation of reproduction as well as sexuality, and the delineation of the virtues that would ensure for Indian women citizenship in the future nation' (2011: 122). Sexual morality was used to anchor 'respectable' ethnic, religious, class and national identities through deliberately erasing narratives of non-conformity (Wahab, 2012; Persadie, 2020). Thus, queer erasure results from modern colonial society's political (legal), social and economic structures.

While African-Caribbean queer men and men-who-have-sex-with-men are hyper-visible, Indo-Caribbean men are comparably absent from discourses, studies and representations of Caribbean queerness. Women are even less visible. African-Caribbean queer scholar, poet and performance artist Rosamond King, terms this 'near-invisibility', whereby queer women are 'implicitly acknowledged while explicitly denied' (2014, 15). Marcus knew several Indo-Trinidadian queer people aged over 50 but few wanted to be interviewed. They were 'near-invisible', having been subject to discursive erasure that absented them from the imagined 'Indo-Caribbean' ethnic identity, despite indications that sexual practices beyond the heteronormative likely existed among indentured servants (Lokaisingh-Meighoo, 2000) and certainly existed in South Asian society and mythology (Vanita, 2005). Ultimately, we interviewed three queer men over 50, each with different education, geographic, religious and socio-economic backgrounds, and one African-Trinidadian queer male activist, who spoke on the distinct ways in which these aforementioned factors influence families, romantic relationships, friendships and participation in activism. All four describe having to employ silence and secrecy as strategies for survival, despite the constraints their invisibility as same-sex-loving has on their opportunities to create and foster intimate bonds. This chapter explores these constraints and how these Indo-Trinidadian men experience sexuality and intimacy throughout their lives.

Contemporary prescriptive sexual ideologies are based on racialised gender binaries established during the colonial period. Contesting white (European and North American), Black and Indian patriarchies influenced gender ideals and realities, basing gender stereotypes on racial assumptions that positioned white settlers and enslaved Africans, and later Indo and African-Caribbean peoples, as antithetical to each other, with incompatible cultural values and ways. Europeans were thought to epitomise civility in every respect, with people of colour needing to prove their respectability by embodying European ideals. In the post-indenture and pre-independence period (early twentieth century), the Indo-Caribbean middle class replaced the colonial image of the indentured woman as lower caste/class, labouring and agentive, with religious conservatism, 'traditional' Indian values, docility and dependence, emphasising their moral superiority to African-Caribbean women, and resisting narratives of Indian acculturation to Creole modernities (Niranjana, 2011). While writing on young Indo-Trinidadian masculinity in the 1980s, Neil Sampath (1993) noted that Indo-Trinidadian youth are caught between notions of honour (traditionally Indian) and reputation (modern Creole); they feel pressured to be 'modern' and adopt Western values that may differ from the values of the older generations, but will earn them respectability among their peers.

Among these values is 'a set of idealised, institutionalised, socio-economic, socio-cultural and political forms of manhood' that men are encouraged to achieve despite it being unattainable to most of them, termed 'hegemonic masculinity' (Reddock, 2004). Reddock notes '[t]he range of acceptable "masculine" behaviours is very limited', and that a show of power is necessary to be considered 'a man' (2004: 4). African-Caribbean men are thought to better embody hegemonic masculinity's sexual prowess, aggression and dominance than other men; Asian- and South-Asian-Caribbean men are deemed less capable of hegemonic masculinity and, as such, have been desexualised and feminised in public discourse. Homosexuality is viewed as antithetical to hegemonic masculinity (Chevannes, 2001), thus, it follows that:

> Indo-Caribbean men have always been read as queer bodies in the context of Caribbean society, where a subtext of non-normativity has underpinned the social construction of their racialization and gender. Polarised against and in relation to dominant Afro-masculinities, their Indian difference renders them always-already queer to the hyperbolic excess of Afrocreole heteromasculinities. (Persadie, 2020: 66)

Additionally, as Reddock asserts, within rural Indo-Trinidadian communities, traditional Hindu values, such as those related to androgyny, may still be understood and accepted, leading to more accepting attitudes towards sexual and gender diversity (2016: 275), thereby reinforcing the view of Indo-Caribbean cultures as 'queer'.

Despite the feminisation and desexualising of Indian masculinity in the wider society, Indo-Caribbean men occupy positions of authority within the private sphere and use sexual dominance and control to establish patriarchal power within Indo-Caribbean family structures (Mohammed, 1998; Niranjana, 2011). Furthermore, Reddock tells us '[t]here were some pathological assumptions about Indo-Caribbean men – alcoholism, [and] violence against women' (2016: 264), that have been accepted for their role in strengthening the patriarchal order. Male patriarchs enforce adherence to the sexual norms, including premarital sexual abstinence, appropriate marriage and reproductive heterosexuality, expected of the family members, especially women, who are viewed as the protectors of their culture (Niranjana, 2011). Although Indo-Caribbean women 'were expected to conform to gender scripts that imagined them as "passive," "docile," "conservative," "respectable," "submissive," and "moral"' (Hosein and Outar, 2012: 1), African-Caribbean embodiments of erotic autonomy, such as wining[1] and participating in Carnival, a nationwide street festival, provided the Indo-Trinidadian community 'with pedagogical tools to reconfigure traditional notions of Indian womanhood and engage in new forms of self-making' (Persadie, 2020: 59), but such creolised Indianness was viewed as a bastardisation of tradition (Hosein, 2012). The shift to maintaining an Indo-Caribbean identity that could arguably be morally superior to African-Caribbean counterparts was dependent on the curtailment of any sexual practices that could be deemed 'unrespectable', including 'queerness'.

Today, the 'postcolonial' state's control over sex, gender and sexuality, includes restrictions placed on same-sex-loving persons, the (il)legality of their sexual practices, their vulnerability to discrimination, and the denial of justice in cases of economic, physical, sexual or other forms of victimisation. Trinidad and Tobago (T&T) decriminalised sexual contact between people of the same sex in 2018, but social attitudes and other legal frameworks do not yet reflect acceptance (Ghisyawan, 2016, 2022). Indo-Trinidadian queer people situate themselves and actively participate at the intersections of these multiple discourses; indeed, it is the ontological and epistemological space from which we write auto-ethnographically, reflecting on the knowledge we hold from our own belonging within Indo-Trinidadian families, queer communities and the nationalist space. For this essay, we interviewed three Indo-Trinidadian men over 50, two of whom identify as 'gay' and one as 'bi-curious', whose lives exemplify various tensions, motives and strategies for seeking intimacy, love, pleasure and erotic fulfilment as queer Indo-Trinidadian men. Yet, they are also charged with maintaining façades of respectability. Their stories highlight how their race and ethnic identifications contribute to their sexual subjectivities, their practices of non-disclosure, respect for family values, secret love, sex and dating encounters. We ask, how does this near-invisible population envision intimacy? What does it mean to them, and how do they actualise it?

Family honour and respectability

'Coming out' and declaring one's sexuality is a Western concept for which there is no cultural equivalent in many other contexts. In fact, research on queer people of colour from around the world (Acosta, 2010; King, 2014; Horton, 2018) shows that non-disclosure is purposeful and intentional when silence can provide more protection. Non-disclosure can reduce the stress of having to cope with erasure, social pressure, stigmatisation and shaming. Ghisyawan's (2016, 2022) work with Trinidadian same-sex-loving women has found that some opt for total compartmentalisation of their lives, keeping their same-sex desire hidden and secret from their families. The choice to 'come out' was also complicated by women's financial independence, ownership of private property, ability to travel regionally and internationally, and the attitudes within their circles of friends and family. None of the three men interviewed were 'out' to their families, and in fact resisted the teleological narratives of queer modernity that required one to go from 'closeted' to 'out' in order to be fully or properly queer. This section details their negotiations as they fostered close familial relationships at the expense of pursuing long-term or consistent same-sex partnerships.

Errol was sure that his family had seen pictures of him on Facebook, dressed in drag, that his friends had posted. "They never said anything," he said. Errol is 61 years old and lives alone in north Trinidad. He is single and practises Hinduism, even volunteering at the local *mandir*, helping with weekly food preparation. Errol did not 'flaunt' his affairs with men or outright admit that he was dating men, but he also did not actively try to keep his drag persona hidden. He said:

> 'Some people ask me why I don't try to change my voice? My answer to that is that I wouldn't be me. I'd be somebody else! Because I would always have to be conscious of making my voice heavier. They say eventually you would get into the habit but, then, I'd be pretending.' (Errol)

He did not want to pretend, but he still wondered whether "it maybe would have been better ... easier. Ah easier life," if he had been open with his family about who he was. He did not elaborate on what he thought might have been easier, but admitted that they had not said or done anything to make him feel they would be homophobic or unkind. Although he accepts that the past cannot be changed, he spoke with sadness in the tone of his voice, quietly reflecting on thoughts he chose not to share.

On the other hand, David was more guarded, cautious not to dispense of any revelations, whether a declaration or a mere suggestion, that he was anything other than 'normal'. David is currently single, 55 years old, and living in rural central Trinidad. He is a self-declared 'home person', saying, "I tend to be home with my mom and I have two of my sisters living near to me, so I will be there spending time with their children and that sort of thing". He preferred dating 'masculine' men, saying, "I would stay away from feminine gays or even bisexual persons, because, for me I think that would embarrass me, because people tend to judge you based on who you, how do I say it? Fraternise with, so yeah." David feels that being seen with a masculine man would eliminate people's assumption about his non-normative sexuality. Gossip is a strong policing force in the Caribbean. The consequences can be life-changing, exposing same-sex-loving persons to verbal and physical violence, shaming and ostracisation from family, peers, community members and even strangers (Ghisyawan, 2022). "The way I would carry about myself in public it may not give the impression it's two gay guys on the road," he said.

As sons within Indo-Trinidadian families, the men were expected to uphold traditional ideals of filial piety, whereby children have a duty to respect, revere, obey and care for their parents, while having a spouse and children of their own. Within Hinduism, Lord Rama is idolised for this fulfilment of his duties as ideal son and husband (Mohammed, 1998). Despite his family's conversion to Pentecostalism, David also felt his parents would be disappointed if he did not fulfil these expectations, even though he had achieved professional success as a lawyer. He said, "Well I'm not what they expect and not what they want in terms of a son." Indeed, Kissoon (2019) found that this expectation of marriage and 'normal' family life was so potent that Indo-Caribbean male survivors of child sexual abuse would keep silent about their abuse for fear of disrupting perceptions of their suitability for idealised domestic life. They feared that people would look at them differently, thinking they failed as men, if, as children, they were abused by a man. Being 'soft' was subtly permitted, like going to the temple and participating in rituals, or Errol's 'feminine' tone and voice, but being ostensibly gay was not allowed. The demanding rigid roles for 'men', such as being provider, protector, husband and father did not leave room for anything non-normative.

In fact, queer men may not even know of an alternative, as they lack models showing what a 'queer life' can be in this context. Drawing on decades of work with the queer community, African-Trinidadian social justice activist and mental health clinical practitioner Mark (late 40s) shared candidly about what it takes to build a life as a queer person in Trinidad. Although African-Trinidadian gay men and trans women primarily seek out his organisation, its longevity means that Mark has worked with various generations of the queer community. He notes that many people in their twenties seek out relationships, but "their thirties are a mid-life crisis for gay people, trying to figure out the fullness of life they are trying to achieve" (Mark, 21 July 2021). This crisis brings many clients to his organisation who need a space to unpack and navigate those developmental crises. He noted that many gay people, especially when not open with elder relatives, lack the support and guidance to deal with their crises of self and self-actualisation. Additionally, being silent about one's sexuality, regardless of one's race or other socio-economic background, forces queer people to perform asexuality, just as David and Errol present themselves in this desexualised way among their families, and are unsure of what kind of family they can create for themselves.

Silencing one's sexuality with family has other consequences, such as sacrificing authenticity and mentorship from elders. Mark highlighted, as Acosta (2010) noted, that his mother avoided conversations for fear of anything 'gay' coming up, preventing them from being truly close and vulnerable with each other. Likewise, the Indo-Trinidadian men we interviewed kept their sex lives secret to abate the risk of rejection. "Even your family does not allow you to evolve in ways that they may have evolved," Mark said, noting that he, and other men his age, felt stagnated, unsure of how to build the "full life" they may have envisioned when younger. Mark suggested that older gay men who continue to "dress young", go to gay parties and pick up young people, did so because they simply did not know how to age as queer men. Concepts of ageing are culturally defined, so without visual representations of queer men building a life together and ageing within the society, these men had no script other than the hetero-patriarchal norms that idealised their heterosexual marriage and fatherhood. David thought he would have a long-term committed relationship, but since his last long-term partner died of illness, he has not been able to establish another such relationship. Contrastingly, even as a young man, drawing the attention of potential sexual partners while walking down the street, Errol never really had a vision for his older life. He did not know what it would be. Was he attempting to hold on to youth by surrounding himself with young men to keep him company and indulge his desires?

Another reason David did not disclose his sexuality to his family was his mother's active involvement in the Pentecostal church, that he occasionally attended with her. He thought she might be disappointed by having a gay son, especially hearing the anti-gay rhetoric within the church. He shared:

> 'I remember going to a church once and I stopped going after because the pastor got up on the pulpit and said if any gay person walked in the church, he would take a chair and beat them and straighten them out. You know? And I found that was so horrible. I never went back and I always say I would have a conversation with him but I never got to have that conversation with him. Not that I was coming out to him but just to let him know who is in the congregation and to be saying things like that, you know, you will push people away.' (David)

David chose to become less religious, following the rules and structure of religion "where you have to do this or have to do that", to instead be more spiritual, doing "more of what I believe in". He said, "It's me being at a place where I am comfortable in what I believe and what I practise." Even though his mother was still an avid church-goer, there was no friction between them, and he did not want to disrupt her relationship with him or the church by disclosing his sexual orientation.

The most secretive man we interviewed was 52-year-old Kishan, who, like David, was invested in maintaining aspects of his life as separate and private. Unlike David, he was a married father-of-one, and practising Hindu. He said,

> 'I would not tell my wife, siblings or child about myself. The simple reason is because I don't think that they will understand, and for who they know I am. They don't know I live a double life but *I know* I live a double life, and that part of my life is totally, totally hidden from the majority of people, from almost everybody. There is [*sic*] very few that know about me. So, I'll keep it hidden for as long as I could, and if at any point in time I think that it could be jeopardised or

anything like that, I would let go of bi-curious and stick with family orientation.' (Kishan)

Kishan grew up in Central Trinidad, in a farming family, the middle child among 11 siblings. Married for 27 years, he has a 25-year-old child and categorises himself as 'bi-curious', a designation that sounds speculative, like an exploration of one's sexuality rather than a term to describe over 40 years of sexual practices. "I'm curious about women just as I'm curious about guys, because on a daily basis I would get my dose of porn clips and naked girls from friends and family and stuff like that, whereas I would chat with gay guys also," he said. Throughout his adult life, Kishan has carried on affairs with men and women, some long-term and others just one-time occasions. Someone with practices similar to Kishan might use a term like 'bisexual' or 'queer', but naming practices are a personal preference. By choosing not to name his sexual practices or claim a sexual identity, Kishan evades confirming either as part of his self-concept. 'Curiosity' means he is free to explore his interests and seek pleasure. Even by saying he can walk away from this 'playing' if he wanted or needed to, he is marking it as a temporary, impermanent facet of himself, not significant enough to be fixed by naming it. Indeed, the naming of sexual praxis is not commonplace in the Caribbean (King, 2014; Ghisyawan, 2022) and is more associated with Western liberal queer politics.

Kishan raised another notable point when he positioned 'bi-curious' orientation as oppositional and exclusionary to 'family orientation' since he perceived them as different worlds of being and acting. He likened it to a 'double life', each posing a threat to the other. He could not let his sexual liaisons become known, as it would crack the 'normative' façade he worked very hard to maintain. His candid sharing of his secret queer pleasures incited questions about the mask's other side. What face was he wearing there? Who was he within his family? Kishan said he was very 'family-oriented', "If I'm going, majority, 95% of the time whenever I going anywhere is with my family. Always a family lime [get-together] or stuff like that." Yet, we know that alcoholism, physical and other forms of abuse are commonly associated with Indo-Trinidadian masculinity (Hosein, 2002, 2011; Reddock, 2016). As Shaheeda Hosein (2002) learned from the lives of elder Indo-Trinidadian women, while the cooperation of labour, pooled incomes and residential proximity of extended families allowed for families to grow wealth, they also exposed the less powerful, such as daughters-in-law and children, to violence. Alcoholism was common among poor Indo-Caribbean farming families (Hosein, 2002), similar to Kishan's, a rural agricultural extended family. "We had cows, goats. We used to milk and sell milk to [excluded information]. So yuh know, it was always like that in farming." Kishan's father was an alcoholic:

'My mother was just a housewife, so every time he come home drunk, we would go through some abuse. Sometimes he would beat us, beat my mother so all hours of the night and stuff she would have to be taking us, taking her kids and passing through the lagoon to go up by her mother's house to stay.' (Kishan)

Nevertheless, he had close relationships with his siblings, saying that despite being the fifth son, he took up the role of head of the family after his parents died, an expectation held for the eldest son. "Everybody used to look up to me," he said, "anything happening, the first person they would call would be me." By saying this, Kishan is demonstrating his status in the family. He has proven himself respectable and dependable, so much so that he has taken on these honoured roles as leader, confidant, protector and adviser.

Kishan has earned respect and built a reputation in the wider society as well, making a career for himself, accumulating wealth and gaining a large business circle. He belongs to many community groups serving workers' unions and human rights interests, and has friends from each of these spheres. He noted that in his close work friendships, "We talk about everything in life. We talk about sex, we make sexual jokes, things like that," but when it came to his other community commitments, "Absolutely nothing sexually oriented goes on there!" He knows thousands of people in every walk of life and tries to maintain professional relationships that can be mutually beneficial. "I would say I'm a loyal friend to whoever I'm friends with," he said, noting his willingness to do whatever he can to help a person in need. Thus, he achieved those aspects of hegemonic masculinity, a family, economic success, political power, a good reputation and respect in the community.

Kishan reflected on his childhood and upbringing, noting that teasing and coaxing among his male cousins led to instruction on masturbation and the sexual experimentation that continued into his adult life. He first learned about masturbation, colloquially referred to as 'jocking', from his male cousins. " 'Yuh know about jocking, boy?' It would have been conversations like that nah," he said. For most of his cousins, he believed, sexual play with each other "was just a growing something because all of them is married now", but he still 'played' and 'had fun' with one other cousin. There was even a moment when he had spent the night at his grandparents' house with other extended family members. He fell asleep on the couch while watching an Indian movie, but woke up to his uncle watching a graphic video of a man and woman having sex. He had gotten an erection, and his uncle touched him. Kishan dismisses the touch as "all well and good", despite it being unexpected and possibly unwanted at that moment. He does not characterise his experiences as abusive in any way, instead accepting them as formative of his own ongoing 'curiosity'.

Kishan has never told anyone about his same-sex desires for fear of being chastised or judged, so instead, he maintains strict compartmentalisation of his social and sexual worlds, never letting his queer sexual partners interrupt or engage with him when he is around family, and never letting his family become aware of the queer persons with whom he interacts. He has disclosed to a few other same-sex-loving persons he knows, including friends he made through an Adult Friend Finder site, where he found "some gay, some bi" persons to have occasional sexual conversations. He did not let them into other parts of his life. Kishan carefully curated his public persona, including his friend's list on social media. He said:

> 'If anybody should look at my profile on Facebook and on Instagram, the persons who I have there, I strictly keep that to family and very, very close friends who my wife will know like my co-workers. Other than that, absolutely nobody else. I have no girlfriends or anybody like that show up on my friend list. … Personal friends, I don't have any gay friends or bi friends coming home, at my home. I don't go out and lime with anybody.' (Kishan)

As head of the family, he tries to maintain an untarnished image.

People often maintain different social circles, as each relationship fulfils specific social and emotional needs, including online relationships (Ben-Ze'ev, 2004). Still, we ask, how does this silence and image management impact the men's happiness and experiences of intimacy? They enjoyed close relationships with their families, even though they kept their sexuality private. David and Kishan shared the belief that secrecy was a barrier to their erotic fulfilment but chose to sacrifice the pleasure and intimacy of long-term partnership to protect their familial relationships. For instance, Kishan said:

> 'It is difficult being married to be able to go out to meet anybody, so it's hardly likely I would go to meet anybody. I've known friends for years and we talk, we chat on camera. We do things on camera but to say, meet? It's difficult, it's hard because I can't host, most of the people I find cannot host, and I can't explain my absence. "Where yuh going?" yuh know? It is difficult sometimes being married.' (Kishan)

Contrastingly, serial-dater Errol did not have as close relationships with his family and said his lack of long-term committed relationships was due to his preference for casual entanglements. These men develop other non-sexual relationships for erotic fulfilment, intimacy and soul-sharing, such as their friendships and community-building work.

Creating queer community

What intimate spaces were available to same-sex desiring men, when relationships and families were not? The men we interviewed shared how they create queer community as a space wherein they can experience authenticity, intimacy and closeness to others. While sourcing contacts for this chapter, veteran activists noted that, to their knowledge, there were no older Indo-Trinidadian persons involved in their groups presently or in the past. David provided insight as to why this might be, saying that typical queer organising alienated people of Indo-Trinidadian descent, especially those from outside the capital, Port of Spain. In recent years, David had become involved in new organisations specifically catering to the queer people of south Trinidad, incorporating Indo-Trinidadian dress, dances and cultural events. Likewise, Errol's occasional drag performance drew on an Indian aesthetic, bringing his cultural experience to the predominantly African-Trinidadian drag spaces. Both Errol and David draw on their Indo-Trinidadian culture to inform their community-building practices, growing the possibilities for intimacy in non-sexual relationships, and expanding potential dating pools.

After T&T's first Pride Parade in 2018, David was invited to a meeting where the dozen attendees shared feelings of exclusion and alienation. They felt the bulk of queer events occurred in north Trinidad, often inaccessible to people in the south due to the distance, time, cost and safety issues associated with travel and accommodations in unfamiliar territory. 'North' in Trinidad typically refers to the urbanised East–West Corridor at the foothills of the Northern Range. 'South' alludes 'to the rural, the Indian, the backward spaces of Trinidad from the vantage point of cosmopolitan Port-of-Spain' (Puar 2001: 1056), even though these areas are racially diverse. David said that "the people of South", suggesting Indo-Trinidadian, were "never given much scope" or invited to put on their activities in the customary spaces and organisations, so by forming their group, "by doing it in South, among ourselves, I think it shows more who we are in South" (David). A second group soon emerged in South, allowing these communities who once felt marginalised from existing queer spaces to make their presence more pronounced. A group from South joined the 2020 Pride Parade in Port of Spain, performing Indian dance and dressed in traditional Indian clothing. "So, you could have actually look and say 'Those are South people there', you know?" (David). Indo-Trinidadian queer communities felt that their sexuality had a space within their culture, but cultural spaces, such as temples or at festivals, or even in day-to-day life, were not distinctly 'queer'. They responded by creating their own spaces, new arenas, such as Divali celebrations and Indo-centric drag personas, wherein gender and sexual transgression can be celebrated alongside cultural identity, allowing for the assertion of 'Indianness' in a queer-affirming space.

David mentioned the increased attendance of people from South and Central participating in the Queen of Queens pageant than when it first started. Jasbir Puar (2001) assessed T&T's drag pageant space in the 1990s, noting just one pair of performers of Indian descent, although audiences were evenly mixed in races and genders, and largely middle class. While the African-Trinidadian performances were seen as drag, the Indian 'couple' mimicked a heterosexual love scene typical of Bollywood movies and were not seen as drag in the same way. The audience was familiar with the performers' gender-bending dance performances, so it was 'normal'. In fact, until the early twentieth century women did not perform in public, so Indo-Trinidadian men dressed as women to perform as dancers and in plays (Gooptar, 2015), so it was not unusual to see this type of performance. The more recent coupling of assumed sexual practices with transgressive gender performances occurred in light of Western narratives of queerness that positioned sexuality within gender. The couple, called Vikram and Sasha, narrated a 'long history of living and working together' in the dance company they ran (Puar, 2001: 1057), and described living in the Central town of Chaguanas 'as "openly" as any gay couple ever could, in a somewhat accepted/tolerated/negotiated transgendered partnership' (Puar, 2001: 1058). The public assumes that their gender transgression includes sexual involvement; even though Puar did not confirm whether they were sexually involved. The men are still read as a couple.

Errol has attended these drag pageants once or twice a year for the last 30 years. He dresses in drag but does not participate in the pageant. He decided to do it "mostly for the experience because I had friends who does [*sic*] it. They were very comfortable with it so I tried. But like in my late years, my thirties, not very young, tender age." He borrowed clothes to debut his drag persona at Queen of Queens, but after that went shopping to equip his wardrobe with the clothes, shoes and accessories needed to "just be(ing) me in an Indian outfit", as he phrased it. Marcus first met Errol, in drag as Savitri, at the pageant. In full Bollywood regalia, she wore intricately beaded skirts (*gharara*) or pant suits (*shalwars*), always with an *orhni*, bangles and a nose ring. Marcus was thrilled to see Savitri reflect his Indian culture within the Westernised mainstream queer spaces where Indian representation was lacking. As a drag artist himself, performing under the stage name Tifa Wine, Indo-Caribbean queer scholar Ryan Persadie draws on the embodied practices and knowledge of Caribbean brown and black *Tanties*, a colloquial term for aunties, who have taught him what it means to 'free up yourself' (Persadie 2021). From queer people, he has learned what it means to 'locate joy as a practice of resistance'. In a video feature, Persadie explains that we perform all the time in all the spaces we occupy, noting that we can examine 'how knowledge that lives in the body is activated through performance'. In this same way, Errol's performance of Savitri is deeply rooted in his own embodied knowledge of himself as a queer Indo-Trinidadian man. Decolonial thinkers such as Audre Lorde, Gloria Anzaldua and M. Jacqui Alexander emphasise the knowledge to be gained from our own embodiment, especially as colonised peoples have been alienated from themselves through colonial violence. Embodied knowledge means reconnecting with the body, the mind and the spirit to know who one is, beyond the external criteria used to define them. For instance, older Indo-Trinidadian women are desexualised to fit the pious image of 'mother', which undermines their sexual desire as living people (Aneja and Vaidya, 2016). As transgressive figures, *Tanties* challenge the prescriptions placed on women's sexuality and gender performance by demonstrating their agency and personhood.

As these Indo-Trinidadian men grew older, they too felt pressured to fit idealised heteronormative roles. It became more difficult for them to claim space in the queer community and meet potential romantic partners. Not being active or visible in the community, David finds it hard to meet people. "I was never that sort of person to just be out there, wearing my sexuality on my sleeve, so that everybody knows, 'aye, there is this fella who is gay and he is looking for a companion' that sort of thing" (David). Keeping private meant remaining hidden from potential dating pools. "Even though I'm active in the group and in the community," David shares, "even with some of the activities the group would have, I would not go because I wouldn't enjoy it." David was more reserved than the group he was serving, calling himself a 'home-body' and relying on gay friends to introduce him to other gay men who he could potentially date. He was not comfortable with having casual sex, preferring to be in a relationship, unlike Errol, who came across as a social butterfly, thriving on the adoration of friends and lovers. Even during our interview, Errol had two or three young male friends in the same room who interjected, despite our suggestion that a private conversation might have been more suitable. However, the men's cajoling drew out Errol's playfulness and encouraged him to share. For instance, when asked who the men were, one of them shouted, "Dais meh man", meaning 'boyfriend'. Errol dismisses him, saying, "We is family." The young man responded, "We is the family from Cunupia [a town in central Trinidad]. We don't have sex," and is met with raucous laughter from the bunch, so he quickly adds, "That's a lie and unprotected too." The joking manner makes it unclear whether these claims of casual unprotected sex were true, but it might have been, as Errol confessed to enjoying the company of younger men and engaging in casual sex, sometimes with multiple partners over a period of time, instead of having long-term relationships. He clarified, "Not like I was dating multiple persons and they don't know. There was always just one person at a time," but these relationships did not become long-term. He said, "I don't know. It seems to me that [a long-term partner] would be difficult to find, especially in the gay community. They are just too promiscuous." He used Facebook to meet friends of friends to have sexual meet-ups but did not form relationships.

Each of the men had their reasons for keeping their circles of friends small and for not pursuing same-sex sexual and romantic relationships. Consequently, they all struggled to form intimate bonds with either romantic partners, members of their communities or their families. Even though social media was a tool for growing community, it was also a space to carefully curate what community looked like in order to maintain the desired public persona. Having community, whether in activism, drag performances or in civil organisations, did not necessarily mean these men had more options for forming intimate bonds, as intimacy requires a measure of emotional vulnerability and openness, and they were all still guarded.

Conclusion: the cost of the veil

Although the men we interviewed shared their thoughts and experiences, we could sense restraint, and much being left unsaid. They allowed us to glance below the veil but did not dare lift it completely. They allowed us to see aspects of their secret lives, but did not dare feel comfortable enough to shed the protective layers they had built up to keep out unwanted attention, shame and disrepute. The metaphor of the veil not only alludes to secrecy, but also to the traditional gender roles that continue to influence these men and their choices. For Caribbean men, regardless of race or class, there is a social penalty to their coming out, and to their keeping silent about their sexuality. As these Indo-Trinidadian men navigate the possibilities for having intimacy outside the 'respectable' order, friendships and family get foregrounded in place of sexual intimacy. David was the only one who thought about how his sexuality might be seen specifically as a failure of his masculinity so tried to uphold an unquestionable masculine image, but Kishan too feared being chastised and treated differently for having sexual desire for men. For him, heterosexuality is his only viable option, as even 'bi-curiosity' would jeopardise his respectability in the society. They all believed family honour was at stake, and it became the most powerful motivator for regulating their public image and behaviours. They did not want themselves or their families to face the shame and social consequences of being sexually transgressive, such as alienation and ill-repute. These feelings, though rooted in traditional ideas of filial piety, are strengthened by the intergenerational socio-economic cooperation that characterises Indo-Caribbean extended family networks. Kishan and David have stronger family ties then Errol and were consequently more protective of their social image and felt obliged to uphold the duties of their social roles, as son, brother, uncle, husband, father, adviser, mentor, and whatever other roles they fulfilled in their families and communities.

Although many younger queer people (in our social and academic experience) still perceive the risk of social and economic consequences of coming out or being openly queer, there is certainly a generational difference as queer communities increasingly create safe spaces, and as society becomes more understanding and accepting of diverse gender and sexual performances. The cultural scripts of the men we interviewed, as 'Indo-Trinidadian', Hindu, Pentecostal or rural, are all based on conservative notions of masculinity that have developed within modern society. Today, young queer men are exposed to multiple scripts, including what is visible on various mass and social media, in the historic and religious narratives of many global cultures, and the lives they see other queer people leading in T&T and abroad. While silence and secrecy remain strategies usable by all, a politics of visibility at least allows for queer possibilities to be seen, modelled and possibly recreated. Additionally, it allows for works like this one to give insight into otherwise unseen and unstudied areas.

Although religious opposition, microaggressions and acts of violence still occur, the 2018 decriminalisation sent a clear message that the state should not condemn the sexual practices of consenting adults in T&T. Although many international funding agencies uncritically bring queer neoliberal ideals with rights and visibility politics to 'postcolonial' spaces such as T&T, their resources also allow local groups to tailor interventions, such as the Sexual Cultures of Justice Project, which involved programming from multiple local organisations for teachers, law enforcement, students and parents, along with public outreach on social and mass media, to destigmatise homosexuality and expand notions of acceptable gender and sexual practices. Embodied queerness and activism, like these projects, work to dismantle ignorance and homophobic intolerance that effect the systematic erasure and dehumanisation of queer people, using local knowledge systems and cultural referents. Together, they envision and co-create spaces wherein queer people can be their authentic selves, can experience love and happiness, can imagine and actualise their life goals and dreams. Indeed, dreaming, imagining and envisioning illuminate the pathways to a decolonial queer future.

Note

[1] Wining, and other Caribbean dance forms, such as 'jukking', daggering, perreo and even twerking, can be traced to enslaved Africans, and result from a combination of interculturation with other ethnic groups, particularly creolisation, the mixing of African and European cultures in the specific context of the plantation societies of the Americas, but also Middle Eastern and South Asian migrants who had significant influence in some territories such as Trinidad. The hip gyrations and bodily movements of these dances were at various times barred, shunned and demonised across the region by European colonists and postcolonial political leaders.

Bibliography

Acosta, K. (2010) '"How Could You Do This to Me?": How Lesbian, Bisexual, and Queer Latinas Negotiate Sexual Identity with Their Families.' *Black Women, Gender & Families* 4(1): 63–85.

Aneja, A. and Vaidya, S. (2016) *Embodying Motherhood: Perspectives from Contemporary India*. New Delhi: Sage Publications.

Bahadur, G. (2015) 'Postcards from Empire', *Dissent Magazine*. Available from: www.dissentmagazine.org/article/postcards-from-empire. Accessed 4 July 2022.

Ben-Ze'ev, A. (2004) *Love Online: Emotions on the Internet*. Cambridge: Cambridge University Press.

Chevannes, B. (2001) *Learning to Be a Man: Culture, Socialization and Gender Identity in Five Caribbean Communities*. Kingston, Jamaica: University of the West Indies Press.

Ghisyawan, K. (2016) 'Queering Cartographies of Caribbean Sexuality and Citizenship: Mapping Female Same-Sex Desire, Identities and Belonging in Trinidad.' Doctoral Dissertation. University of the West Indies.

Ghisyawan, K. (2022) *Erotic Cartographies: Decolonization and the Queer Caribbean Imagination*. New Brunswick: Rutgers University Press.

Gooptar, P. (2015) *The Ramleela of Sangre Grande*. Port of Spain: NALIS.

Horton, B.A. (2018) 'What's So "Queer" About Coming Out? Silent Queers and Theorizing Kinship Agonistically in Mumbai.' *Sexualities* 21(7): 1059–1074.

Hosein, G. (2012) 'Modern Navigations: Indo-Trinidadian Girlhood and Gender-Differential Creolization.' *Caribbean Review of Gender Studies* 6: 1–24.

Hosein G. and L. Outar (2012) 'Indo-Caribbean Feminisms: Charting Crossings in Geography, Discourse, and Politics.' *Caribbean Review of Gender Studies* 6: 1–10.

Hosein, S. (2002) 'Until Death Do Us Part? Marriage, Divorce and the Indian Woman.' *Oral History Journal* 30(1): 63–72.

Hosein, S. (2011) 'Unlikely Matriarchs: Rural Indo-Trinidadian Women in the Domestic Sphere.' In *Bindi: The Multi-faceted Lives of Indo-Caribbean Women*, edited by R. Kanhai, 101–120. Kingston, Jamaica: University of the West Indies Press.

King, R. (2014) *Island Bodies: Transgressive Sexualities in the Caribbean Imagination*. Gainesville: University Press of Florida.

Kissoon, M. (2019) 'Processes of Disclosure and Gender Negotiations amongst Indo-Caribbean Male Survivors of Child Sexual Abuse/Sexual Assault.' Master's Thesis. Institute for Gender and Development Studies, UWI, Trinidad.

Lokaisingh-Meighoo, S. (2000) 'Jahaji Bhai: Notes on the Masculine Subject and Homoerotic Subtext of Indo-Caribbean Identity.' *Small Axe* 7: 77–92.

Mohammed, P. (1998) 'Ram and Sita: The Reconstruction of Gender Identities among Indians in Trinidad through Mythology.' In *Caribbean Portraits: Essays on Gender Ideologies and Identities*, edited by C. Barrow, 394–441. Kingston, Jamaica: Ian Randle.

Niranjana, T. (2011) 'Indian Nationalism and Female Sexuality: A Trinidadian Tale.' In *Sex and the Citizen: Interrogating the Caribbean*, edited by F. Smith, 101–124. Charlottesville: University of Virginia Press.

Persadie, R. (2020) '"Meh Just Realize I's Ah Coolie Bai": Indo-Caribbean Masculinities, Chutney Genealogies, and Qoolie Subjectivities.' *Middle Atlantic Review of Latin American Studies* 4(2): 56–86.

Persadie, R. (2021) 'Meet U of T Student Ryan Persadie.' YouTube. www.youtube.com/watch?v=WAwP6xxYHGA

Puar, J.K. (2001) 'Global Circuits: Transnational Sexualities and Trinidad.' *Signs, Globalization and Gender* 26(4): 1039–1065.

Raghunandan, K. (2012) 'Hyphenated Identities: Negotiating "Indianness" and Being Indo-Trinidadian.' *Caribbean Review of Gender Studies* 6: 1–19.

Reddock, R., ed (2004) *Interrogating Caribbean Masculinities: Theoretical and Empirical Analysis*. Kingston: The University of the West Indies Press.

Reddock, R. (2016) 'Indo-Caribbean Masculinities and Indo-Caribbean Feminisms: Where Are We Now?' In *Indo-Caribbean Feminist Thought: Genealogies, Theories, Enactments*, edited by L. Outar and G. Hosein, 263–282. New York: Palgrave Macmillan.

Sampath, N. (1993) 'An Evaluation of the "Creolisation" of Trinidad East Indian Adolescent Masculinity.' In *Trinidad Ethnicity*, edited by K. Yelvington, 235–253. London: Macmillan.

Vanita, R. (2005) 'Homosexuality and Hinduism.' *Gay & Lesbian Vaishnava Association (GALVA-108) Information & Support for LGBTI Vaishnavas & Hindus*. Accessed 5 January 2015. www.galva108.org/hinduism.html

Wahab, A. (2012) 'Homophobia as the State of Reason: The Case of Postcolonial Trinidad and Tobago.' *GLQ* 18(4): 481–505. https://doi.org/10.1215/10642684-1600707

3

Older *kinnars*, ageism and sexuality during the COVID-19 pandemic

Anushkaa Arora अनुष्का अरोड़ा

Introduction

'*Dharma*' (righteous conduct), '*Artha*' (the pursuit of material success and wealth), '*Moksha*' (ultimate salvation) and '*Kama*' (sensual pleasure) are the four '*Purusharthas*' (vital expressions of human life), which have, since ancient times, been considered in India as essentials of existence (Roy, 2021). In India, '*Kama*' has been depicted widely and historically through eroticism, is evident in temple sculptures and, some may be surprised to know, in ways that depict various forms of sexuality.

In effect, diverse sexual expression was widespread and largely accepted in India until colonial rule, which increased gender disparities in a society where women had, at least, enjoyed some measure of equality in being credited for and encouraged to work. Following the colonial encounter, they came to be regarded more as instruments of reproduction (Thakur, 2012), and preferably of male children, which reinforced the patriarchal misogyny enmeshed with colonial racism. Women were henceforth excluded from authority or as belonging in public spaces and became associated with the private spaces of domesticity, fitted for household chores, leaving education, culture, science and politics to men (Thakur, 2012). This era not only witnessed women's subjugation to domestic drudgery, but, perhaps unsurprisingly, it also saw the worsening of the social conditions of *kinnars* (what we might term trans people), who had been hitherto generally respected (Wadhwa, 2018). Colonial rule criminalised, pathologised and thus excluded those thought to represent non-normative forms of 'gender' and 'sexuality', such as transgender individuals or the third gender ('*tritiya prakriti*') of *kinnars* or *hijras*. Following Mayer et al (2008: 990), the term 'transgender' (or trans) is used inclusively to describe individuals embodying 'gender identities, expressions, or behaviors not traditionally associated with their birth sex'. Life could be tougher and even more unjust for *kinnars*. While women and *kinnars* were both subjected to sexual assault, natal women still had a voice in law. *Kinnars* have, until very recently, lacked any legal status or support and have experienced limited spaces where their concerns could be articulated and heard and mutual support could be developed.

Despite the widespread depiction of erotica since ancient times, which has been explicitly displayed in sacred places such as temples, and verse such as the 'Kama sutra', written by ancient philosopher, 'Vatsyayana', to explain the art of sex and sexual gratification, Indian society has still largely considered sex to be a taboo or a practice which is not to be talked about openly (Kalra and Shah, 2013). Such stigmatisation of sexual matters, along with the derogation of women and kinnars, seen as gender non-conforming, has been linked, during the colonial era, to sexual assault, violence and other forms of reputational inequality in public spaces (Talwar, 1999). In a country where sex was already considered to be taboo, *kinnars* were considered 'pariahs' worthy of being ostracised. Even though they managed to survive the opprobrium of Indian society during the colonial era, their situation today appears equally gloomy. Despite legal recognition of *kinnars* as a 'Third Gender', the decriminalisation of homosexuality (ending the 1861 colonial-era law, which remained in force for 157 years), the passing of The Transgender Persons Act 2019 (giving protection to the *kinnars* in India against atrocities), *kinnars* still struggle to achieve due recognition and respect for their gender difference. The law may have changed in India more recently but, as will be seen, the legacy of 'patriarchal colonialism' casts a long shadow, and public attitudes to gender and sexual difference may lag behind legal change for some time to come. It took Britain at least 30 years from the decriminalisation of homosexuality for public attitudes to soften towards lesbian and gay people (Weeks, 2007). The status of trans people there and elsewhere in the post-industrial global North and West remains contested, given fierce debates about the ontology of gender related to campaigns for legal self-recognition by trans people to legitimate control over definition and to avoid over-medicalising aspects of the transition process.

For millennia, *kinnars* and later life sexuality in India have been neglected, literally as unspeakable subjects. If one's ageing, gendered sexuality is so unspeakable, it is not surprising that *kinnars* would be rendered more vulnerable to mental health difficulties and, as a consequence, deterioration of physical health. This chapter will, then, focus on what is it like to live as an older *kinnar*, and the pressures they face in a society that marginalises them. In particular, and in view of the dearth of studies addressing older *kinnars* in India (and older trans people in other global regions), I set out to understand how age played a vital role in shaping the sexual outlook of the *kinnars* in northern India during the COVID-19 outbreak, which worsened their situation. With the aid of Colaizzi's (1978) phenomenological approach (explained later on in the chapter), I attempt to identify and describe the intersecting forms of age-related, gendered and sexual stigmatisation and its impacts on older *kinnars'* accounts of sexuality. The findings are based on semi-structured interviews with 20 *kinnars*, who ranged in age from 23 to 68 years old. Interview questions revolved around: general outlook on life (life chances); how they defined later life; what difficulties they faced (or expected to face) during later life and especially in terms of sexual practices and pleasures during the COVID-19 outbreak; whether any decline in sexual activity has led to trauma during sexual confrontations; and any other concerns about a sexual future.

By way of contextualising the empirical analysis, I begin with a discussion of ageing and ageism in relation to *kinnars*, followed by consideration of their social, legal and aesthetic-sexual context. I then move to address, in more detail, the particular complex situation of older *kinnars* during the pandemic. The latter issue includes some consideration of how declining health can affect sexual activity and the ability to secure a livelihood necessary for survival in a nation where health and welfare provision is piecemeal, underfunded and over-reliant on voluntary services and individualised responsibility.

Ageing and ageism: fears of loss and decline

A famous poem (verse 200), by ancient poet Bhartrihari (1967: 147), sums up fear of growing older (as presentiment of mortality) that can involve physical 'suffering' and 'the anguish of estrangement and disease'.

The verse of Bhartrihari succinctly elucidates the denigration faced by individuals across the lifespan, especially in old age when confrontation with emotions and physical incapacities becomes an unavoidable part of quotidian life. If ageing is seen as a natural, inevitable phenomenon that affects us all, we might well question why people in later life should be subjected to ageist (and other forms of) discrimination, which affect their well-being. As intimated, the situation is far worse for trans individuals, and older ones especially, who face multiple exclusions from any health and welfare services because of hostile attitudes based on ignorance and prejudice concerning their ageing, gendered difference.

For the purposes of this chapter, ageism is described as an individual and societal stereotype that results in prejudice and discrimination based on age. In addition to 'race', and sexual bigotry, ageism permeates Indian society (Achenbaum, 2018). This process intensifies when focused on older *kinnars* who are confronted with the complexly enmeshed and fissile influences of ageism, cisgenderism and heteronormativity that serve to distinguish between acceptable and unacceptable forms of gendered sexual expression deemed pathological (Vance, 1991).

As Colaizzi's approach deployed later in the analysis helps to reveal, older *kinnars* are the most frequent victims of hate crimes in India. It is surprising and sad to note that, for older *kinnars*, their own community offers little support, and individual *kinnars* are forced to rely on their individual capacity for resilience that they may (or may not) have developed in the face of public hostility. Given that *kinnars* are obliged to rely on sex work for survival, this can be very difficult beyond the age of about 40. Indeed, insecurity looms around the age of about 35 for *kinnars* when their beauty is seen as beginning to fade. Indeed, the study on which this chapter is based, indicated that a clear majority (18 of 20) of *kinnars* deploy various beautification practices such as toning of skin, hair treatments, cosmetic surgeries, all to resemble femininity and maintain the semblance of youth to prolong sexual marketability. Study participants reported that such practices increased their chances of attracting male counterparts (customers) who would desire to have intercourse with a *kinnar* who looks beautiful, as opposed to a regular or old, plain-looking *kinnar*. Hence, cosmetic surgeries are undergone, despite the risks and discomfort, to prolong the ability to attract the male attention necessary for survival.

Global catastrophes such as the COVID-19 pandemic present serious socio-economic and political challenges and nowhere more acutely than in less industrial global regions where income and wealth are more unevenly distributed and welfare systems are less developed. In India, intensive care algorithms and triaging for the treatment of COVID-19 with limited resources meant that younger people affected by the illness were prioritised over older people, some of whom were effectively abandoned, if not sacrificed (Choi and Taylor, 2020). Furthermore, mental health problems that were triggered by preventive measures such as lockdowns, became major issues for discussion on global social media platforms. Young or older, such discussions completely ignored the situation and economic, social, emotional and sexual needs of *kinnars*, who, as will be seen in the later empirical discussion, were hit very badly by the pandemic.

The context of *kinnars* during the pandemic

In India, and because they find it difficult to secure regular employment, *kinnars* are obliged to rely on '*badhai dena*' or sex work and begging as their main sources of income. By the onset of COVID-19, such sources of income came to a halt, causing anxiety for this section of the community and particularly for older *kinnars*. Today, *kinnars* are largely disrespected and ill-treated, which has had even greater impact on older *kinnars* who encounter ageism mixed with cisgenderism, which means that they have to deal with considerable socio-economic and psychological challenges resulting from prejudice and discrimination. Despite legalisation of *kinnars* as a third gender in India, decriminalisation of same-sex activity as an offence, and formalisation of The Transgender Persons (Protection of Rights) Act 2019, there is still a long way to go before older trans people will be able to experience peace of mind and the ontological security of being able freely to express their authentic selves.

Furthermore, much less has been spoken about the sexual outlook of older *kinnars* during the height of the pandemic. Not only is there a dearth of studies on *kinnars*, because of hostility and stigmatisation, but also, consequently, older *kinnars* especially are reluctant to talk to researchers. However, the pandemic did direct some attention towards this multiply oppressed segment of society (though, as stated earlier, the greying minority was generally neglected) (Banerjee and Rao, 2021). Nevertheless, it is worth bearing in mind that there are at least three million older *kinnars* among the Indian population (Rhude, 2018). This is nearly equivalent to the population of Jaipur and more than Manchester.

Just as significantly, in our study, older *kinnars* generally considered themselves to be old after the age of 40. The majority (18 out of 20 study participants) reported becoming anxious about their conjoined sexual and economic futures from around the age of 35. Such anxiety was generally reflected in concerns about being abandoned by a partner, loss of sexual allure and performance, possible health and vitality concerns, all of which are tied to the ability to generate an income for survival. Mixed in with this anxiety are cultural and aesthetic concerns that society would start to look on *kinnars* with fear and disgust upon losing their 'artificial' beauty. The question, who is an old *kinnar*, is, then, a matter internalised by *kinnar* culture (including clients or lovers) but reflecting wider cultural concerns, of a kind impacting upon older women generally about the loss of beauty, vitality and, hence, social value.

The context for older *kinnars*

From interviews with young, middle-aged and older *kinnars*, the fears mentioned earlier further exacerbate the tendency towards disinterest in sexual activities expressed by older *kinnar*. Living in constant fear of hostility and with economic struggle and precarity can lead to mental health problems that can incapacitate sexual performance (Cramer et al, 2012). Such oppressive circumstances can lead to social withdrawal, reinforcing the marginalisation and isolation and possibly risking being outcast or shunned by the wider community. One of the few significant studies on the Indian greying minority is by Banerjee and Rao (2021) whose research addresses the psychosocial challenges during COVID-19. These authors conclude that during the pandemic, older *kinnars*, who are generally unheard, were exposed to extreme emotional and social risks. The only solution to address their health and well-being issues is to implement the necessary policy/policies for the welfare of the community that spread awareness and empower the elderly gender minorities. This subject is politically overlooked rather than novel per se and I concur with the view of Bannerjee and Rao, but recognise that persuading a wider public to accept policy measures further supporting *kinnars* would be very challenging in the present political climate created by a socially, culturally and economically conservative government.

However, while Indian scholarship remains largely silent on the concerns of older *kinnars*, there is some literature from outside India that can help illuminate the vulnerabilities of older *kinnar*, such as work by Fredriksen-Goldsen et al (2014). This study elaborates on internalised stigma and victimisation as mediators of the relationship between gender identity and health outcomes. Unfortunately, this study confines itself to the mental health of older trans people in a global North context at a particular point in time. Hence, our aim here is to analyse the first-hand accounts of *kinnars*, young and old, and both concerned with the impacts of ageing sexuality on overall well-being. In terms of overall health and well-being in older persons, sexual health is an essential but underappreciated component (Bannerjee and Rao, 2021).

Despite the tenor of the discussion earlier in this chapter, there are glimpses of hope in the guise of more agentic sexual possibilities for some older people. Indeed, Bannerjee and Rao (2021: no page number) discuss sexuality in older Indian adults and observe some possibilities for 'sexuality as a mode of resilience' and 'emotional stability and intimacy as attributes of sexual pleasure'. However, such possibilities appear to be quite gendered. The same authors describe how majority men (cisgender and heterosexual) once refrained from discussing sexuality but, more recently, have begun to consider it to be a vital aspect of well-being and to welcome the idea of a companion/s with whom they can openly discuss sexual matters. Majority men in later life tend to reduce sexual activity with their partners on account of difficulties achieving and/or maintaining erection, or else premature ejaculation, which may benefit from discussion. In contrast, the older majority of Indian women commonly have learned to consider it wrong to indulge in sex and rather tend to immerse themselves in religious and family duties. Further, the older *kinnars* in our study reported difficulty in maintaining sexual activities with age due to health issues and especially performing anal sex during old age. As analysis of the stories of the oldest *kinnars* will show, mobility difficulties (such as arthritis) can impede or even make sexual activity impossible.

Analysis: fear of loss of youth, distancing from 'old', and desexualisation

To extend understanding, Colaizzi's (1978) phenomenological approach was deployed, which helped identify the impact of 'stigmatisation' on the study participants. This strategy concerns whittling down of interview materials to the core or essential structures of the phenomenon in question – in this case, *kinnars*' concerns about sex and sexuality in later life. It involves stripping away all aspects of study participants' accounts to reach a core or what is central to the main research puzzle concerning *kinnars*' experience of sex and sexuality in later life. More specifically, this method was applied following Colaizzi's seven-step approach, which involved:

1. familiarisation with all participant stories, reading across accounts twice;
2. identification of the most relevant statements in relation to the main research question from the wider dataset;
3. initial interpretation of accounts, which required formulating 'early' meanings;
4. clustering the initial interpretations into key themes;
5. summarising of all themes identified;
6. developing a wider structure from the identified themes;
7. final verification of the salient themes.

In more practical terms, 20 *kinnars*, who ranged in age from 23 to 68 years in northern India, were recruited as interviewees with the help of colleagues in a local college of music and dance, bearing in mind the connection with *kinnars*' skills in these cultural activities. Further, a set of interview questions was asked of young, middle-aged and older *kinnars* revolving around: outlook towards life; how they understand old age; difficulties faced during old age, especially in terms of sexual activity; how satisfying sexual activities are; how/whether they feel they have aged; energy post-midlife; challenges faced during the COVID-19 outbreak; whether/how decline in sexual activity leads to trauma or whether trauma leads to decline in sexual activity; risks involved during sexual encounters; and desire in the possible context of the decline in sexual activity.

Discussion in this section is divided into key motifs in the case of each age-grouping: young(er); middle-aged (a group between younger and older as understood within *kinnar* culture); and old(er) *kinnars*. It involves analysis of themes that clustered around gender and sexual stigmatisation combined with the effects of (increasing) ageism. In doing this, I have attempted to create a means for older *kinnars* to voice their problems and articulate solutions to the challenges that confront them.

Young to middle-aged kinnars *(aged 23–35): fear of loss*

In response to the question, 'At what age is a *kinnar* considered old', there was a clear consensus among the cohort (ten younger *kinnars*) that a *kinnar* of 45 years is 'a very old *kinnar*'. Such accounts were embedded in various other aspects of life experience that concerned the challenges of ageing and sexual well-being and concerns for their future. Indeed, study participants had no doubt about what their future would be like. Older *kinnars* were viewed as a cautionary tale and younger *kinnars* spoke of taking precautions not to repeat the mistakes of their old/er counterparts who suffer the revenge of old age and are also shunned by the wider community, which results not only in isolation, but also deprivation of any sexual opportunity and hence income.

Given the fears mentioned earlier, it perhaps comes as no surprise that younger *kinnars* were painfully aware of the transitory nature of beauty, youth and vitality. While they may not have used such terms, such awareness, along with use of beauty regimes and cosmetic surgeries, such discourse indicates the culturally constructed character of categories such as age, femininity/gender and beauty itself. However, considering the younger participants' accounts just described, it could be concluded that fear around loss of youth and beauty, reflects ageist/youth-oriented, cisgenderist and heteronormative expectations of femininity that redound to the detriment of all *kinnars*' experiences of sexuality and that this fear/process takes root at an early age. Such discursive regulation also has tangible consequences for access to the sex work that forms a vital part of *kinnars*' income and sociality (isolation even from other *kinnars*), and the lack of both of which can result in mental and physical health problems. In a competitive scenario or sexual marketplace, which places older subjects at the bottom of the *kinnar* hierarchy and with the least sexual capital, the latter can also be displaced from sex work by their younger counterparts.

The isolation just described appears to have been exacerbated by the COVID-19 pandemic. In effect, no one was allowed to enter the 'Dera/Basera', a place allotted to older *kinnars*, and no financial support or food was provided to them. Even the young *kinnars* were unable to help older ones due to restricted entry to older *kinnars*' spaces. Of course, the sequestration of older *kinnars* meant that they were deprived of opportunities for sex with any partner and from sex work itself. As a consequence, younger study participants observed that such forms of deprivation had contributed to the deaths of older *kinnars*, exacerbated by COVID-19, and primarily those belonging to the '*Gharana*': a social group who make a living through entertaining and with fewer socio-economic and cultural resources.

Middle-aged kinnars (38–45): distancing from the category 'old(er)'

Similar questions to those put to the younger participants were asked of this middle group of eight interviewees and there was some overlap in the answers from both groups, who identified common themes and issues in terms of ageism in relation to their gendered sexuality and its effects on their ability to make a living. Nonetheless, it may come as no surprise that this middle group registered feeling such ageism more acutely than their younger counterparts. If the latter largely anticipated sexual redundancy, the former spoke of actually experiencing it. Participants in this group could appear traumatised, insecure and distinctly uncomfortable when discussing their experiences of later life sexuality.

However, what also emerged as significant and distinct, and, again, underscoring the discursive power of gendered ageism, was how *kinnars* in this age group felt the need to distance themselves from the category 'old' or 'older' by applying such epithets to *kinnars* aged 50 plus. From such strategic avoidances (or perhaps defence mechanisms), it could be concluded that *kinnars* are implicated in a form of queering and relativising of age and later life. But, this occurs less in resistant, questioning ways than ways that partly reflect lower life expectancy in India and the wider constraints of a gendered ageism that would sound familiar to older women in global North and 'Western' contexts to whom valid sexual status is often denied. Whether this instantiates or stems from neocolonial relations or is now largely a phenomenon peculiar to modernising India is a point worthy of further debate and separate treatment.

Besides, there were familiar concerns expressed by this middle group about loss of allure with age and precarious income. For instance, one study participant opined: 'We enjoy sex, as we know more years and we would not be even needed.' Another participant phrased the issue even more bleakly when she asked: 'Who would want to have sex with his or her grandparents?' Such statements show that even if *kinnars* retain vitality and vigour in later life, they still risk being seen as redundant as sex partners. Further still, such remarks are redolent of what Simpson (2021: 36–45), writing in an English context, has called 'ageist erotophobia'. This represents a form of phobic discourse or negative aesthetic that can involve visceral disgust at the idea of older people as sexual beings. In particular, it constructs older people as unsexy (they are neither desiring subjects nor worthy of being desired), which thus positions them in an abject, 'post-sexual' status that is considered beyond any sexual expression or practice.

However, despite the commonly held concerns mentioned earlier, differences of education (markers if not a proxy for status and class) among *kinnars* were also invoked. Indeed, one participant, who held a Master's degree in English Studies (where queer theory has established a strong foothold), was able to speak of relative economic security and how her education could be used to question heteronormative, cisgenderist ageism. Despite her cultural resources, the participant remained concerned about the impending loss of social value and economic deficit for *kinnars* that can come with ageing, and especially much later in life. This study participant explained: "Our partners are just using us. They are only [wanting] to have fun. There is nothing called love. We know once we grow old or old age signs start being exhibited, they will leave us. They will anyway leave us because of society's pressure and/or their own family pressure."

Insecurity is the word which aptly describes all *kinnars* irrespective of education. The more educated study subject did not involve herself in sex work for earning her livelihood. Rather, she was a teacher and taught English language to fellow *kinnars*. Despite having a stable job for the time being, she was very perturbed about her ageing, and categorically mentioned that her partner only remains with her while her body displays the essence of youth. The same participant spoke of being secure for the time being with respect to her job but was more sceptical as to whether she could retain such employment in later life, and worried how she would provide for herself in the future. Further, she expressed fears about losing her partner and thus her sex life, which impacted on the quality of her sex life in the present: "Due to so much stress, at times, I am unable to perform well during sex with my partner. Hence, he leaves."

Older kinnars *(aged 65 and 68): abjection, rejection, violence and symbolic annihilation*

Given the problems described earlier in relation to recruiting participants because of their distrust in the face of widespread public hostility based on ignorance, it was perhaps no surprise, and even a small wonder, that two *kinnars* aged 65 and 68 were recruited for interview.

The main theme that emerged during interviews was a complete lack of inclination towards sexual activity and evidence of further withdrawal from any public life. Indeed, the participants' accounts were dominated by the theme of alienation from any significant others, including biological family, lovers, former clients, their local community and younger *kinnars*. Furthermore, eight of the 20 *kinnars* reported having been raped, either by customers, police or partners. One older *kinnar* declared: "It is painful when they force themselves upon us. They do not even leave alone the old."

The disinclination to talk about sexual matters, if not total exclusion from sexuality, was also exacerbated by poor health status that could make sexual activity virtually impossible. While 68 is not considered old in the more affluent parts of the globe, the situation just described recalls what Gilleard and Higgs (2015), in a British context (where the evolution of 'subaltern' relationships traced back to the colonial era), have termed a 'fourth age', a status of the 'abject' oldest old, who represent the most excluded of all aged groups, if not a form of social death.

For the two oldest study participants, sexual activity, whether for love, money, or any other reason, was very much consigned to the past and involved very negative accounts invoking rape by men they had known and trusted, as well as violent rape by male police officers, which lead to anal trauma and permanent ruptures (which had occasioned heavy bleeding) and HIV infection. Lacking the funds for medical treatment caused further deterioration of well-being. The two participants took it for granted that *kinnars* were so reviled as sub-human that not even doctors or other medical staff (notwithstanding the Hippocratic Oath) would help them. Both study participants expected to be forgotten after death, fearing that they would be denied dignity on death of a proper funeral.

Both the study participants elaborated upon the subjugation in the form of sexual violence in their early lives:

> 'We do not have much to sustain ourselves, due to COVID-19, as it is "badhai dena" (ritual carried out by *kinnars* to bless a newborn baby and in return receive money and food) came to a halt and now people do not call *kinnars* to their homes, we have no choice but to struggle in activities of sex work with anyone even at our age.'

However, considering the age of such *kinnars* and their loss of youth, beauty, physical capital and energy, earning a livelihood via sex work becomes increasingly difficult and, consequently, they are more prone to sexual abuse and violence. As one *kinnar* explained: "We are subjected to sexual assault, forceful sex, sexual abuse, under the pretence that the person will give us money in return. No money is ever received. Considering our age, we are used and thrown aside. … We just rot and die eventually."

In sum, and considering the situation post-COVID-19, the means for older *kinnars* to earn a livelihood such as '*badhai dena*' has become more tenuous and riskier and their sex lives with partners may become highly precarious. We might, then, conclude that older *kinnars* are practically rendered abject and, as such, are obliged merely to exist rather than live a viable life. It is abundantly clear that ageing and later life represent a phantom which haunts even young *kinnars*.

Examining recent legislation on gender and sexuality

Having described *kinnars*' exclusion from valid sexual citizenship (and other forms thereof), I move to consider the contradictions thrown up by the more recent legal reforms that attempt to liberalise the status of non-normative expressions of gender and sexuality. Such reforms could be thought consonant with the neoliberal ideology of India as a modernising, industrial nation consisting of diverse, rights-bearing citizens.

It is worth noting that *kinnars* have obtained legal recognition only as an afterthought by the Indian Judiciary. In 2019, the Indian Parliament passed The Transgender Persons (Protection of Rights) Act with an aim of protecting transgender persons' identity and to prescribe their rights. Though the policy implementation has been slow, at minimum its enactment is intended to serve as a safeguard for trans-identified individuals. Nonetheless, the concerns of vulnerable older trans people are not recognised within the legislation. The inclusivity of the Indian Transgender Persons Act is therefore questionable and ambiguous. Section 2(k) of the Act defines the 'transgender person' as 'a person whose gender does not match the gender assigned to that person at birth' and includes trans men, trans women irrespective of gender-affirmation surgeries and people with intersex variations, defined as genderqueer. The definition also encompasses people with sociocultural identities, for example, '*hijra*' and '*aravani*' (the names accorded intersex individuals in Tamil Nadu State) and '*jogta*' or '*jogappas*' who are intersex individuals who devote their lives to 'Renukha Devi' ('Yellamma'), whose temples are located in Maharashtra and Karnataka. Both the male and female servants of that goddess are referred to as '*jogta*' and '*jogti*' (sometimes referred to as '*Devadasi*'). If it is part of one's family tradition or if one finds a '*Guru*' (or '*Pujari*') who accepts them as a '*Chela*' or '*Shishya*', one can become a '*jogta*' (or '*jogti*') disciple. When referring to male-to-female transgender people who are followers of Goddess 'Renukha Devi' and members of the *hijra* communities, the name '*jogti hijras*' is often used (Das, 2017).

While the categories just mentioned can include older *kinnars*, they lack special attention to them and thus fall short of addressing the cultural, political and socio-economic concerns of older *kinnars*. Further, medical healthcare facilities for trans people, which would be especially important for older ones, are absent from the Act and there is no punishment prescribed for raping a *kinnar* (though such violations have been condemned). This situation can be contrasted with The Maintenance and Welfare of Parents and Senior Citizens Act 2007, which guarantees constitutional rights and provides welfare measures to the older citizens of India. No constitutional mandate has been granted to the senior citizens belonging to the third gender.

While colonialism created problems for the first time for *kinnars*, leading to pathologisation and demonisation, perhaps ironically, more recent liberalisation around gender and sexuality in 'the West' or global North (including Britain), could provide *kinnars* in India with some encouragement and the vision to identify themselves positively and articulate their own demands about recognition as particular gendered sexual beings and their needs in public spaces, including those organised around health and well-being. One of the study participants was of the view that specific/special section/rooms for the trans individuals, including hospitals for the security and protection of *kinnars*, should be provided by the government. Other participants recommended including older *kinnars* in the definition of 'senior citizen' with a need for financial assistance commensurate with that status.

Another middle-aged *kinnar* was of the view that there should be penal provisions in the criminal laws of India, which punish crimes against trans individuals and for those who sexually violate and/or exploit them. Further, she rightly suggested that *kinnars* should have the right to choose the groom/bride of their choice to marry as they can be forced by their parents to marry someone whom they are not sexually attracted to, as well as rights in relation to live-in relationships. In cases of marriage, the same participant advocated for law enabling entitlement towards maintenance in case of financially abusive relationships. Sadly, while such protections are required as minima, the more 'local' stigmatisation of *kinnars* reduces the chances of such positive developments in the foreseeable future, though this makes the need for advocacy by self and allies all the more urgent and necessary.

Conclusion

To the best of my knowledge, this is the first study to examine ageism and sexuality in relation to older *kinnars* (living in northern India). Despite the difficulties caused by societal stigma and taboo surrounding the subject, the authors were able to recruit a respectable sample and, using Colaizzi's phenomenological approach, could examine participant accounts to extend and deepen understanding of how ageism, cisgenderism and heteronormativity combine to set serious constraints on the sexuality of older *and* younger *kinnars*.

In particular, Colaizzi's method was used to funnel down to the essentials not only of commonly experienced problems across *kinnars* of different ages, but also some of the differences between them. The main concerns/themes by age group were: younger *kinnars*' anticipatory fear of loss of youth, beauty and thus income, as well as status within *kinnar* culture (and beyond); the felt obligation to distance the ageing self from the category 'old/er' (a defensive strategy of the middle group); and the keenly felt abjection of the two oldest *kinnars* who had internalised a completely desexualised status. In addition, there are intimations that *kinnars* themselves are so divided by internalised ageism that this may prevent the mutual support and solidarity prerequisite for a movement that could articulate and militate for proper respect, effective legal rights and recognition within a spectrum of valid sexual citizenship.

The study's findings reveal that older *kinnars* are obliged to become invisible and lose, or rather are prevented from gaining, a sense of themselves as valid sexual beings. They desire security, leading a decent life and a life with dignity at the time when they grow old. However, their rejection and marginalisation militates against such possibilities and has been exacerbated by COVID-19, which has served to intensify their ostracisation, despite the recent legal reforms discussed.

Further, this study has sought to address the vulnerabilities of the 'greying minority' of older *kinnars*, especially in light of the extreme paucity of scholarship on the subject in India and beyond. Addressing and resolving the problems faced by older *kinnars* is an urgent issue; the legislative and executive wings of state governments should act upon these problems via the creation and effective implementation of robust laws and policy measures that protect the interests and promote the welfare of older *kinnars*. Such measures should include those articulated by our study participants concerning legal penalties for violation of the person, a right to bodily, sexual and relational autonomy, and protection from abusive relationships or abandonment by a long-term partner, leaving the person without financial support or any security in later life.

Further, there is an urgent need for welfare systems to include and address the sexual health needs of older *kinnars*. Recognising sexual health as a natural component of health measures should be adopted by the government to introduce awareness programmes so that the taboo around sex and older *kinnars* can be gradually eroded. The sexual needs of *all* older adults should be acknowledged, respected and accommodated in healthcare education, services, research and policy interventions. Regardless of their area of expertise, doctors need to be made aware of the need to acknowledge older people's sexual rights across the range of gender, sexual and age differences. Considering later life sex as taboo in India, our chapter, via first-hand knowledge of older *kinnars* during the crisis of COVID-19, has provided an in-depth insight into the complex enmeshments of a heteronormative cisgenderism (with roots in colonialism) with (local) ageism. Just as importantly, I also hope to have extended understanding of the conjoined legal, political, socio-economic and cultural solutions to the many obstacles placed in the way of a highly oppressed social group.

Finally, and perhaps suggesting the long shadow of complex, 'neocolonial' relations, *kinnars*' accounts variously show the use of and replicate accounts of cross-cutting gendered ageism familiar in Western and global North contexts and complicate these knowledges in certain ways, such as the negative relativisation of ageing and later life, which is felt earlier by younger *kinnars*. Further research could be usefully organised around *kinnars* and building resilience through community and inclusion as well as how their accounts might offer alternatives to Western and global North epistemologies and ontologies of gender and sexuality and other categories of identity and experience.

Acknowledgements

Thanks are accorded to Ms Pratibha Singh, Secretary of Kala Mandali of Bharatiya Kala Kendra, New Delhi, India along with Mr Ajay Bose, Director, Dhruv Bose Foundation, for their invaluable assistance in helping to recruit study participants. Thanks are also given to Ms Navya Prathipati, Research Associate, ABA Law Office for assiduously working on this chapter with me.

References

Achenbaum, W.A. (2018). 'Ageism, Past, and Present', in Treviño, A.J. (ed) *The Cambridge Handbook of Social Problems*, Cambridge: Cambridge University Press, pp 441–58. Doi: 10.1017/9781108656184.025

Bannerjee, D. and Rao, T.S.S. (2021). '"The Graying Minority": Lived Experiences and Psychosocial Challenges of Older Transgender Adults During the COVID-19 Pandemic in India, a Qualitative Exploration', *Frontiers in Psychiatry*, 11(1): 5–6. Doi: 10.3389/fpsyt.2020.604472

Bhartrihari. (1967). *Bhartrihari: Poems* (translated by B.S. Miller). New York: Columbia University.

Choi, J. and Taylor, S. (2020). 'The Psychology of Pandemics: Preparing for the Next Global Outbreak of Infectious Disease', *Asian Communication Research*, 17(2): 98–103.

Colaizzi, P. (1978). 'Psychological Research as a Phenomenologist Views It', in Valle, R.S. and King, M. (eds) *Existential Phenomenological Alternatives for Psychology*, New York: Open University Press, pp 48–71.

Cramer, R.J., McNiel, D.E., Holley, S.R., Shumway, M. and Boccellari, A. (2012). 'Mental Health in Violent Crime Victims: Does Sexual Orientation Matter?', *Law and Human Behavior*, 36(2): 87–95. Doi:10.1037/h0093954

Das, W. (2017). *Tritiya-Prakriti: People of the Third Sex* [online], New York: Xlibris. Available from: https://books.google.com/books?id=gRjGApZVwPIC&printsec=frontcover [accessed 12 August 2022].

Fredriksen-Goldsen, K.I., Cook-Daniels, L., Kim, H.J., Erosheva, E.A., Emlet, C.A., Hoy-Ellis, C.P., Goldsen, J. and Muraco, A. (2014). 'The Physical and Mental Health of Transgender Older Adults: An At-risk and Underserved Population', *The Gerontologist*, 54(3): 488–500. Doi: 10.1093/geront/gnt021

Gilleard, C. and Higgs, P. (2015). 'Social Death and the Moral Identity of the Fourth Age', *Contemporary Social Science*, 10(3): 262–71. Doi: 10.1080/21582041.2015.1075328

Kalra, G. and Shah, N. (2013). 'The Cultural, Psychiatric, and Sexuality Aspects of Kinnars in India', *International Journal of Transgenderism*, 14(4): 171–81.

Mayer, K.H., Bradford, J.B., Makadon, H.J., Stall, R., Goldhammer, H. and Landers, S. (2008). 'Sexual and Gender Minority Health: What We Know and What Needs to be Done', *American Journal of Public Health*, 98(6): 989–95. Doi:10.2105/AJPH.2007.127811

Rhude, K. (2018). 'The Third Gender and Hijras', Harvard Divinity School, (online) nd, Available from: https://rpl.hds.harvard.edu/religion-context/case-studies/gender/third-gender-and-hijras [accessed 20 November 2022].

Roy, S. (2021). 'Indology (Indological Perspective): Meaning, History and Founders', *Sociology Group [blog]* 1 July. Available from: www.sociologygroup.com/indology-2/ [accessed 7 August 2022].

Simpson, P. (2021). 'AT YOUR AGE???!!! The Constraints of Ageist Erotophobia on Older People's Sexual and Intimate Relationships', in Simpson, P., Reynolds, P. and Hafford-Letchfied, T. (eds) *Desexualisation in Later Life: The Limits of Sex and Intimacy*, Bristol: Policy Press, pp 35–51.

Talwar, R. (1999). *The Third Sex and Human Rights*, New Delhi: Gyan Publishing House.

Thakur, D.N. (2012). 'Feminism and the Women's Movement in India', *Research Journal of Humanities and Social Sciences*, 3(4): 458–64.

Vance, C.S. (1991). 'Anthropology Rediscovers Sexuality: A Theoretical Comment', *Social Science & Medicine*, 33(8): 875–84. Doi: 10.1016/0277-9536(91)90259-f

Wadhwa, P. (2018). 'The Third Gender in India: Reconfiguring Identity', *International Journal on Multicultural Literature*, 8(1): 39–46.

Weeks, J. (2007). *The World We Have Won*, London: Routledge.

4

Doing complex intimacy in the later life of Chinese gay men in Hong Kong

Barry Lee 李文偉 *and Travis S.K. Kong* 江紹祺

Introduction

This chapter presents a qualitative study investigating intimacy among nine older Chinese gay men (aged 60 and above) and how experiences of sex and intimacy are manifested in their lives. The categories 'being single' and 'long-term couple/committed relationship', with their various subcategories, are employed to illustrate their stories. The findings indicate how older gay men 'do' sex and intimacy in a Chinese context. Most of them embrace one-to-one, committed, long-term relationships. Informants involved in a relationship negotiate between romantic and sexual adventures. Together or separately, openly or secretly, and with explicit or implicit agreement, they explore involvement in a variety of relationships, from brief casual sexual encounters to 'quality' but secondary relationships. The narratives of these older gay men in relation to sex, love and ageing bodies suggest that their intimate lives are affected by heteronormative culture intersecting with the homonormativity and ageism embedded in a Confucian cultural context.

Hong Kong society: homosexuality, Confucianism and doing intimacy in the Chinese context

The Hong Kong population is predominantly of Chinese lineage, with a significant influx of people from mainland China during the 1940s and 1950s. As a consequence of over a century of British colonial rule, Hong Kong culture has become a hybrid of East and West (Lu, 2009). With a population that is more than 90 per cent ethnically Chinese, however, Chinese culture remains the dominant influence on Hong Kong society. Confucianism has had a profound influence on the idea of filiality, which focuses on family-centredness. The individual and the family are commonly conceived as a 'unit' in Chinese culture (Chou, 2000). The predominant influences associated with Hong Kong culture, then, combine colonialism, Confucianism and the latter's emphasis on family-centredness.

Homosexuality in Hong Kong

Until 1991, male homosexual acts were criminalised under the British Offences Against the Persons Act of 1861, which was incorporated into Hong Kong law (Chou, 2000). Beyond the illegal status of homosexuality in Hong Kong, anti-gay sentiment was further exacerbated by the medicalisation of homosexuality and fundamentalist religious condemnation of homosexual acts, resulting in homosexuality being deemed immoral, unnatural and pathological, as well as illegal (Ho, 1995). In light of historic and current circumstances of homophobia and heteronormativity, Chinese gay men in Hong Kong have tended to adopt non-confrontational strategies, sculpted mainly by local politics and Chinese harmonious values and contrasting with Western gay liberation movements (Kong, 2004). Many older gay men hid or ignored their same-sex desires and chose to marry when they were young. Many began exploring their sexual identity only after reaching their 50s, after they had accomplished their filial duties of procreation and forming a family (Kong, 2012, 2019). In addition, the Confucian focus on familial harmony creates a hurdle for gay men seeking intimacy in later life.

Heteronormativity and homonormativity

International research shows that older gay men struggle within heteronormative spaces (Pilkey, 2014) and that heterosexuality is constituted as the default sexuality. Heteronormativity can be defined '[as] institutions, practical orientations, and structures of understanding, making heterosexuality seem coherent and privileged' (Berlant and Warner, 2000: 312). Moreover, it positions heterosexual relationships as the basis of society and a means of reproduction (Warner, 1993). Being non-heterosexual in a heteronormative culture, gay men encounter not only systemic heteronormative oppression manifested at the community level, but also the effects of heterosexism ingrained within at the personal level (Ahmed, 2014). Heteronormative culture forces many older gay men to conceal their sexual identity (Heaphy and Yip, 2003). In Hong Kong, heteronormativity, via British colonialism and Western religion, Christianity in particular, defined homosexuality as a crime, a sin, an unhealthy lifestyle and unnatural behaviour, exerting a strong impact on older gay men during their youth (Kong, 2012, 2019, 2023).

Expanding on the concept of heteronormativity, homonormativity is defined as '[a] politics that does not contest dominant heteronormative assumptions and institutions, but upholds and sustains them, while promising the possibility of a demobilised gay constituency and a privatised, depoliticised gay culture anchored in domesticity and consumption' (Duggan, 2002: 179). Moreover, homonormativity exhorts non-heterosexuals to embrace oppressive sexist and heteronormative systems that inherently turn on binary ways of thinking about gender and sexuality. Homonormative practices also foster a youth-obsessed culture, which can be challenging for older gay men (Simpson, 2013). Ageism within the gay community is often a contributing factor when older gay men seek sexual partners (Gott, 2005). In Hong Kong, homonormativity, which emerged in the 1980s with the rise of gay subcultures, is stratified along the lines of class, gender performance, race and ethnicity, and body type, with older gay men seen as undesirable, self-loathing, closeted and sad (Kong, 2012). Kong (2023) fused the idea of homonormativity with hegemonic masculinity, coining the term 'homonormative masculinity' to capture the essence of current gay subcultures. This new concept characterises Chinese gay men who increasingly seek to conform to traditional notions of masculinity by emphasising such qualities as appearing straight (cisgender), youthfulness (age), physical fitness (body) and a desire for monogamous relationships or exclusive emotional connections within a couple (monogamy). Additionally, they embrace a consumption-driven, cosmopolitan lifestyle to achieve middle-class status. These individuals often support a private, domestic and apolitical way of life that lacks radical or subversive elements. Homonormative masculinity can thus be understood as prioritising four key aspects within the realm of sexual identity: 'body and gender performance, coupled intimacy, middleclass sensibility, and political conservatism' (Kong, 2023: 92).

Confucianism

Originating in ancient China, Confucianism is a system of thought that emphasises the significance of personal ethics and morality. Among its beliefs, relational harmony and filial piety are highly relevant to intimacy in the lives of Chinese gay men. *Wu lun* (five relations) focuses on the five cardinal human relationships: that between father and son; ruler and minister; husband and wife; elder and younger brother; and between friends. The notion of *wu lun* not only privileges heterosexual relationships, but also promotes the virtue of respect for one's parents. Marrying and bearing children are essential parts of the filial piety that children owe to their parents (Dau-lin, 1970). Failure to produce a son to carry on the family name is not only the most unfilial of all acts (Chan, 1963), but is also thought to damage the foundation of family harmony (Dau-lin, 1970). The damage of unattainable filiality can cause a 'loss of face'. Face (*mianzi*) can be understood as both individual face (that is, showing one's integrity) and social face (showing one's social prestige). The effect of losing face may be the loss of personal and family reputations and social connections through relational separation from families and communities (Hua et al, 2019).

The Euro-American model of the individual presupposes an autonomous and freestanding inner self, and thus the Euro-American 'coming out' model is based on a free self who first confesses to the self, then to the family, and finally to the world as a form of self-development. Such a model assumes that growing up and coming out usually mean leaving the natal family, with coming out perceived as a personal matter. The Chinese notion of the self, in contrast, is more relational, with the self embedded in a socially reciprocal relationship network in a family-centred culture informed by Confucianism (Kong, 2023). Many Chinese gay men find it difficult to come out because they are very concerned about breaching filiality, which would lead to relational disharmony within the family, and because coming out is seen as a family rather than personal matter (Wang et al, 2009).

Doing intimacy in a Chinese context

The construction of intimacy in Western sociology is framed by the notion of the 'pure relationship' based on choice, equality and mutuality (Giddens, 1992). Berlant (1998) highlights practices of intimacy that are often implicated in practices in the political and personal spheres. She challenges the clear distinction between the private and public, viewing them as blended and mutually influencing, especially as public discourse strongly influences private sexual activity. The concept of intimacy is heavily focused on couple intimacy (see Ferreira et al, 2013), and the concept of the couple remains understood largely in heterosexual terms.

Studies show that older LGBT-identified people rely more on 'friendship families' for support, while older heterosexuals are more dependent on their family of origin, with older gay men also indicating that 'friends as family' play a crucial role in caregiving and social support (Kosberg and Kaye, 1997).

Both heteronormative and ageist culture affect the intimacy of older gay men in Hong Kong. The historical background of criminalisation and discrimination against homosexuality, combined with ageism in the gay community and the possible loss of gay friends and partners as one ages, builds complexity into older gay men's intimate lives (Oswald and Roulston, 2020). Intimacy for older Chinese gay men in Hong Kong is not only strongly influenced by heterosexual practices, but is also closely connected to familial relationships. The term 'familial heteronormativity' is used to describe how the conflation of heteronormativity and Confucianism operates to silence homosexuality and privilege heterosexual intimacy (Kong, 2012: 901). Family and intimate relationships can be indistinguishable because remaining unmarried and childless is contrary to filiality.

However, homosociality is highly valued in Chinese culture, possibly even more so than spousal love (Chou, 2000). The story of 'the bitten peach and the cut sleeve' illustrates the way in which traditional Chinese culture consents to men becoming such close friends that they even share clothes. The term 'sworn brotherhood' refers to deep friendships between men built on loyalty, trust and mutual assistance, but is also expressed in shared closeness and intimacy (Jordan, 1985). To avoid the stigma attached to same-sex affection between men and minimise negative outcomes, 'sworn brotherhood' has often been neutralised as mere friendship (Wang et al, 2009).

The study and participants

This chapter is based on a continuing study of older Chinese gay men's stories, but the current focus is on investigating their intimate lives in Hong Kong. With several informants drawn from a previous project by the second author (Kong, 2012), a total of nine men were interviewed between March and May 2022 by the first author. The data were collected via semi-structured, in-depth interviews. Categories and subcategories were developed from broader themes derived from the men's narratives, with attention paid to key points or phrases occurring in their stories.

The informants, all aged 60 or above, self-identified as gay men. Ethical approval was obtained from the Human Research Committee of the first author's institution, the Education University of Hong Kong, prior to conducting the interviews. The study employed a qualitative approach involving interviews focusing on the development of a deeper understanding of the lived experiences of the informants and the meaning they assign to those experiences (Creswell, 2012).

Findings

Nine older Chinese gay men shared accounts of their intimate lives, which were classified into diverse categories and subcategories of 'being single' and in 'long-term couple/committed relationships' primarily derived and modified from Kong's (2011: 111–17) model of doing intimacy among gay men in Hong Kong. The categories arising from the data were extracted from the informants' narratives. Their views on intimacy appeared to be influenced by their experiences, and thus our analysis references their past familial and same-sex relationships while focusing on their recent lived experiences. The informants' stories illustrate how they negotiate intimacy and ageing experiences. The names of all interviewees given below are pseudonyms to protect their identity.

Being single

In this broad category, participants were categorised into two subcategories, 'being single and preferring monogamy' and 'being single and preferring polyamory', as illustrated below.

Being single and preferring monogamy

Nam, Jimmy and Tam were all single at the time of the interviews, but longed for a long-term monogamous relationship. Although Nam (age 76) wanted an exclusive relationship, it had not yet happened for him. He had completely devoted himself to his late partner, Ah Sing, who was over ten years younger than Nam and insisted on multiple relationships. Nam was willing to compromise, as made clear in the following statement: "I loved him, but he loved other men. ... He invited two other men into our relationship. I was okay with it because I was the 'principal wife'. ... I looked after his mother, and she liked me ... as her daughter-in-law."

Nam recognised that his relationship with Ah Sing had been fairly one-sided. He had invested all of his emotion, time and even savings in his partner. Interestingly, Nam seemed accepting of this imbalanced relationship, and the sacrifices he had made to maintain it, which he justified to himself using phrases such as, "I was the principal wife". Nam's adaptation to heterosexual-type relational practices is interesting. He was exceptional among the interviewees in being influenced by heteronormative ideology, which assumes a binary masculine or feminine role in a relationship, as reflected in his adoption of the stereotypical female role in his same-sex relationship. Most of the informants, in contrast, did not adopt the concept of husband and wife in their same-sex relationships. In addition, Nam's narrative also reflected a sense of a hierarchical family structure, as conveyed in the use of terms such as 'mother-in-law'. When asked why he had been willing to settle for an open relationship, Nam said: "I am old-fashioned. ... Also ... as I told you, my down there [his penis] is very small, and I am a bottom. If I were a top, I could have as many men as I want. ... Who wants an old, not-pretty bottom?"

Here, Nam signalled that penis size matters within the gay community (Drummond and Filiault, 2007). His narrative indicated a close relationship between penis size and the role of masculinity in same-sex behaviours, such as being assertive or submissive (Moskowitz and Hart, 2011). It was also clear that he had internalised a stereotypical belief concerning ageing, including a felt lack of autonomy in negotiating power within relationships (Hoy-Ellis and Fredriksen-Goldsen, 2016). Hence, heteronormative and ageist assumptions made him willing to sacrifice himself within an unequal intimate relationship.

Jimmy (age 74) also longed for a monogamous relationship. He explained that his concept of monogamy originated from the dominant marriage-type practices in his heteronormative environment. When discussing ageing and relationships, Jimmy declared: "I am getting old; I have changed a bit. If I [continue to] stubbornly ... insist on a monogamous relationship, and do not give myself a chance to meet other guys, I will never have someone to share my life."

Ageing seemed to be a factor in Jimmy's lack of insistence on an exclusive one-to-one relationship. Although his preference was still for a monogamous relationship, he had realised that finding someone with whom to share his life was more important. Among the many forms of relationship possible, for example, casual, open and so on, Jimmy found companionship to be the most important, particularly as one grows older. He was thus prepared to explore more possibilities for a relationship.

The idea that a sense of intimacy can be transformed or culminate in companionship rather than in a sexually and emotionally based relationship was shared by most of the study participants. Tam (age 62), for example, found it satisfying to share intimacy with his partner, but discovered that having an intimate relationship comes with a cost: "I used to think I was more valuable if I was in a relationship! ... Now, I still want a partner, but it takes a lot of hard work. ... I am not as 'accommodating' as I was when I was young. I am not sure now [how to form a relationship as he grows older]."

Jimmy shared a similar idea about couple-hood, but noted that ageing had given him new insight. His narrative reflected the heteronormative framework whereby 'couple-hood is implicitly privileged over singlehood' (Kates, 1999: 33). Jimmy pointed out that the privilege of couple-hood status was less important than his psychological need for companionship. Tam's narrative indicates that he has been influenced by heteronormative regulations, which privilege heterosexual couple relationships. In addition, he considered that time was running out for him to pursue the type of relationship he really desired beyond couple-hood intimacy.

Being single and preferring polyamory

Simon (age 78) has had multiple partners, most of whom live in mainland China, and he is not emotionally involved with any of them. When asked what counts as intimacy, he replied: "Intimacy? ... Do you mean emotional intimacy or sexual intimacy? I think emotional intimacy and sexual intimacy are two different things. ... I have both, but with different guys. I don't see any problem with that, and why would it be a problem?"

Simon is able to have emotional intimacy without sexual intimacy and vice versa. He can have a deep emotional connection with one man without engaging in a sexual relationship, and then, with another, have a sexual relationship without any sense of emotional closeness. The two forms of intimacy thus seem distinct in his life, and they do not always go hand in hand. Furthermore, Simon's view on intimacy is clearly different from that of the other informants, as he made a clear distinction between the binary of sex and love, which is common within both the gay and straight communities (see Bonello and Cross, 2009). Polyamory involves an agreement between two or more people to engage in a non-exclusive sexual and/or romantic relationship. Simon questioned why polyamory is a problem in a society where exclusive sexual relationships are the norm. He both enjoyed and accepted a polyamorous relationship. When asked to compare himself to an older heterosexual Chinese man, he said he was pleased not to be constrained by the marriage system. He also thought that it would have been problematic for him to be forced into a heterosexual marriage like other older gay men.

With respect to ageism within the gay community in Hong Kong (Kong, 2012), Simon reported experiencing it at saunas in Hong Kong, prompting him to seek out more elder-friendly sexual venues in mainland China: "I never thought I could be attractive when I got old, but it is not the case in China. There, the gay scene is much better than in Hong Kong!"

Other informants, including Nam, also reported experiencing ageism within the gay community in Hong Kong. Simon said that his experiences in mainland China, where he has been able to find sexual opportunities, have given him a positive outlook. The experience of discovering gay-friendly spaces for older gay men in mainland China was shared by other informants interested in physical and emotional intimacy with younger gay men. Gay-friendly venues for older men in China is an under-researched area, although the informants' experiences can be associated with the growing phenomenon of sex tourism in China (see Mao et al, 2018).

Simon has actively resisted both heteronormative (that is, he rejects binary gender and sexuality beliefs) and homonormative (he refuses same-sex monogamous relationships) trends. Moreover, his account suggests that he has fought back against ageism within the local gay community and embraced homonormativity by seeking intimacy in mainland China.

Long-term couple/committed relationships

Four subcategories are identified within the broader category of long-term couple/committed relationships, as outlined below.

'1+1: Negotiated monogamy'

At the time of the interviews, Park (age 76) had been in a relationship with his same-sex partner for over 15 years, but the two men lived separately because Park was still in the closet. He reported telling various lies to his family and heterosexual friends over the years. Park was the only informant in a long-term, exclusive same-sex relationship and conceded that it was an ideal relationship for him. However, he indicated that physical intimacy with other men was tempting: "I am lucky to have a one-to-one long-term partner, but it is not easy, as there is so much temptation within the gay community. I have been trying hard to stay faithful."

When discussing intimacy, a one-to-one relationship was the phrase that arose most often among the informants. Park seemed to know what type of intimacy he wanted and knew how to control himself to maintain it despite the temptation he often felt. He did admit, however, that there were exceptions to the exclusive intimacy he enjoyed with his partner: "We agree to allow ourselves 'holiday sex' when we travel. It is casual sex, but we end up becoming friends with them."

'Holiday sex' can be conceptualised as consensual non-monogamy, with both or all partners giving explicit consent to engage in romantic, intimate and/or sexual relationships with multiple people (Conley et al, 2017). Park attempted to embrace homonormativity by remaining in a monogamous relationship, but his polyamorous desires were punished by homonormativity. He was concerned about the stigma attached to his and his partner's sexual agreement, as he knew that the predominant culture praises monogamy as the 'ideal'. In fact, studies have shown that polyamorous sexual agreements can confer positive benefits on couples in terms of sexual health (Mitchell, 2014), relationship satisfaction, trust, commitment and psychological health (Rubel and Bogaert, 2015).

'2+1: Heterosexual marriage plus homosexual romance'

Chow (age 78) and Danny (age 74) were both in heterosexual marriages when they were young but had both had gay relationships in later life. Despite having divorced their wives long ago, seeking same-sex intimate relationships was difficult owing to their family responsibilities. Both remained closeted to their families. Chow lived with his son, daughter-in-law and grandson, while Danny had lived with his same-sex partner for about five years before recently moving into a care home because of his deteriorating health. Their stories reflect how filiality remained a major influence in their lives. Chow also shared his struggle with the conflict between a straight marriage and gay romance:

> 'Getting married is the duty of ... a Chinese man, especially as I am the eldest son in the family. ... I always envy gay couples [who] liv[e] together, but I know I cannot. ... My son probably knows I am gay, but not my daughter-in-law and grandson. ... Being gay is not a personal matter. I cannot be selfish by burdening my son with my secret.'

Danny had a similar background to Chow. In addition to fulfilling his filial duty to marry and have offspring, his concerns extended beyond the family circle. He explained:

> 'My ex-wife and my son probably know I am gay, as I have been living with a man, but we never discuss it. I am still in the closet. I cannot

face my friends, relatives, ex-colleagues, especially my two sons. How can I tell them the truth after lying to them for so long?!'

Danny and Chow are representative of many older Chinese gay men, who grew up in far more restrictive and intolerant times. Even though they had formally exited their heterosexual marriages through divorce, their intimate lives remained restricted. Their narratives on heterosexual marriage reflected the way in which the heteronormative and Confucian culture of Hong Kong has ingrained itself into their personal and social lives. Both men feared that coming out would bring about negative consequences for their family members because of the prevailing homophobia in society. Moreover, they were equally concerned about being humiliated or 'losing face', as defined earlier (see Lee, 2022). Under the influence of their Confucian beliefs, Chow and Danny married and had children, thereby fulfilling their filial duties. Although they had fulfilled their filial responsibility to their parents, however, as fathers and grandfathers, they remained anxious about their own families, as they knew that homophobia might affect them. In addition, Chow's statements about being 'Chinese' and about being gay not being 'a personal matter' seem to position his Confucian belief in family harmony as one of the main challenges preventing him from developing a cohabiting intimate relationship.

'2+1: Gay couple relationship plus gay secondary relationship'

Among the informants, Johnson's (age 72) intimate life was rather complex. He married a woman when he was young, but had always been sexually attracted to men, although he did not dare to explore his same-sex desires until later in life. At the time of the interviews, Johnson was living a double life. Like other closeted gay men in a heterosexual marriage, he had gone through a period of cruising in public toilets (to be discussed under the next subcategory). Although he eventually found a gay partner, he continued to play the role of husband with his wife. In addition to his wife and gay partner, he had also developed a relationship with another man. Johnson shared the joys and struggles of being involved with two men:

'My gay partner asked me to find another man when he got married [to a woman]. … I had casual sex with the second man, but it turned out I was attracted to him romantically. Since I started having … relationships with men, I [have] realised I really enjoy having male company. That is why I have … stayed in touch with most of my ex-lovers as "sworn-brothers/fathers".'

Johnson started just having casual sex with the second man, but, over time, he began to develop a romantic relationship with him. Furthermore, Johnson and his first gay partner seem to have come to a sexual agreement, that is, an explicit agreement between two people concerning whether other sex partners are allowed and, if so, under what conditions (Hoff and Beougher, 2010). However, Johnson's partner does not seem to have been explicit about whether his encouragement 'to find another man' referred to a purely sexual experience or otherwise. Sexual agreements are common within Hong Kong's gay culture, although they take different forms. For example, partners can explicitly consent to one another engaging in romantic, intimate and/or sexual relationships with multiple partners. These are consensual relationships, not to be confused with infidelity. Another form of sexual agreement might include three or more people in a relationship remaining romantically and sexually exclusive. Common forms of such agreement include polyamory, open relationships and swinging relationships (Moors et al, 2021). Johnson said he used the term 'sworn-brothers/fathers' to refer to his gay sexual and romantic partners in public. The term can be useful for gay men to resolve their same-sex relationships without fear of stigmatisation, as intimacy can be interpreted as 'close and intimate' or 'close, but not intimate'.

'2+ many: heterosexual marriage plus lots of anonymous sex'

Prior to engaging in a gay relationship, Johnson went through a period of cruising public toilets that gay men frequent for sexual satisfaction because he knew nothing about the gay scene at the time and, more importantly, was a married man:

> 'Toilets were the only place I could have sex with men at that time. I did not know how to find other men in any other way. Even if I had known, I would not have dared to do so because I am a married man. What would happen if I got caught?! I would lose everything, my family, my work, and my life.'

Johnson stated that he still loved his wife, although his sexual interest lay only in men. Secretly exploring their same-sex attractions while remaining married is difficult for many gay men. Johnson believed that, as a married man, he faced greater pressure than single older gay men. Despite cruising toilets being highly risky, Johnson kept doing it because he did not know anywhere else to go to meet 'people like him'. Johnson's story is typical of this cohort, that is, older gay men who married when they were young and are just looking for quick sex rather than a relationship, because they have not been able to reconcile their own gay identity. Heteronormativity forces many gay men like Johnson to experience the impact of heterosexism (Lee, 2022) and, consequently, many remain in the closet to avoid homophobia and heteronormativity (Kong, 2012).

'2+ many: gay couple relationship plus lots of anonymous sex'

Donald (age 70) had a 10-year relationship with a same-sex partner from whom he lived separately, and often visited gay saunas during the relationship. When asked whether it had been an open relationship, he said: "No, we were in a one-to-one relationship. Sometimes he [my ex-partner] knew I went to saunas but just for chatting with other guys, not for sex. He was okay with it."

When asked whether he would have had sex with another man if he had been the right man, Donald remained silent. It appears that Donald and his partner had had a sexual agreement whereby Donald could go to gay saunas purely to socialise with other men. Similar stories occur among gay men who cruise public toilets (Johnson, for example). However, Donald's silence about whether he would have had sex with another man if he had been the right man speaks volumes. Like Park, Johnson and Simon had a sexual agreement within their relationships that was self-defined by the partners. However, the sexual agreement between Donald and his partner seems to have constituted a classic 'don't-ask-don't-tell' situation, whereby one partner knows about but does not wish to acknowledge his partner's indiscretion.

When asked for his views on anonymous sex on the side, Donald expressed his understanding of a one-to-one relationship as follows.

> 'I was 10 years older than my partner and had tried everything! If my partner had wanted to have sex with others, I would have been okay with it. I don't think you need to tell your partner everything; not telling everything to your partner [can] be a good thing.'

Throughout the interviews, there were many responses that seemed to be in accordance with 'don't-ask-don't-tell' strategies, for example, 'only chatting in saunas', 'my partner knew sometimes', and 'not telling everything to your partner can be a good thing'. They bring into question some men's understanding of one-to-one relationships and may reflect a state of self-denial they have adopted to deceive themselves into believing that their actions are acceptable. There is nothing wrong with Donald, or any other of the informants, practising non-monogamy and wishing to maintain privacy. Some people may find 'don't-ask-don't-tell' situations contradictory, although it is not uncommon for gay couples to have rules regarding sex (Ramirez and Brown, 2010). Anderson (2012) explains that the natural diminution of sexual excitement within a relationship is not the same as losing sexual desire. However, it could explain the desire to seek sexual gratification outside the relationship.

Donald's pursuits outside his relationship, which were restricted to sex and did not involve emotion, are not unheard of. Similar to Park and Simon,

Donald resisted heteronormativity (that is, he rejected binary gender and sexuality beliefs), but struggled with homonormativity (he was uncertain whether he embraced the idea of a one-to-one relationship). Donald's mention of his age seemed a way to justify his flexible approach to his relationship with his partner.

Discussion and conclusion

The narratives reported in this chapter suggest that the intimate lives of older gay men in Hong Kong are shaped by heteronormativity, homonormativity and ageism embedded in a Confucian cultural context. This final section discusses issues relevant to the findings and links them with comparable results in existing studies.

The Confucian cultural context in Hong Kong shares many similarities with that in mainland China, despite the Western influences on Hong Kong. Although homosexuality remains a private matter for Chinese gay men, the notion of family-centredness and concerns with relational disharmony connect their personal issues to family matters. In accordance with the concept of filiality, Chinese gay men are expected to maintain strong ties of mutual support with their parents into adulthood and to preserve the collectivity of the natal family. As a result, many find it difficult to come out to their family and take ownership of their personal intimacy.

The study participants' narratives demonstrate how older gay men 'do' intimacy in one-to-one, committed and long-term relationships within a Chinese context. Among all of the needs satisfied by a relationship, such as sex, love, passion, a sense of security and companionship, the last seemed to be equally important to the others. Those informants who were in a relationship had to negotiate between romantic love and sexual adventure. Together or separately, openly or secretly, and with explicit or implicit agreements, they explored a variety of relationships, from brief casual sexual encounters to 'quality' but secondary relationships (Adam, 2006; Kong, 2011: 111–17). Indeed, they also tried out various ways of 'doing' intimacy, challenging the primacy of the mainstream couple relationship, that is, of sexual and emotional exclusivity. They also 'modified' the traditional idea of monogamy into a new form of relationship with rules such as 'disclosing intimacy' (Giddens, 1991).

Research has revealed that Chinese male sexualities are multiply formed and complex (Kong, 2012). In the present study, the informants' accounts of intimacy exhibit a similar pattern. Some of the men practised subversive intimacy by remaining single, entering into a marriage of convenience or a same-sex relationship, or adopting the '2+1' model or '2+many' models or some combination thereof. The informants who formed '2+1' or '2+many' non-monogamous relationships did not challenge the idea of coupledom.

Indeed, some tried to 'negotiate with monogamy' (for example, Park) by engaging in consensual non-monogamy or exploring 'cheating' in secret (for example, Donald). Their narratives show that their views on 'gay couples' are consistent with the concept of homonormativity (Brown, 2012). Fighting against the double stigma of a heteronormative and ageist culture is challenging. This research reveals a rejection of binary gender and sexuality beliefs and a refusal to conform to monogamous relationship styles. Studies in the West have shown a similar resistance within the older LGBTQ community (Pilkey, 2014; Oswald and Roulston, 2020).

Most of the informants were influenced by filiality when they were young. Some were forced into marriage and to have children to fulfil their filial duties to their parents. However, the expectation that they maintain a harmonious familial relationship also exerted an impact on their intimacy in later life. Chow, for example, continued to feel responsible for maintaining family harmony. This Confucian belief can become an impediment to pursuing one's ideal same-sex relationship (Huang et al, 2017).

The concept of filial piety carries a certain degree of reciprocity, with its emphasis on obligations, and goes far beyond it in its purest form (Whyke, 2023). Linking this idea to the stories of Johnson, Danny and Chow, the question arises of how their children and grandchildren respond to the filial duties expected of them towards their father/grandfather. Learning from recent studies on the acceptance of homosexuality, and given that public conceptions of homosexuality have improved dramatically (Suen and Wong, 2017), the core nature of filial piety has shifted from absolute obedience to parental views towards egalitarian care and respect within the parent–child relationship in Hong Kong (Yeh et al, 2013). However, homosexuality remains a sensitive topic in Hong Kong, and further research investigating the meaning of homosexualities, the significance of coming out, and dyadic relationships within the Chinese family is therefore needed. The Confucian principle of friendship helped Johnson, as he could use the term 'sworn-brother/father' to refer to his same-sex relationships without fear of stigmatisation. The use of similar strategies was described by Ho (2006).

Many older Chinese gay men hide their identity and intimate relationships from their families, often because they do not know how their families will respond. It is not uncommon for older gay men to suffer abuse from and even be ostracised by their families (Cook-Daniels and Munson, 2010). In Hong Kong, heteronormative culture intersecting with homonormativity and ageism is embedded in the cultural context of Confucianism, which, in many cases, causes older Chinese gay men to engage in self-blame and to internalise homophobia (Huang et al, 2020). The connection between sharing one's intimate relationship with family members and the current lack of anti-discrimination legislation for sexual minorities in Hong Kong may be a contributing factor to older gay men's reluctance to seek advice and/or counselling for relationship and sexuality issues. When older gay men are exposed in their daily life to a heterosexist culture without any protection, it poses a significant threat to their mental health (Hoy-Ellis and Fredriksen-Goldsen, 2016). It is thus unsurprising that many older Chinese gay men in Hong Kong suffer similar stresses to those reported in studies of older gay men in other parts of the world (Kuyper and Fokkema, 2010).

This study has demonstrated how sex, intimacy and the ageing bodies of older gay men are primarily affected by heteronormative sexual norms. Nonetheless, their sexual encounters signify how they navigate and manage their lives between the oppression of heteronormativity and the local youth-dominated gay (homonormative) culture. The categories and subcategories of relationships discussed here provide insight into the complex intersection between ageing, intimacy and sexuality in a Chinese context.

The study is constrained by the small number of informants. The authors do not intend to affirm any claim of a universal stance based on their narratives. Nevertheless, the rich narratives of these nine older Chinese gay men show that their lives and the circumstances in which they negotiate intimacy and ageing are valid. There are many ways in which older Chinese gay men can engage in intimacy. However, in the current climate influenced by heteronormativity and ageism, their intimate lives remain closeted for the most part, resulting in society-imposed constraints on their basic rights. Older gay men are entitled to and must be encouraged to live a life enhanced by positive ageing experiences within both gay society and the wider society.

References

Adam, B.D. (2006) 'Relationship innovation in male couples', *Sexualities*, 9(1): 5–26.

Ahmed, S. (2014) *The Cultural Politics of Emotion* (2nd edn), Edinburgh: Edinburgh University Press.

Anderson, E. (2012) *The Monogamy Gap: Men, Love, and the Reality of Cheating*, Oxford: Oxford University Press.

Berlant, L. (1998) 'Intimacy: a special issue', *Critical Inquiry*, 24(2): 281–8.

Berlant, L. and Warner, M. (2000) 'Sex in public', in L. Berlant (ed) *Intimacy*, Chicago, IL: University of Chicago Press, pp 311–30.

Bonello, K. and Cross, M.C. (2009) 'Gay monogamy: "I love you but I can't have sex with only you"', *Journal of Homosexuality*, 57(1): 117–39.

Brown, G. (2012) 'A metropolitan concept that denigrates "ordinary" gay lives', *Journal of Homosexuality*, 59(7): 1065–72.

Chan, W.T. (1963) *A Source-Book in Chinese Philosophy*, Princeton, NJ: Princeton University Press.

Chou, W.S. (2000) *Tongzhi: Politics of Same-sex Eroticism in Chinese Societies*, New York: Haworth.

Conley, T.D., Matsick, J., Moors, A.C. and Ziegler, A. (2017) 'The investigation of consensually non-monogamous relationships: theories, methods and new directions', *Perspectives on Psychological Science*, 12(2): 205–32.

Cook-Daniels, L. and Munson, M. (2010) 'Sexual violence, elder abuse, and sexuality of transgender adults, age 50+: results of three surveys', *Journal of GLBT Family Studies*, 6(2): 142–77.

Creswell, J.W. (2012) *Qualitative Inquiry and Research Design: Choosing among Five Approaches* (3rd edn), Thousand Oaks, CA: Sage.

Dau-lin, H. (1970) 'The myth of the "five human relations" of Confucius', *Monumenta Serica*, 29(1): 27–37.

Drummond, M.J. and Filiault, S.M. (2007) 'The long and the short of it: gay men's perceptions of penis size', *Gay and Lesbian Issues and Psychology Review*, 3(2): 124–9.

Duggan, L. (2002) 'The new homonormativity: the sexual politics of neoliberalism', in Castronovo, R. and Nelson, D. (eds) *Materializing Democracy: Toward a Revitalized Cultural Politics*, Durham, NC: Duke University Press, pp 175–94.

Ferreira, L.C., Narciso, I. and Novo, R. (2013) 'Authenticity, work and change: a qualitative study on couple intimacy', *Families, Relationships and Societies*, 2(3): 339–54.

Giddens, A. (1991) *Modernity and Self-Identity: Self and Society in the Late Modern Age*, Cambridge: Polity Press.

Giddens, A. (1992) *The Transformation of Intimacy: Sexuality, Love and Eroticism in Modern Societies*, Cambridge: Polity Press.

Gott, M. (2005) *Sexuality, Sexual Health and Ageing*, Buckingham: Open University Press.

Heaphy, B. and Yip, A.K. (2003) 'Uneven possibilities: understanding non-heterosexual ageing and the implications of social change', *Sociological Research Online*, 8: 1–12.

Ho, P.S.Y. (1995) 'Male homosexual identity in Hong Kong', *Journal of Homosexuality*, 29(1): 71–88.

Ho, P.S.Y. (2006) 'The (charmed) circle game: reflections on sexual hierarchy through multiple sexual relationships', *Sexualities*, 9(5): 547–64.

Hoff, C.C. and Beougher, S.C. (2010) 'Sexual agreements among gay male couples', *Archives of Sexual Behaviour*, 39(3): 774–87.

Hoy-Ellis, C.P. and Fredriksen-Goldsen, K.I. (2016) 'Lesbian, gay, & bisexual older adults: linking internal minority stressors, chronic health conditions, and depression', *Aging & Mental Health*, 20(11): 1119–30.

Hua, B., Yang, V.F. and Goldsen, K.F. (2019) 'LGBT older adults at a crossroads in mainland China: the intersections of stigma, cultural values, and structural changes within a shifting context', *The International Journal of Aging and Human Development*, 88(4): 440–56.

Huang, Y.H.C., Bedford, O. and Zhang, Y. (2017) 'The relational orientation framework for examining culture in Chinese societies', *Culture & Psychology*, 24(4): 477–90.

Huang, Y.T., Chan, R.C.H. and Cui, L. (2020) 'Filial piety, internalized homonegativity, and depressive symptoms among Taiwanese gay and bisexual men: a mediation analysis', *American Journal of Orthopsychiatry*, 90(3): 340–9.

Jordan, D.K. (1985) 'Sworn brothers: a study in Chinese ritual kinship', in J.C. Hsieh and Y.C. Chuang (eds) *The Chinese Family and Its Ritual Behaviour*, Taipei: Institute of Ethnology, Academia Sinica, pp 232–62.

Kates, S.M. (1999) 'Making the ad perfectly queer: marketing "normality" to the gay men's community?', *Journal of Advertising*, 28(1): 25–37.

Kong, T.S.K. (2004) 'Queer at your own risk: marginality, community and Hong Kong gay male bodies', *Sexualities*, 7(1): 5–30.

Kong, T.S.K. (2011) *Chinese Male Homosexualities: Memba, Tongzhi and Golden Boy*, London: Routledge.

Kong, T.S.K. (2012) 'A fading tongzhi heterotopia: Hong Kong older gay men's use of spaces', *Sexualities*, 15(8): 896–916.

Kong, T.S.K. (2019) *Oral Histories of Older Gay Men in Hong Kong: Unspoken and Unforgotten*, Hong Kong: Hong Kong University Press.

Kong, T.S.K. (2023) *Sexuality and the Rise of China: The Post-1990s Gay Generation in Hong Kong, Taiwan, and Mainland China*, Durham, NC: Duke University Press.

Kosberg, J. and Kaye, L. (1997) *Elderly Men: Special Problems and Professional Challenges*, New York: Springer.

Kuyper, L. and Fokkema, C.M. (2010) 'Loneliness among older lesbian, gay, and bisexual adults: the role of minority stress', *Archives of Sexual Behavior*, 39(5): 1171–80.

Lee, B.M.W. (2022) 'Growing old with stigma: a case study of four older Chinese gay/bisexual men living with HIV in Hong Kong', in M. Henrickson, C. Charles, S. Ganesh, S. Giwa, D. Kwok and T. Semigina (eds) *HIV, Sex, and Sexuality in Later Life*, Bristol: Policy Press, pp 136–59.

Lu, T.L.D. (2009) 'Heritage conservation in postcolonial Hong Kong', *International Journal of Heritage Studies*, 15(2–3): 258–72.

Mao, J., Tang, W., Liu, C., Wong, N.S., Tang, S., Wei, C. and Tucker, J.D. (2018) 'Sex tourism among Chinese men who have sex with men: a cross-sectional observational study', *BMC Public Health*, 18(1): 1–12.

Mitchell, J.W. (2014) 'Characteristics and allowed behaviors of gay male couples' sexual agreements', *The Journal of Sex Research*, 51(3): 316–28.

Moors, A.C., Schechinger, H.A., Balzarini, R. and Flicker, S. (2021) 'Internalized consensual non-monogamy: negativity and relationship quality among people engaged in polyamory, swinging, and open relationships', *Archives of Sexual Behavior*, 50(4): 1389–400.

Moskowitz, D.A. and Hart, T.A. (2011) 'The influence of physical body traits and masculinity on anal sex roles in gay and bisexual men', *Archives of Sexual Behavior*, 40(4): 835–41.

Oswald, A. and Roulston, K. (2020) 'Complex intimacy: theorizing older gay men's social lives', *Journal of Homosexuality*, 67(2): 223–43.

Pilkey, B. (2014) 'Queering heteronormativity at home: older gay Londoners and the negotiation of domestic materiality', *Gender, Place & Culture*, 21(9): 1142–57.

Ramirez, O.M. and Brown, J. (2010) 'Attachment style, rules regarding sex, and couple satisfaction: a study of gay male couples', *Australian and New Zealand Journal of Family Therapy*, 31(2): 202–13.

Rubel, A.N. and Bogaert, A.F. (2015) 'Consensual nonmonogamy: psychological well-being and relationship quality correlates', *Journal of Sex Research*, 52(9): 961–82.

Simpson, P. (2013) 'Alienation, ambivalence, agency: middle-aged gay men and ageism in Manchester's gay village', *Sexualities*, 16(3/4): 283–99.

Suen, Y.T. and Wong, M.Y. (2017) 'Male homosexuality in Hong Kong: a 20-year review of public attitudes towards homosexuality and experiences of discrimination self-reported by gay men', in X.D. Lin, C. Haywood and M. Mac an Ghaill (eds) *East Asian Men: Masculinity, Sexuality and Desire*, London: Palgrave Macmillan, pp 69–81.

Wang, F.T., Bih, H.D. and Brennan, D.J. (2009) 'Have they really come out: gay men and their parents in Taiwan', *Culture, Health & Sexuality*, 11(3): 285–96.

Warner, M. (1993) *Fear of a Queer Planet: Queer Politics and Social Theory* (Vol 6), Minneapolis, MN: University of Minnesota Press.

Whyke, T.W. (2023) 'Discourses of heteronormativity and power: the ethical position of Confucianism on same-sex behaviour in China', *Journal of Homosexuality*, 70(9): 1787–806.

Yeh, K.H., Yi, C.C., Tsao, W.C. and Wan, P.S. (2013) 'Filial piety in contemporary Chinese societies: a comparative study of Taiwan, Hong Kong, and China', *International Sociology*, 28(3): 277–96.

PART II

Women questioning age/ing intergenerationally and intragenerationally

5

Deep within the eye of the beheld: exploring hidden accounts of intimacy in the lives of older Indian women in urban Malaysia

Sally Anne Param

Studying the Indian community in Malaysia is a contested field. Although this chapter focuses specifically on gendered accounts of intimacy, the personal is situated against a backdrop of deep-seated social and economic vulnerability among the Indian minority community in Malaysia. This community battles between maintaining their culture and (not) having ownership of the landscape they belong to.

The central idea in this chapter is to explore and understand the taboo discourse on sex and intimacy among older Indian women in urban Malaysia. These women are the first or second generation of Indians born in the host country, to diasporic parents from India. However, several discourses need to be examined before the positioning of these women's socio-subject identity can be revisited and identified with more honesty. Only after the social, cultural and historical contexts have been established, would the examination of the women's complex, multi-layered narratives make better sense. It is necessary to study the voices of the younger generation, which capture the voices of the older generation, so the latter can be recorded. This dialogic challenge includes making audible and knowable the unspoken issues of intergenerational silences.

The inter-ethnic diasporic past

Indians as a migrant population left India and arrived in Malaysia (then called Malaya) in the 1800s, when the colonial East India Company decided to increase its revenue by trading with Malaya (Sandhu, 2006). Although the blanket term 'Indian' is used in this research, it must be mentioned that these Indians have historical roots in 'North' India (as Sikhs, Hindustanis, Sindhis, Gujeratis, Bengalis), or in 'South' India (as Tamils, Telugus, Malayalees, Chettiars and even Sri Lankan Tamils). The usage of the generic 'Indian' is convenient and is evidenced in all national narratives that seek to represent a united front for multiracial Malaysia (Sandhu, 2006; Manickam, 2010).

Although the majority of Indians were brought in to work on rubber plantations, 'substantial numbers of English-educated Indians' also began to arrive, as those who benefitted from the colonial education policy (Sandhu, 2006: 154). The two separate sets of arrivals eventually created a class divide among the Indians, where the educated ones became the middle class, and where the manual labourers remained working class.

As sociological accounts of class-based communities tend to evidence, poverty-induced social ills among the working class tend to be highlighted; resulting in deviance amplification (Muzaffar, 2006; Manickam, 2010). For example, despite making up only seven per cent of the total population, a newspaper article has cited that more Indians are shown to have died in police custody than any other race (one in four deaths) (The Rakyat Post, 2020). While 'death' seemed the initial concern, the rest of the article strongly implicates the issue of deviance – being found in 'police custody'. A more recent article claims that it is 'about time' that the Indian community is 'taken more seriously' (The Malay Mail, 2022). However, the mention of 'poverty-reduction processes' can be interpreted as mere rhetoric when subject to a contextual analysis of social ills highlighted in various other local narratives.

Such media portrayals eclipse successful narratives of middle-class Indians, whose lived reality of educational and economic progress remains obscured at national and popular levels. These silences are exacerbated with the arrival of another diasporic group: Chinese people from mainland China.

Historians have referred to the Chinese as the more stable population in comparison to the Indians (Muzaffar, 2006). With a strong business acumen, and free of a divisive caste hierarchy, the Chinese are 'much more homogenous culturally' (Muzaffar, 2006: 215). Both factors worked in the favour of the Chinese and hastened the process of reduced Indian employment opportunities in the public service sector. The preference for the Chinese as a diasporic presence contributed further to the muting of Indians, explaining the 'marginalisation of sorts of the Indian middle class' (Muzaffar, 2006: 226).

Apart from a race- and class-based eclipse, national narratives have remained dominantly male-centred, with rare and sporadic mention of 'wives and children' (Sandhu, 2006). The domesticated role of Asian women has been exacerbated by political ideology that seeks to preserve 'Asian values' through women's silenced roles as nurturers of 'households' (Quah, 2009: 113). Female labour contributions to the household economy continue to receive little attention (Douglass, 2012; Hirschman, 2016). This explains the larger milieu within which the women of this research are positioned. The silences these urban Indian women face cut across diasporic, racial, class-based and gendered lines.

The older Indian women in this research have one more peripheral experience to account for: their age. These women did not have a recognised social space even when they were younger (Param, 2016). In spite of Malaysia being considered an ageist society that favours the elderly over the young (Yiing et al, 2021), perceptions of being marginalised are what the elderly strongly feel (Ooi et al, 2021). Due to this multi-layered void that shades the backdrop of these older women's lives, the proverbial elephant in the room is not so much issues pertaining to intimacy or sexuality in their later years. Rather, it is these women's aspirations, hopes and significance that have not had the space to be acknowledged or recognised.

These contexts explain why the voices of these women's daughters had to feature in the research process; to facilitate, in a realistic manner, the hearing of the quiet(ed) lives of their mothers. This indirect method of gaining knowledge has been a blessing in disguise, as this process has opened up an intergenerational conversation about stories of sex and intimacy. This gives depth and rich insight into Indian female lives in Malaysia, enabling an intergenerational, familial relationality to be examined at the same time.

The research participants, the daughters of these older mothers, represent the younger generation who are more willing to talk about sex and intimacy. They may not fully understand the anthropological significance or necessity of capturing the othered voices of their mothers. They may not be able to process how ideas on sex and intimacy can be relevant in studying the hidden meanings of a minority ethnic community. Yet, it is interesting to note that these daughters were willing to participate in the research. These younger women thanked the researcher for the opportunity to talk about personal issues in an open, validating manner. The eagerness on their part reiterates the reality that space for such casual yet self-affirming narratives has been absent in the lives of female Indians.

Feminist theory frameworks

The women in my research experience inequalities that cut across the numerous delineations of race, class and gender, and in the nexus of relationships these women have, patriarchy is the basis. Two feminist theories are selected to help explain the lives of the women, both structurally and in lived reality. Marxist-feminist theory (Walby, 1990; Gottfried, 2013) helps establish the structural and contextual background. Muted Group Theory (Ardener, 1975; Barkman, 2018) is foregrounded more, as it explains current restrictions the women face, and how their voices remain muted. These related theories prove useful in accounting for how macro-level structures and ideologies impact upon discussions of intimacy at the everyday micro level.

Marxist-feminist theory deals with the inequalities women face both in the labour market and in the household, under the capitalist system (Armstrong,

2020). At the workplace, the women face subordination due to unequal social and power relationships. At home, they contend with unpaid and reproductive 'women's work'. The 'dual burden' outcome for women in capitalist settings fits the description of the younger women in this research perfectly, as both public and private versions of patriarchy define them.

The Marxist-feminist preoccupation with female labour, both paid and unpaid, is a suitable and necessary theoretical framework for this chapter because the entire diasporic essence of this gendered community is based on migratory work patterns. The older women came as wives to husbands who worked under colonial rule. Although many were allowed to come as housewives, other women were allowed migration access due to the occupations they could be employed in in the host nation (Sandhu, 2006). This workforce trajectory also explains why it is a 'success' when the daughters of these women are able to take up paid employment. These intergenerational work patterns have been reshaped to provide upward social mobility.

Usefully, Sylvia Walby (1990) has identified six structures that create the matrix of both private and public patriarchy; how the interrelationships between paid work, housework, sexuality, culture, violence and the state create different forms of patriarchy. Her six-dimensioned theorising explains the how and why it is 'essential to capture the depth, pervasiveness and interconnectedness of different aspects of women's subordination' (Walby, 1990: 1–2). In Marxist-feminist thought, patriarchy and the structure of a capitalist economy go hand-in-hand. When discussing the theme of sexual silencing later, Marxist-feminist thought on work identity will be revisited as a resource.

Although indebted to a Marxist-feminist analysis, Muted Group Theory (Ardener, 1975, 1993) provides a clearer light on the women's lived reality, delineating how certain groups of people remain powerless compared to others. Like Marxist-feminism, this theory also relies on an understanding of relationships, a study of interactions between dominant and subordinated groups (Wood, 2005). In analysis of this theory, Barkman (2018) refers to the subtle and overlapping power relations that occur in the everyday, which cause minority groups' issues to be unvoiced.

Developed by anthropologists Shirley and Edwin Ardener, Muted Group Theory found that women's voices were 'often more "inarticulate" than men['s]' (Ardener, 1975: viii), exposing the subtle reasons for how women are marginalised even in everyday conversations, both at home and at the workplace. The discourse can be taken to a broader structural level that considers the role of the state in facilitating discourses that favour men.

Second wave feminist scholars Mitchell and Oakley (1976) had pointed out how muted invisibility (double metaphor intended) had been identified as the main problem in women's position and status as a distinct social group.

In their study on news media coverage, Okiyi, Odionye and Okeya (2020) confirm how prime time is reserved for issues relating to the dominant group (men), while that of the othered communities (female and children) remain muted.

Muted Group Theory is thus about 'power dynamics' and the unequal 'relationships' which are 'responsible for muting voices' (Barkman, 2018: 4). Patriarchy naturalises male and female divisions, making it seem natural and right that women's voices are subordinated to men's. These 'subtle' power issues are what I would like to probe into in this chapter; dynamics which keep the voices of these Indian women silenced. Muted Group Theory also helps explain the hesitancy the older women in this research have in talking about personal elements of their lives due to an upbringing which established their 'othered' identity. Discussing sex and intimacy with younger people (even if it is their own daughters) would be the worst of cultural taboos in an ageist Indian community.

Research design

The empirical research on which this chapter is based sought to evaluate the impact of actual rather than assumed responses from eight urban Indian women living in Malaysia who are willing to talk about the lives of their elderly mothers who have a diasporic background. Most of these women are mothers themselves, living in nuclear households, and all of them are professionally employed in a full-time capacity (meaning that they are not housewives or working in volunteer or part-time engagements). The recruitment of these women was achieved through word-of-mouth. To avoid researcher bias, I could not interview my own circle of Indian female friends who fit the description. However, I could use the snowballing method to ask my friends whether they knew of other Indian females who would fit the description. My friends were given the list of requirements: women who are Indian and of the diasporic descent, engaged in various forms of full-time employment, had mothers they were in close contact with, and most importantly, who would be willing to talk about the personal lives of their mothers.

The methodology used falls within the 'feminist allegiance' where the philosophy underlying the methods and approaches highlight and champion 'women's experience' (Bart, 2000: 209). This is possible because all the participants in this research are females, and the research is committed to two important criteria that follow what is called a gendered framework (including women's lives and concerns): minimising potential harms to women in the research process, and supporting value-based research that can improve women's status (Metso and Le Feuvre, 2006). Within this framework, a qualitative lens is used.

Qualitative data aim to capture the quality of people's lives, and how they feel or think, or why they make certain decisions (Rossman and Rallis, 2016). Qualitative research takes place in the natural setting and uses methods that solicit active participation from the participants, while maintaining sensitivity to their privacy (Creswell, 2003). Unlike quantitative data, which prioritise statistical information devoid of deeper interpretations and meanings, qualitative research seeks to explore the richness of the responses at hand, advocating 'the inclusion of women's experience' in reported and recorded accounts of lived reality (Bart, 2000: 209). My study was exploratory, like a small-scale case study that provides a snapshot of the older Indian women's lives, as they talk (or not) about sex and intimacy to their daughters. The two research tools that are used are semi-structured interviews and the practice of reflexivity.

The older mothers were aged between 60 and 84, and the daughters' ages ranged between 30 and 57. The research participants, daughters of the older women, had agreed in advance to a scheduled meeting with the researcher. All participants were met in quiet public places (mostly restaurants or cafés), and notes were jotted down during the time of all conversations. The purpose of the research was outlined in a pre-interview phone call, and before the start of the interview, informed consent was confirmed. Informal chatting was used as the 'door-opener' to deeper conversations. The semi-structured interview style is perfect for the research design. This is because even though the main questions are pre-determined, other digressive aspects are also able to be visited through the openness of the exchange. The semi-structured interview enables a 'conversation', where 'the stories told' by the participants encourage a more open-ended dialogue to proceed (Kvale, 1996: 124).

As part of the gender-sensitive methodology, researcher reflexivity was also consciously used, where the researcher's positioning and role in the process of gaining data, is acknowledged (Alvesson and Skoldberg, 2017). Reflexivity enables researchers to examine 'the broader social landscape' within which the research participants live and where they are located in hierarchies, so that this knowledge of 'context, power, and historical circumstances' can deepen the intersecting relationship between researcher and research participants (Alvesson et al, 2008: 485).

From my own experience with previous research on Indian women, the common identity markers of gender and ethnicity shared between researcher and participants helped facilitate a closer bond between us, enabling a more open discussion. In sharing a somewhat similar lived experience, participants unconsciously have a taken-for-granted perception that the researcher understands the local cultural sensibilities which they experience (Jackson et al, 2017). This practised 'familiarity' facilitates the participants feeling understood, causing them to open up more about the unspoken subjectivities of their mothers' lives. Reflexivity also enables a quick yet conscious observation of other details about the participants which can add to the meaning-making process of their spoken words.

Reflexivity as a tool empowers the researcher to map the interviewees' responses against larger perspectives, thus enabling more open, authentic responses (Ryan-Flood and Gill, 2010; Alvesson et al, 2008). Although 'researcher bias' is levelled at qualitative research, its use of intersubjectivity is, nonetheless, the most productive way of getting closer to participant meanings. Indeed, reflexivity functions as a marker of academic rigour in qualitative research (Alvesson and Skoldberg, 2017).

During the research process, the creation and use of ice-breaking conversations, carried out in a warm and relaxed way, proved essential. Without these conscious practices, the participants could have felt that they needed to put on their best behaviour and give responses which they think the researcher regards as 'correct' or 'good enough'. The unspoken power relations had to be made more equal, so that the 'realness' of the researcher could encourage the 'realness' in the women. Only then would the opportunity to glean more detailed nuances of their mothers' lives be possible. This understanding foregrounds the importance of why reflexivity can 'never be seen as an individualised practice, detached from the social dimensions in which we (researchers, researched, and the phenomena we are investigating) are inserted in' (De Paula, 2021: 442). Rather, reflexivity is inevitably socially sensitive and thus context-dependent (De Paula, 2021).

Despite the richness that reflexivity provides in garnering data about the older mothers' lives through the younger women's lives, it must be acknowledged that the actual interiority of the older women cannot be gleaned from talking to the daughters alone. My 'positioning practice' – as a fellow Indian female who has a diasporic past, is a mother, and being engaged in the employment sector – enables me to reflect on the tensions within the narratives of the younger women's relationships with their mothers, and not from the mothers' actual lives per se. This research is therefore a story of how the younger women manage their mothers' expectations in their personal interior lives, in terms of what is said, implied and left unsaid. This is the closest the researcher can get, in terms of addressing the research gap on the intimate experiences of older Indian females in Malaysia.

Findings

The 'hidden curriculum'

By way of context, it is worth bearing in mind that the mothers of the younger women live in geographical spaces that are relatively close by to their daughters. Only one mother lives further than the rest, in a town 270 kilometres away.[1] All other mothers' homes are only 40–70 kilometres away. Geographical proximity informs the analysis later.

The respondents and their mothers come from backgrounds where being or becoming middle class was the main aspiration. Some of the respondents' grandparents were the first to set foot in Malaysia, where having respectable jobs and educating their children were essential priorities (Jayasooria and Nathan, 2016). Getting married was part of the process leading to a successful life.

The respondents were asked if their parents showed affection to one another in their formative years. Four of the respondents denied seeing any show of affection or intimacy between their parents. Indra (age 52) said her father was rarely at home, and when she got older, she understood that her absent father was the main reason for her mother's eventual divorce. The other respondents qualified the lack of evident intimacy, although they wanted to justify a broader understanding of intimacy. Giita (age 36) claimed that "the cultural barriers they overcame speaks of their love", while Sham (age 57) claimed there were "amicable conversations" and Tamilarasi (age 30) said "they showed trust and respect" to each other.

A few of the women reported that parental affection was evident. "My parents hugged in front of the children, and we knew that romance is important in marriage", said Shivani (age 36). Diana (age 48) remembers how her parents used to "hold hands while crossing the road, sit close while they watched TV, or even how dad would yell for mum to come scrub his back while he was showering".

However, what many of these women remember more about their mothers is the way a routinised lifestyle was implemented. "My mum was the tiger mum. We children used to get whacked [physically punished], and even made to eat chilli and onions", says Shivani. "Mum was very strict, she used to beat us often with whatever she gets in her hand", stated Sangeetha (age 40).

The concept of the 'household' is evident through the imposing of these negative sanctions. Douglass (2012) mentions how capitalism repositions the home into 'an institution' charged with 'the reproduction of labour' and as 'a unit of consumption' (Douglass, 2012: 7). The mothers of the women represented here represent the 'exigencies of a modern economy' where children are brought up to toe-the-line in adhering to the discipline of school, homework and house chores (Quah, 2009: 110). Within the context of middle-class Indian homes in Malaysia, the 'growth of education … for their children' has become 'an acute necessity' for parents (Arasaratnam, 2006: 197), and the mothering role is the one that holds the family and the home together (Param, 2016). Apart from the random 'hug and kiss' affection that measures intimacy between parents (as told by Shivani), what comes closest to intimacy seems to be strict household management by the mothers.

'Study hard' versus 'Playboy magazines'

In recollecting their own adolescent years, interviewees were asked about their mothers' attitudes and knowledge about intimacy and sexuality at that time. With the assumption that these are the more formative years when romantic inclinations are overt, the researcher had hoped that this may have been an appropriate time for the mothers to share personal intimate secrets with their daughters.

Unfortunately, what all the younger women remember most at this formative stage of their lives was how they were made to study hard at school. "My mother had only one advice: focus on your studies, marriage will come later", says Sham. Tamilarasi only remembers the 'study hard' mantra in her adolescence: "Dad was the sole bread-winner as a sundry shop owner, the four of us siblings needed scholarships and loans to get by." For others, there were traces of leniency in relation to boyfriends. "I could talk to boys on the phone, but the 'finish studies first' was still more important", says Sangeetha. Diana reported that her mother actually arranged for her to meet 'nice boys' at this time: "We could joke about romantic innuendos and all, but the bigger picture was being independent for my studies and all."

Even when their daughters were ready to date and have boyfriends, the mothers did not use this time to talk about their own sexuality or intimacy. The interviewees had to make sense of such things on their own. "Because my parents had to overcome cultural barriers to get married, I guess that reflects how deep their love is", stated Giita. For a few women, all knowledge of sexual intimacy was from the gutter. Indra says, "Nothing sexual was openly discussed but there were a lot of books in the cupboards and drawers, from Mills & Boons, Harrold Robbins and even *Playboy* magazines. My ideas about sex were from these 'hidden away' materials". For 39-year-old Ruba, she was allowed to bring boys home, but the message from her grandmother (not even her mother) was clear: "Be careful. Boys only want one thing. Never come back with a baby. Your life will be ruined." Sangeetha was also sanctioned but in a more instructional manner: "My mum taught me the difference between a good touch and a bad touch."

These findings show an absence of the older women talking about their own sexual intimacies. Such a knowledge gap (on the part of academics rather than the women themselves), however, does reveal their quotidian preoccupations; their daughters' educational futures (which should not be hindered by romantic inclinations). Meeting boys or talking to them on the telephone were the closest these mothers came to creating space for the unspoken topic of romance and intimacy. Hidden literature, as in Indra's case, and sanctioned advice as in Ruba's (from her grandmother) provide evidence that the subsumed topic of sex is not important; mothering techniques prioritising educational trajectories are.

Marriage

The interplay of culture and kin relationships in defining marriage is highly significant among the Indian community. The researcher had hoped that within this element of historical conjuncture, the older mothers would perhaps reveal parts of their own intimate lives when their daughters hit 'marriageable years'.

Again, the daughters of these mothers remember other elements rather than sexual intimacy when they approached the time to marry. Sham's mother talked about whether the bridegroom was 'worthy' of her daughter in terms of dowry-giving, or whether the wedding plans fit communal expectations. Still single, Tamilarasi was hassled about 'finding a husband' so that cultural propriety would be adhered to. Some of the respondents faced other forms of resistance or compulsion. Indra's choice of husband was accepted with pretended candour and Diana's first husband was not accepted at all. Sangeetha's hopes for marriage seemed to elude her to the point her mother asked her to consider an arranged marriage through migration. Ruba was pushed towards marriage when six years was seen as too long to be going steady with her boyfriend. Most of the daughters could not recall conversations regarding sexual intimacy with their mothers when they were 'preparing' for marriage. In fact, some of the respondents had other family members who were more involved in their lives at this point, and not their mothers. It was her mother-in-law who talked to Giita about the cultural aspects of the marriage union. Ruba declared: "My grandmother talked to me about using the condom, and told me to 'enjoy' myself between having children. My aunts also played a role in educating me about sex, although one of them knew I wasn't a virgin."

Some study participants said they were the ones who broached the topic of sex, and not their parents. Shivani proffered: "I actually share sexual secrets with my mum instead, not the other way around. Mum is open for me to talk about it and listen. Mum even heard me out as I talked about how I was not a virgin before marriage, and she was fine with it." Tamilarasi commented: "I am the one who talks about sex. In fact, I talk more to dad than mum about it. Like there was this one time while we were washing dishes, and I asked dad what he thought about shaving pubic hair!"

These instances show that the older women did not reveal sexual secrets of their own lives, even when their daughters hit marriageable years. The resistance that they exuded, or the cultural propriety that they seemed to highlight through this silence, shows that sexual identity is constituted as secondary compared to cultural-discursive influences of the Indian community. The mothering role in maintaining the 'appropriate' elements of family life, such as making their daughters study hard, is a learned construct that they saw fit to maintain. Sex and intimacy seem to be superficial concerns that should continue to be prohibited even in private conversations.

Discussion

The responses of the younger women in this research reveal that they view the workplace versions of patriarchy as systemic and something they have to undergo. Applying a Marxist-feminist framework, Walby's identification of public patriarchy is something that remains a given in the current context. Women's participation in the workforce is a common feature in all local narratives of economic development (as reflected in the Twelfth Malaysia Plan),[2] and being part of these narratives is not only normalised but viewed as successful. In the younger women's conversations with the researcher during the interviews, concerns about the employment structure, the boss, co-workers or any other gender-based grievance were acknowledged merely as something they had to endure, in order to maintain their middle-class jobs and salaries.

Three factors could explain this mindset. The first could be the constant push towards educational success their mothers have instilled in them (Jackson et al, 2017; Yeoh and Huang, 2010). Having respectable jobs in a capitalist economy is identified as part of having a successful life. The second could be the 'marginalisation of sorts' which the 'Indian middle-class' experience (Muzaffar, 2006: 226). Due to the presence of other races with advantageous leverage in middle-class employment positions, middle-class Indians have felt the need to develop a resolve to maintain a share of the economic pie. A third factor could be avoidance of association with ills commonly linked with working-class Indians (Manickam, 2010). Social ills among the Indian community tended to be normalised in public narratives and perhaps there was an unspoken resolve to undo this unjust label. Whatever the combination of reasons, these women's attitudes can be seen as a rebuttal of gendered discrimination within the capitalist workforce. Through their involvement in 'paid job obligations' (Quah, 2009: 124), the younger women were living out their roles as daughters of a generation of diasporic parents who saw their work identities as crucial beginnings to their migratory experience. Unconsciously, this was their way of maintaining class position.

As regards private patriarchy, it was clear that the younger women had learned cultural representations of womanhood from their mothers. The women in this research had minimal or no explicit complaints regarding 'child care', and thus refuted the 'dual burden' syndrome of paid and domestic labour (Walby, 1990). 'Child care' is something the older Indian women wanted to engage in, judging by their daughters' accounts. They viewed the process of nurturing children to grow up, get married and have children of their own as part of the complex reciprocal relationship between being female and subscribing to Indian cultural norms. In other words, heterosexual expectations and demands for normative behaviour were met, both by older and younger women.

Within participant accounts, it seems that sex and sexual intimacy are the means of having children, period. All the younger women who were interviewed spoke about child-bearing and motherhood as though these experiences are essential to their marriage. Narratives that the older women lived by seemed to be perpetuated in their daughters' lives. The only reason (still single) Tamilarasi is spared disapproval is because 'finding a husband' is still her mother's dream for her. One of the reasons Giita is pregnant with her second child is because her mother had kept asking when her son would get a sibling to play with. Sangeetha is 40 years old but she is still hopeful for a pregnancy after her late marriage, as encouraged by her mother. Diana is happily married to her second husband, who has two children of his own, but her mother's words still make a difference: "There is nothing like having your own." Indra's marriage was her own choice amid her mother's reluctant acceptance, but she admitted that her mother's negative opinion affected her for many years after. Therefore, the connective strength the women depict in their mother–daughter dyads can be seen as a powerful tool to live by. The 'distinct' ways in which 'women's social location shapes their lives can thus be seen as a subversion of patriarchy (Wood, 2005: 61).

Moreover, the younger women have important relationships with other female members within the extended family. Grandmothers (Sangeetha), mothers-in-law (Giita), sisters (Indra) and aunts (Ruba) formed a network of support for the younger women's growth. This phenomenon celebrates the importance of kin within the Indian community. This aspect of the younger women's lived reality clearly evidences how intergenerational, kin-based female empowerment can overcome private patriarchy. Borrowing a Bourdieusian lens via 'cultural capital' – embodied knowledge of society that is 'clearly bound up with social class' (Swingewood, 2000: 214) – it can be said that the women's cultural capital is crucially shaped by intergenerational knowledge and support among females, which they use to counter the hegemony of patriarchy. Through this sense of female power, they are able to demonstrate resilience and agency that talks back to household-based patriarchy.

Open discussions on sex and sexual intimacy are still absent among this community. While individuation and personalised social networks in 'First World' cultures may facilitate open expressions of sexual intimacy, this research reveals that kin-based female friendships in a South Asian diasporic community stops at familial cohesion and emotional support. Existing research on another Malaysian community reveals how proximity of women to their natal family can be a source that helps disperse inequalities between men and women (Hirschman, 2016). This was true for the women featured in my research, as well. Living close by can be an important resource, where the 'geography of power' between men and women can be diminished in the light of female solidarity (Gottfried, 2013: 37). The women featured in this chapter could display independence in female familial practices more than independent expressions of sexual freedom.

Both Marxist-feminist and Muted Group theories can further understanding of relationships or domination and subordination. While forms of public and private patriarchy seem to be overcome at some levels, the silences in sexual expressions remain unvoiced. This seems to align with what is normative for Indian women, as sex-related conversations can be seen as inappropriate and even taboo. Such silences were suspected before the research began and have been vindicated in the results.

Sex and intimacy are largely viewed as the means of having children, and if it is ever 'enjoyed', it is never spoken about. Whatever power dynamics may have been present, it seems that the older women have not restructured traditional cultural expectations of gendered relations in their own marriages, continuing their subordinate roles as wives. The older women's viewpoints on sex and intimacy remain something secret in their own hearts and lives. Perhaps the call for their daughters to 'study' hard' (Tamilarasi) could be a defence mechanism against having to remain silenced about sexual desires. Perhaps the 'finish studies first' (Sangeetha) could be displacement of personal sexual fantasies that have to remain muted.

However, despite the covert possibilities just mentioned, this chapter has acknowledged how the older women have viewed mothering practices above and beyond any other self-expression, sexual or not. Their 'success' has been in raising 'good daughters', first in education, and then as members of society with their own families. This echoes extant research on Asian families where focusing on children's educational and future needs is heavily prioritised (Jackson et al, 2017; Quah, 2009; Donner, 2008). All research questions to the younger women were devised to glean finer detail of elements of their mothers' accounts of sexual intimacy. Yet, there was no whisper of such hidden accounts of experience. The last research question asked what the daughters' own views were, of what is important to their mothers. All interviewees echoed a similar chord in their responses – that their mothers wanted them to be "well and independent, running their own homes" (Shivani) or "having their own family, and leading a stable life" (Giita).

While hegemonic masculine control may continue, and may need more research to probe its effects, the women in this research have shown that they are able to subvert patriarchal 'conditions' that mute them through their own 'practice' of intergenerational norms and values (Donner, 2008: 177). Unlike 'First World' scenarios which would probably entail a distinct breaking away from controlling relationships (Jackson et al, 2017), this situation presents more of a navigation through the continuing existence of a strong patriarchy.

While 'subordinating' in nature, perhaps these very 'conditions' and 'practice[s]' are able to provide 'the conditions of agency' (Donner, 2008: 177) in the future. Perhaps this pioneering research of sorts is only the teaser for future research that may evidence more telling accounts of private sexual experiences. The older women have brought up their daughters to live according to class-based propriety (Param, 2016, 2019). Perhaps the daughters will one day be able to talk back to their community's lived sexual reality.

Conclusion

The key point of this chapter is that older Indian women in Malaysia maintain sexual silence in their married lives. Living in a society that practices the hegemony of masculine control, female subordination is normalised. These women have not even transmitted their viewpoints on sex and intimacy to their own daughters. The small-scale study on which this chapter is based has evidenced that older women cannot yet break sexual silences. Unlike individuals from the 'First World' that can celebrate assertions of sexuality in later life (Simpson et al, 2018), the women featured in this chapter cannot. Living within the safe confines of heterosexual monogamous marriages, only a few of the older women voiced marginal accounts of intimacy with their husbands, such as hugging openly or holding of hands publicly. The majority of them remained muted about private intimate encounters.

Moreover, against this scholarly knowledge gap concerning conversations about sexuality and intimacy, there are small but important shifts in intergenerational dynamics to be noted. The daughters of the older women talked about liberties their mothers did not experience. Seemingly insignificant elements such as learning about the use of a tampon during menstruation (Indra), watching X-rated films together with mum (Sangeetha), talking about the loss of virginity before marriage (Shivani), being advised on the use of a condom before marriage (Ruba), or hearing her sister talk about sex to her mother (Giita), are probably experiences the elder mothers never had. Within a community that has treated conversations about sex as taboo, these daughters get to explore on the periphery of sexual intimacy, implying that some modest intergenerational shifts are taking place.

The younger women featured in this chapter are part of the populace who epitomise Malaysia's gendered socio-economic transformation. These women keep homes and feed the global market economy (Douglass, 2012). They are educated, professionally employed, middle class and (with the exception of one interviewee who is still single), constitute dual-income households. This is the sought-after category in the nation's national economic policy.[3] This is the success that the older mothers dreamed about for their daughters. Taking the diasporic past into consideration, where work identities were the key element that defined the migratory experience, the lives that these daughters now live are a fulfilment of generational dreams that can overcome the 'marginalisation of sorts' (Muzaffar, 2006: 226).

Muted Group Theory addresses silencing and specifically how the powerful in society are 'responsible for muting voices' of the powerless (Barkman, 2018: 4). This sums up the psychological, cultural and socio-economic aspects of being urban, older, female and Indian in Malaysia. These older women have lived through the historicity of multiple silences imposed on them, and have been encouraged rather to maintain intergenerational familial culture in order to raise successful daughters. The older women may not have been able to discuss their own sexual experiences, but their mothering techniques in maintaining their households and sustaining the community's class identity can perhaps be seen as creating an ambivalent space for their daughters, simultaneously enabling accommodation and resistance. Despite knowing that the interview questions would attempt to probe their deeper thoughts on sexual intimacy, the younger women did display an eagerness to be part of the research. Socio-cultural change happens more slowly than we think but perhaps the evidence of a few participants keener to talk about sex and intimacy foreshadows the development of greater opportunity for agency in such matters.

In closing, I use a participant quote of 'not a virgin'. This short phrase represents a bold statement by one of the younger women as she accounted for her lifestyle choices before marriage that were not normative in the community. She had shared this experience with her mother, who was actually supportive of her daughter's 'othered' experience. This mother–daughter exchange symbolises the beginning of unsilenced expressions in this community. It speaks of a potential intergenerational gendered shift where conversations about sex and intimacy are more freely expressed. This possibility alone is a more significant finding than what the researcher set out to discover.

Notes

[1] The furthest distance of a mother's residence is a town called Taiping, about 270 km away from the capital, Kuala Lumpur.
[2] *Twelfth Malaysia Plan*, www.malaysia.gov.my/portal/content/31186
[3] *Twelfth Malaysia Plan*, www.malaysia.gov.my/portal/content/31186

References

Alvesson, M. and Skoldberg, K. (2017) *Reflexive Methodology: New Vistas for Qualitative Research* (3rd edn), Thousand Oaks, CA: Sage.

Alvesson, M., Hardy, C. and Harley, B. (2008) 'Reflecting on Reflexivity: Reflexive Textual Practices in Organization and Management Theory', *Journal of Management Studies*, 45(3): 480–501.

Arasaratnam, S. (2006) 'Political Marginalization in Malaysia,' in Sandhu, K.S. and Mani, A. (eds), *Indian Communities in Southeast Asia*, Singapore: The Institute of Southeast Asian Studies, pp 190–210.

Ardener, S. (1975) *Perceiving Women*, London: Malaby Press.

Ardener, S. (1993) 'Introduction: The Nature of Women in Society', in Ardener, S. (ed), *Defining Females: The Nature of Women in Society*, London: Routledge, pp 1–16.

Armstrong, E. (2020) 'Marxist and Socialist Feminism', in Naples, N. (ed), *Companion to Feminist Studies*, Malden, MA: Wiley Blackwell, pp 35–52.

Barkman, L.L.S. (2018) 'Muted Group Theory: A Tool for Hearing Marginalised Voices', *CBE International*. Available from: www.cbeintern ational.org/resource/article/priscilla-papers-academic-journal/muted-group-theory-tool-hearing-marginalized [accessed 25 September 2022].

Bart, J. (2000) *Women Succeeding in the Sciences: Theories and Practices across Disciplines*, West Lafayette, IN: Purdue University Press.

Creswell, J. (2003) *Research Design: Qualitative, Quantitative, and Mixed Methods Approaches* (2nd edn), Thousand Oaks, CA: Sage Publications.

De Paula, B. (2021) 'Reflexivity, Methodology and Contexts in Participatory Digital Media Research: Making Games with Latin American Youth in London', *Learning, Media and Technology*, 46(4): 435–450.

Donner, H. (2008) *Domestic Goddesses, Maternity, Globalization and Middle-class Identity in Contemporary India*, London: Routledge.

Douglass, M. (2012) 'Global Householding and Social Reproduction: Migration Research, Dynamics and Public Policy in East and Southeast Asia', *ARI Asian Research Institute Working Paper Series No. 188 East and Southeast Asia*, Singapore: National University of Singapore.

Gottfried, H. (2013) *Gender, Work and Economy: Unpacking the Global Economy*, Cambridge: Polity Press.

Hirschman, C. (2016) 'Gender, the Status of Women, and Family Structure in Malaysia', *Malaysian Journal of Economic Studies*, 53(1): 33–50.

Jackson, S., Ho, P.S.Y. and Na, J.N. (2017) 'A Tale of Two Societies: The Doing of Qualitative Comparative Research in Hong Kong and Britain', *Methodological Innovations*, 10(2): 1–12.

Jayasooria, D. and Nathan, K.S. (2016) *Contemporary Malaysian Indians: History, Issues, Challenges and Prospects*, Selangor: Institute of Ethnic Studies (KITA), National University of Malaysia (UKM).

Kvale, S. (1996) *InterViews: An Introduction to Qualitative Research Interviewing*, Thousand Oaks, CA: Sage Publications.

Manickam, J.R. (2010) *The Malaysian Indian Dilemma: The Struggles and Agony of the Indian Community in Malaysia* (3rd edn), Selangor: Nationwide Human Development and Research Centre.

Metso, M. and Le Feuvre, N. (2006) *Quantitative Methods for Analysing Gender, Ethnicity and Migration*, York: University of York.

Mitchell, J. and Oakley, A. (1976) *The Rights and Wrongs of Women*, London: Penguin Books.

Muzaffar, C. (2006) 'Political Marginalization in Malaysia', in Sandhu, K.S. and Mani, A. (eds), *Indian Communities in Southeast Asia*, Singapore: The Institute of Southeast Asian Studies, pp 211–236.

Okiyi, G., Odionye, C. and Okeya, A. (2020) 'Socio-cultural Variables and Media Coverage of Girl Child Marriages', *Nnamdi Azikiwe University Journal of Communication and Media Studies*, 1(2). Available from: www.rex.commpan.com/index.php/naujocom/article/view/93 [accessed 13 February 2024].

Ooi, P.B., Ong, D.L.T., Peh, S.C., Ismail, S.F., Param, S.A., Siew, A.H.L., Lean, K.S. and Chan, N.N. (2021) 'Active Aging, Psychological Well-being and Quality of Life of Elderly and Pre-elderly Malaysians during Movement Control Periods', *Educational Gerontology*, 47(8): 353–368.

Param, S.A. (2016) 'Sustaining Middle-Classness: Studying the lives of Indian Working Mothers and their Children in Malaysia', Doctoral Thesis, Kuala Lumpur: University of Malaya, Malaysia.

Param, S.A. (2019) 'Responding and Adjusting: Exploring the Friendship Dilemma through the Qualitative Lens of Educated Indian Women in Malaysia', in Bromwich, R., Ungar, O. and Richard, N. (eds), *Critical Perspectives on 21st-Century Friendship: Polyamory, Polygamy, and Platonic Affinity*, Bradford, ON: Dementer Press, pp 13–28.

Quah, S.R. (2009) *Families in Asia, Home and Kin*, New York and London: Routledge.

Rossman, G.B. and Rallis, S.F. (2016) *Learning in the Field: An Introduction to Qualitative Research*, Los Angeles, CA: Sage Publications.

Ryan-Flood, R. and Gill, R. (2010) 'Introduction', in Ryan-Flood, R. and Gill, R. (eds), *Secrecy and Silence in the Research Process: Feminist Reflections*, London: Routledge, pp 1–11.

Sandhu, K.S. (2006) 'The Coming of the Indians to Malaysia', in Sandhu, K.S. and Mani, A. (eds), *Indian Communities in Southeast Asia*, Singapore: The Institution of Southeast Asian Studies, pp 151–189.

Simpson, P., Brown Wilson, C., Brown, L., Horne, M. and Dickinson, T. (2018) '"We've Had Our Sex Life Way Back": Older Care Home Residents, Sexuality and Intimacy', *Ageing and Society*, 38(7): 1478–1501.

Swingewood, A. (2000) *A Short History of Sociological Thought*, New York: St. Martin's Press.

The Malay Mail (2022) 'Time we take the Indian community in Malaysia seriously – Charles Santiago'. Available from: www.malaymail.com/news/what-you-think/2022/07/05/time-we-take-the-indian-community-in-malaysia-seriously-charles-santiago/15795 [accessed 26 September 2022].

The Rakyat Post (2020) 'Indian Malaysians are over-represented in police custody deaths'. Available from: www.therakyatpost.com/living/2020/06/04/indian-malaysians-are-over-represented-in-police-custody-deaths [accessed 12 October 2022].

Unit Perancang Ekonomi Jabatan Perdana Menteri (nd) *Twelfth Malaysian Plan (RM12)*. Available from: www.malaysia.gov.my/portal/content/31186 [accessed 27 September 2022].

Walby, S. (1990) *Theorising Patriarchy*, Oxford: Basil Blackwell.

Wood, J. (2005) 'Feminist Standpoint Theory and Muted Group Theory: Commonalities and Divergences', *Women and Language*, 28(2): 61–72.

Yeoh, B.S. and Huang, S. (2010) 'Mothers on the Move: Children's Education and Transactional Mobility in Global-city Singapore', in Chavkins, W. and Maher, J.M. (eds), *The Globalization of Motherhood: Deconstructions and Reconstructions of Biology and Care*, Abingdon: Routledge, pp 31–54.

Yiing, J.L., Ee, S.L. and Senadjki, A. (2021) 'Health Promotion and Active Aging among Seniors in Malaysia', *Journal of Health Research*, 36(5): 444–456.

6

From age of despair to window of opportunity? Reframing women's sexuality in later life in the Middle East and North Africa

Shereen El Feki and Selma Hajri

Naming and reclaiming

In Arabic, the common term for female menopause is *sinn al ya's*, 'age of despair'.[1] Although there are more precise clinical terms in Arabic (*inqata' al tamth*, 'cessation of menstruation', for example), it is despair that dominates popular and medical discourse across the Middle East and North Africa (MENA).[2] Language speaks volumes as to how societies view sexual acts and sexual beings. And so 'age of despair' says it all: a dim and distant shelf to which cultures, uncomfortable with female sexuality in general and ignorant of older women's sexuality in particular, consign women past their reproductive (and, by extension, sexual) best-before date.[3]

Similarly, while Arabic has a wide array of words to denote homosexuality, from the Qur'anic (*liwat*, 'sodomy') to global human rights terminology (*al-mithliyya al-jinsiyya*, 'sexual sameness'), the expression most commonly used and most readily understood for a male who engages in same-sex relations is *shadh*, 'deviant' (Amer, 2012).[4] This term, however, has met its match in LGBTQ activists across MENA who have spent more than a decade trying to shift usage to the more neutral and apposite *mithliyy* (Abdelmoez, 2021; Semerene, 2019.

It is a measure of political and economic transitions in MENA since the Arab Spring that efforts to reclaim 'menopause' in Arabic are now led, not by civil society (which has seen its room to manoeuvre shrink dramatically in many countries over the past decade), but rather by the private sector. In 2021, TENA, a global manufacturer of incontinence products, launched its #DespairNoMore social media campaign in an attempt to shift attitudes towards menopause – and presumably, its own products as well (TENA, 2021a). According to a survey of 600 Saudi Arabian women aged 40 and above conducted by YouGov and TENA, while almost a fifth of post-menopausal respondents were so embarrassed by their reproductive transition that they kept silent about their experiences, more than 80 per cent of participants wanted to see the term 'age of despair' updated to more accurately reflect their active lives (TENA, 2021b).

Central to the campaign was a call for women across the region to submit their ideas for better terminology. UNFPA (United Nations Population Fund) formally endorsed the winning entry, *sinn al-tajdīd* or 'age of renewal', as the new-and-improved Arabic term for menopause with a high-profile launch at EXPO 2022 (UNFPA, 2022). Al Maany, an online Arabic dictionary, is among the first to offer it as an alternative entry under 'age of despair', defined as the 'age at which a woman's menstrual blood and ovulation stops, and her energy is renewed for a new and promising stage of her life, usually between forty-five and fifty' (El Chaer, 2021).

Whether 'age of renewal' will find fertile ground in MENA remains to be seen. What is clear, however, is that this initiative related to menopause is part of a wider flowering of conversations on hitherto hidden aspects of female sexuality in communities across MENA. As one gynaecologist from the region put it a decade ago: 'In the Arab world, sex is the opposite of sport. Everyone talks about football, but hardly anyone plays it. But sex – everyone is doing it, but nobody wants to talk about it' (El Feki, 2014a).

Thanks to the internet, however, this silence is increasingly filled by Arabic-speaking voices. Topics long the subject of private whisperings are increasingly finding an audience in social media, that no-man's land between private and public discourse (El Feki et al, 2014). It is not just experts or activists who are speaking up, but also 'ordinary' individuals who are busy online questioning, if not outright challenging, received wisdoms as they relate to sexual and reproductive life: the primacy of female virginity (Eich, 2010); the (im)permissibility of homosexuality (Walsh-Haines, 2012) or contraception and abortion (Wynn et al, 2009) or sexuality education (Müller et al, 2017); the social desirability of female genital mutilation or early marriage (Shaw and Silverio, 2021); the stigma of unwed motherhood or infertility; the acceptability of sexual harassment and gender-based violence (Abdelmonem, 2015), among other hotly debated issues. Also, while menopause increasingly features in this online dialogue, given the demographic profile of internet users in MENA – mainly young and male – female sexuality in later life is not a trending topic – at least not yet (Reffat, 2022).

This virtual sex talk follows a well-worn path. At their pinnacle in the 9th to the 11th centuries, Arab scholars were the masters of sex, producing works that not only offered an exhaustive examination of sexual problems, but also a celebration of the full spectrum of sexual pleasure and intimacy (El Feki, 2015). Indeed, as seen and selectively interpreted by generations of Westerners, it is this tradition of frank discourse on sex that helped to fuel centuries of Orientalist views of the Middle East, with all their political, economic and cultural consequences (Saïd, 1995; Tabahi, 2020).

Much of this Arabic literature – poetry, medical treatises, and self-help books – was written by Islamic scholars who saw nothing incompatible in striking a balance between the needs of the flesh and the demands of the faith (El Feki, 2014b). This historical record reflects a framing of female desire in Islamic texts as far more powerful than that of men, and reveals a deep well of male anxiety as to how to rise to the occasion of women's full-throttle sexual drive. For all the primacy of virginity in religious and cultural discourse, Arabic erotica also celebrates female sexual experience and features a long line of older women (the remarkable character of Hubba Al Madiniyya, for example) who share their intimate advice, and sexual favours, as they please (Myrne, 2019). This chapter provides a twenty-first-century update, in the form of a critical assessment of how menopause is managed in the MENA, through a review of the academic literature and selected clinical experience.

Menopause under the microscope

In contrast to the increasingly active dialogue online, presentations of sexuality in 'official' fora across MENA – be it mainstream media or education or research – are far more controlled and constrained, not only in comparison with the region's social media but also with analogous spaces in other parts of the global South.

Clinical research on SRHR (sexual and reproductive health and rights) across MENA by-and-large focuses more on the 'R' than the 'S' and tends to frame both as problems to be solved – diseases (for example, STIs), disorders (such as vaginismus), deficiencies (for example, erectile dysfunction).[5] In the context of sexuality, the white coat of public health is seen as lending legitimacy and respectability (not to mention official authorisation and funding) to interrogate otherwise taboo topics. So, it is unsurprising that the majority of research on sexuality and intimacy in the later lives of women in MENA focuses on that bookend of female reproduction – menopause.

For the record, menopause is defined as the permanent cessation of menstruation as a result of the loss of ovarian activity; natural menopause is recognised after 12 months or more of amenorrhea in the absence of a pathological cause (World Health Organization, 2022). Where such data are collected across MENA, the average age of natural menopause is estimated to be between 46 and 49 years (see Reynolds and Obermeyer, 2001, 2003; Greer et al, 2003; Sallam et al, 2006; Ceylan and Özerdogan, 2015; Naz et al, 2019; Busami et al, 2021), on the lower end of the internationally accepted range of 45–55 years old and younger than the rising trend in many Western countries.

The hormonal alterations that accompany menopause are associated with a number of physical and psychological changes, among them vasomotor symptoms (temperature changes due to hormones); urogenital atrophy; vaginal dryness and dyspareunia (genital pain during or after sexual intercourse); sexual dysfunction; joint and muscle pain; sleep disturbances, depression, mood alterations; as well as an elevated risk of a range of chronic disorders such as cardiovascular disease, osteoporosis and diminished cognitive function. While a universal phenomenon, experience of menopausal symptoms has been shown to vary from woman to woman according to individual characteristics, including the usual suspects such as age and underlying health status, as well as less obvious contributors such as education, employment and marital status (Namazi et al, 2019).

Analysis of global datasets has shown that an estimated 50 per cent of women aged 40–64 experience sleep and mood disorders, with around 60 per cent reporting vasomotor symptoms, muscle and joint pain and some form of sexual dysfunction (Makara-Studzinska et al, 2014). But these averages veil intriguing geographic variations: for example, significantly higher percentages of European women going through menopause report more sleep, mood and sexual disorders than their North American counterparts, who, in turn, appear to suffer more commonly from hot flashes and excessive sweating than their South American peers.

Women's attitudes towards menopause also differ considerably, with some perceiving it as a release from the complications associated with menstruation and contraception, opening the door to more liberated lovemaking; while others lament the onset of age and the end of childbearing, as well as a perceived loss of attractiveness and a loss of sexual desire. Not surprisingly, symptomology of and attitudes towards menopause are intimately entwined: women with more positive perspectives on menopause tend to report fewer symptoms, and vice versa.

Conventional framings of menopause and sexuality emphasise deficit and dysfunction – vaginal dryness and dyspareunia, combined with assorted other physical symptoms, depression and anxiety – as having an impact on arousal and orgasm and, by extension, frequency of and satisfaction with sexual activity. This school of loss chimes with broader societal framings of older life as a winding down in the bedroom, despite ample evidence to the contrary (Taylor and Gosney, 2011). In contrast, feminist perspectives that shift from a narrow biomedical lens to a broader biopsychosocial approach yield a different picture by understanding menopause in the context of a woman's life course and how both she and the world in which she lives change over time (Yisma and Ly, 2018). Seen from this angle, menopausal women can and do enjoy sex and intimacy, given the growing body of research showing that relationship quality (including communication and adaptation over time) and a host of other social factors affect women's sexual experience as much or even more than menopause's medical sequelae, and how women perceive changes in their post-menopausal lives in general, and their sexual function in particular, is as much a function of societal norms as it is of individual circumstances (see Winterich, 2003; Hinchliff et al, 2010).

In this regard, conventional wisdom holds that in traditional societies, which place high importance on childbearing and rearing, depreciation in social value associated with the end of fertility is offset by the rising status of the women with age (and the presence of adult sons), which in turn gives women more authority. In contrast, it is posited that, Western societies, while placing less importance on fertility, valorise youth and beauty, thereby posing greater challenges for ageing women (Namazi et al, 2019).

As an example of this contrast, earlier studies comparing women in Asian and European settings suggested that women living in Eastern cultures who view menopause as a natural process reported fewer symptoms and held more positive views than women living in the West (Pitkin, 2010). However, recent reappraisals have noted the complexity of international comparisons due to cultural factors which may lead to under-reporting of symptoms and satisfaction (particularly as these relate to sexuality) and are subject to shifting positions due to globalisation and education, which expand women's understanding not just of their own experience of menopause, but of how their counterparts elsewhere in the world are experiencing the same change of life (Baber, 2014).

MENA in the middle

At the crossroads of East and West, MENA offers an interesting testbed for such cross-cultural theories. The region is vast and varied, with as many differences within countries as there are between them. Nonetheless, there are red lines running right across the region, and the ones related to female sexuality and sexuality in later life have woven together to create a veil which has until recently covered the intimate and sexual experiences of women going through menopause.

This situation is now changing, thanks in part to demographics. For decades, discussions of population trajectories in MENA have focused on the 'youth bulge' of under-30s; the region is now shifting to an 'age bump' of over-50s thanks to longer lifespans and lower fertility rates (Abyad and Hammami, 2021). The average life expectancy for women in MENA is 73.5 years, which means they will spend roughly a third of their lives post-menopause (ESCWA, 2019). Those numbers add up: globally there will be 1.2 billion women post-menopause by 2030, with more than 10 million in Egypt and Iran alone (see, for example, Sallam et al, 2006; Namazi et al, 2019).

This demographic momentum, combined with an increased focus on women's rights in the region post-Arab Spring, is reflected in a small but growing body of research on menopause in MENA. The majority of studies are strictly quantitative, measuring physical and psychological symptoms and quality of life; this is particularly true of emerging work on menopause in the Gulf States. Where sexuality is considered, it is mainly measured by scales and scores, rather than applying more nuanced approaches to understanding the full spectrum of women's experiences.

Among the exceptions is Tunisia, which is widely seen as an outlier on women's rights and sexual and reproductive health in the region. This reputation dates to its independence from France in 1956, and then-President Bourguiba's modernising project which included greater integration of women into the nation-building process. In one of its first post-independence breaks with the past, Tunisia introduced a new personal status code which represented a significant departure from earlier laws grounded in *shari'a*, including the abolition of polygamy, a ban on repudiation and the introduction of a minimum age of marriage. Additional rounds of legal reform included the legalisation of contraception in 1964 and abortion in 1973, criminalisation of gender-based violence in 2016, as well as further levelling of the playing field between men and women when it comes to voting rights and political representation, equal pay and the right to divorce.

However, patriarchy dies hard in Tunisia, all the more so after the 'Jasmine Revolution' of 2010 and subsequent rise of religious conservatism in public and private life. While laws punishing same-sex relations and extramarital sex are still on the books, marital rape is not yet criminalised. Abortion services – though legal – are increasingly hard to access because of pushback from conservative providers (Raifman et al, 2018). By law, inheritance favours men over women, creating an ever more challenging economic situation for women given that only one in four is formally employed.

It is against this backdrop of steps forward and steps back, that Hajri and counterparts have spent almost two decades probing the meaning of menopause in Tunisian women's lives in their clinical practice and research. In 2005–2008, Ferrand, Hajri and colleagues conducted the first large-scale study of more than 1,000 women aged 45–64 in Tunis and surrounding rural areas, looking at the physical and mental health of peri- and post-menopausal participants and its impact on their quality of life (Ferrand et al, 2013).

A high proportion of Tunisian women in this groundbreaking survey reported adverse physical and emotional effects of menopause. Women living alone reported more somatic symptoms, reduced memory, anxiety and sleep disturbance than their married peers – not surprising given the social value placed on marriage, and its status as the only socially accepted context for sexual life in Tunisian society (El Feki, 2014a). However, the factor most strongly and widely associated with poor quality of life in this sample of women was a low level of education and low socio-economic status. Compared with university-educated women in the study, illiterate respondents (who made up the majority of the sample) had a significantly elevated risk of physical symptoms and signs of depression and anxiety (Benzineb et al, 2013).

Tunisia is one of the few countries in MENA to have explicitly examined women's experiences of menopause in cross-cultural context, specifically in comparison with counterparts in France, with which Tunisia has significant historical connections and current relations. Hajri and colleagues further compared results from the Tunisian survey with findings from 700 women in France aged 48 to 53 years. Tunisian women scored lower in every dimension of Quality of Life, including elevated somatic and vasomotor symptoms, depressed mood and anxiety, than their French peers, with a greater gap seen between Tunisian and French women in lower socio-economic classes than between their middle-class counterparts (Ferrand, 2013).

Less is known about the impact of menopause on Tunisian women's sexual lives. Small-scale clinical studies suggest that more than 70 per cent of peri- or post-menopausal women have some form of sexual dysfunction, mainly in the form of diminished desire and excitement, accompanied by lower frequency of intercourse (Ati et al, 2018; Siala et al, 2019). Not surprisingly, fewer women with positive attitudes towards menopause and better relations with their husbands experienced such symptoms; interestingly, the majority of women in such studies reported being satisfied with their sexual lives, even those who scored as experiencing some form of sexual dysfunction.

Qualitative research reveals a spectrum of attitudes among menopausal women in Tunisia (Delanoë et al, 2012). Working-class participants in greater Tunis reported strong physical and emotional symptoms (pain in particular), accompanied by a sense of loss through ageing and feelings of uselessness. Some were also concerned about the health effects of what they mistakenly thought was 'impure' menstrual blood being retained in the body in the absence of menstruation. For these women, sex was framed as a religious obligation. Interestingly, their rural counterparts had a greater sense of social value in older age, possibly through their greater physical activity and employment.

In contrast to the working-class participants, middle-class Tunisian women noted few physical symptoms, but were deeply concerned about changes in their appearance (especially body fat), leading to a sense of lower physical and sexual attractiveness and worries about diminished sexual appeal. A third group – educated, middle-class women – took menopause in their stride, describing it as emotionally and sexually liberating, free of the social constraints of their youth; the change of life most worrying to them was retirement, not menopause.

The takeaway message from this work in Tunisia, consistent with experience elsewhere in the world, is that differences in menopausal experiences are not biologically determined, but rather linked to social class and patriarchal norms. A certain level of economic and social independence and emancipation appears to allow women to have an identity beyond their reproductive function and, therefore, to retain their status after menopause.

Further, in a follow up with peri- and post-menopausal women (aged 48 to 65) in Greater Tunis in 2022, Hajri and colleagues found that less-educated women still cited multiple menopausal symptoms (mainly pain and depressive signs) but few thought such physical problems had any impact on their sexual lives. They were more likely to attribute a drop in sexual activity to other factors – their husbands' own sexual dysfunction or crowded living conditions and the presence of adult children. Few spoke of pleasure, but few also considered a dip in their sexual activity to be a problem.

Some women, in fact, framed this shift as a benefit: an excuse to finally evade sexual intercourse with husbands whom they did not like and did not choose, their marriages having been arranged for them by their families 'like a pair of shoes' that failed to fit. While a few spoke about menopause in general terms with their husbands, friends or family peers, none felt comfortable broaching the sexual side of their life change. As one woman explained: "It's too intimate, we don't discuss this kind of thing. Menopause yes, old age approaching [yes], people close to us who are ill or dying [yes]. But not sex" (Hajri, personal communication, 2022).

While it is tempting to ascribe limitations in research about menopause and sexuality in MENA – even in more ostensibly open Tunisia – to religion and culture, a look just beyond its borders offers a challenge to such framing. Two of the region's nearest neighbours – Turkey and Iran – while sharing to differing degrees a similar climate of entrenched patriarchy, religious conservatism and authoritarian governance found across MENA – are clear illustrations of how progress can be made in understanding such socially sensitive subjects even in challenging contexts.

With its intertwined history, Turkey shares many cultural features with Tunisia, including a tendency to reticence on intimate life, especially as this relates to female sexuality. Nonetheless, clinical research on menopause and quality of life in Turkey goes beyond 'polite' measures of physical and psychological symptoms frequently to include wide-ranging assessments of sexual function and satisfaction.

Between 40 and 70 per cent of Turkish women in multiple studies of urban and rural participants between the ages of 35 and 65 have been classified as experiencing sexual dysfunction as gauged by problems with desire, arousal, lubrication, orgasm and experience of satisfaction and pain (Yağmur and Orhan, 2019). Among the factors associated with women's reports of symptoms consistent with sexual dysfunction in some, but not all, studies is lower education and lower income, with menopause consistently featuring as a major correlate of diminished female sexual function (see, for example, Oksuz and Malhan, 2006; Aslan et al, 2008; Verit et al, 2009).

Focusing on peri- and post-menopausal women in Turkey reveals upwards of 80 per cent with impaired sexual function and sexual quality of life, unsurprisingly correlated with severity of menopausal symptoms, as well as lower income and education (see, for example, Gozuyesil et al, 2018; Yanikkerem et al, 2017). After menopause, women also reported decreased frequency of sexual activity, diminished sexual desire and pleasure during intercourse (see, for example, Biri et al, 2007).

Studies exploring women's own attitudes towards menopause reveal mixed views. A minority of women welcomed menopause for the end of menstruation (for a number of reasons, among them an end to period-related restrictions on prayer) and the need for contraception, along with a perceived rise in societal status as an official 'older woman'; majorities of women surveyed, however, held negative views of assorted physical symptoms and the loss of fertility (Kisa et al, 2012), but firmly rejected the notion that it represented the end of femininity. The more educated, employed, socially supported and sexually active women were pre- and post-menopause, the more positive were their attitudes (Yangin et al, 2010; Erbil and Gümüsay, 2018).

As in Tunisia, few women in Turkey use HRT, and then only sporadically. Some studies have postulated that women do not seek professional treatment for menopausal symptoms (including their attendant sexual problems) – not only out of fear of practitioner or wider societal judgement – but because they consider this to be the 'natural' order of things rather than a source of distress; women who hold such views also tend to regard menopause (including its impact on their sexual lives) in a more positive light (Bülbül et al, 2021; Yanikkerem et al, 2012).

While bringing sexuality into the picture, research on Turkish women's experiences of menopause is still largely seen through a medicalised and quantitative lens. The limited body of in-depth interviews with women adds shadow and light – for example, concerns at loss of attractiveness and sense of personal responsibility to maintain sex appeal (lest a decline in sexual activity send their husbands astray), balanced with relief 'that business with men ends after menopause' (Erol, 2014).

In qualitative investigations, women on either side of menopause spoke achingly of their sadness at the loss of reproductivity (particularly among those who are unmarried) and an accompanying sense of 'uselessness', while at the same time celebrating the end of all the discomfort and inconvenience associated with menstruation (Fenercioglu, 2017). Women also pointed to a triple bind, in which physiology (vaginal dryness), taboo (discouraging them from seeking medical help) and cultural expectations (a sense of duty to have intercourse with their husbands) combined to produce a Gordian knot of sexual discomfort and marital problems (Erol, 2014).

As in Turkey, an extensive body of clinical research in Iran reveals a comparable prevalence of sexual dysfunction, with 70–90 per cent of menopausal women experiencing at least some symptoms (see, for example, Heidari et al, 2019). In the wider MENA, however, Iran stands out for a more detailed appreciation of the complexity of women's sexuality in later life, with the most extensive body of qualitative research into older women's intimate lives providing nuance that cannot be captured by indices and indicators.

Attitudes towards menopause among Iranian women studied range from positive perspectives related to the end of menstruation (and the attendant freedom to participate in religious practices whenever they want, wherever they want, without having to resort to oral contraception to suspend menstruation) to a neutral perspectives (God's will/fact of life) to negative views related to the impact on their personal appearance and body image as well as concerns about the onset of old age and ill health. Given conservative norms in many parts of Iranian society, women rarely mentioned the impact of menopause on their sexual lives as in any way affecting their attitudes towards this transitional phase (see, for example, Hakimi et al, 2016).

Studies among Iranian urban women on either side of menopause, reveal a clear impact on desire, due to physiological changes (too hot, too dry, too painful). But when probed on sex, women quickly pivoted to focus their concerns on physical and emotional intimacy – or the lack of it – with their husbands, whom they felt did not understand their needs in this time of transition (Javidivala et al, 2018). In essence, women were looking for communication, companionship and romance, and saw a clear link between husbands supporting and helping them through menopause with their own levels of sexual desire.

Desire, however, was not the sole determinant of sexual activity; many women also saw a need to conform to sexual scripts that frame women's fulfilment of their husbands' sexual needs as a religious duty and therefore continued sexual relations irrespective of their own waning desire. As in Tunisia, women with older children thought it unseemly to continue sexual relations when they had children old enough to have sexual needs of their own, and preferred to define themselves in asexual terms as mothers, rather than as sexual beings (Gharibi et al, 2019).

Similar views were expressed by older post-menopausal women. They saw their own desire as a means to a better life (more satisfied husbands, religious duty fulfilled) rather than in terms of their own sexual pleasure, and rarely initiated intercourse at any stage of their sexual lives for fear of being branded immodest, in part, and a common understanding that it is the man's role to do the running (Bahri et al, 2017). Menopause aside, past experiences – arranged marriages, and in particular episodes of sexual violence – also clearly coloured current levels of sexual desire.

As in Tunisia and Turkey, some women found menopause to be a useful pretext to finally refuse sex with their husbands, particularly in cases of unhappy arranged marriages or histories of intimate partner violence (Hashemiparast et al, 2022). Others leveraged sex as a tool of empowerment and agency to keep husbands in line and treating their wives well, thereby maintaining marital harmony and family stability (Ravanipour et al, 2013; Amini and McCormack, 2019).

Room for improvement

Health and social support systems across MENA are clearly not fit for purpose in dealing with the challenges that menopause poses for women in the region. COVID-19 has shown the need for the strengthening of health systems (including greater affordability) across MENA, particularly as such care relates to the vulnerabilities of women. It is a double challenge – health and welfare services are not yet adapted to meet the needs of an ageing population (especially as traditional family structures shift under the forces of modern life), and struggle to address the sexual concerns of their patients at any age.

Care providers represent a substantial part of the problem. For example, despite a history of wider SRHR service provision in Tunisia than in other countries of the region, medical practitioners are still ill-prepared to probe questions of sexuality with older patients. Even a younger generation of medical students has been to shown to hold frankly ill-informed views on sexuality, with stereotypically negative opinions of sexual function and desire in older populations, more so for the impact of menopause than andropause (Maâlej et al, 2018).

As in Tunisia, Turkish physicians are often at a loss when it comes to the sexual well-being of older patients, with little knowledge and a considerable degree of reluctance proactively to question older adults, combined with a reductionist approach that conceptualises sexual problems in menopause as purely physiological to be solved through HRT (Dogan et al, 2008; Erol, 2014). This is reflected in the rarity of women seeking assistance for sexual problems, particularly in later life (Ayranci et al, 2010; Yücel and Eroglu, 2013). A younger generation of healthcare professionals, however, appears to be better equipped to engage in such issues, with a growing appreciation of the importance of sexuality throughout the life course (Reyhan et al, 2022).

While its extensive body of clinical research offers Iranian practitioners greater insight into the sexual concerns of their menopausal patients, it remains difficult for healthcare providers to act upon it, with only a minority of doctors, nurses and midwives feeling adequately informed and sufficiently unembarrassed to engage in such conversations with patients (Ghazanfarpour et al, 2017; Azar et al, 2022).

Healthcare practitioners attributed this in part to a lack of experience: with only a minority of women consulting practitioners on matters related to menopause, opportunities for healthcare professionals to hone their skills are limited and, even when the occasional patient does appear, it is usually for an urgent complaint the immediate treatment of which crowds out discussion of the bigger sexual picture. An equally formidable challenge is patients' own embarrassment, not just with their physiological complaints related to sexual function, but also their culturally conditioned shame at discussing either their waning or waxing sexual desire. Other women, by contrast, considered their sexual problems to be a fact of ageing life and thus not a problem worthy of medical attention. When they did seek help, it was as often as not related to their concerns about the impact on their husband's sexual pleasure and family stability (Azar et al, 2016).

While there is a growing recognition of the need to improve sexual healthcare in MENA, the needs of older women (particularly their rural, poor, less-educated and migrant sisters) are still largely neglected in terms of actual service improvements or policy reform – and that is just in terms of the basics such as HRT, let alone the more nuanced problems of sexuality in later life (Rashad et al, 2021). The emerging field of primary care in the region would do well to incorporate the needs of this population from the start – and that begins with training healthcare professionals on how to initiate conversations with their patients on these sensitive subjects and how to respond with evidence-based, judgement-free assistance (Khadivzadeh et al, 2018; Abuidhail et al, 2021).

On the other side of the equation, raising women's awareness of what to expect during menopause and how to smoothly transition to this new phase of their lives is urgently required. Given the absence of comprehensive – or indeed, even rudimentary – sexual education for young people across MENA, it is hardly a surprise that significant proportions of women across the region on the edge or in the middle of menopause are ill-informed about the changes in store and how to manage what this means for their lives (see, for example, Elkazeh and El-Zeftawy, 2015).

Experience from across the region shows that educational programmes delivered in clinical settings can improve peri- and post-menopausal women's knowledge and attitudes towards menopause and the severity of their symptoms, in and out of the bedroom (see, for example, Eiz-Elregal et al, 2019; Khoshbooii et al, 2021). The missed opportunity here is to reach out to women where they actually seek information and assistance – from other women (mainly friends and relatives) or traditional healers – with community-based education and services (see, for example, Tayyem et al, 2022). While women's rights groups across the region are increasingly engaged on issues of sexuality, especially as these relate to young women's bodily autonomy, few show the same enthusiasm to embrace older women's rights to a safe and satisfying sexual life. This needs to change.

Men remain something of a mystery in our understanding of female sexuality in later life in the region. Research from a number of settings across MENA has demonstrated a connection between marital satisfaction and positive attitudes towards menopause (see, for example, Bülbül et al, 2021); the severity of physical symptoms and husbands' support of, and attitudes towards, menopause (Aksu et al, 2011; AlQuaiz et al, 2013); the preoccupation women have with fulfilling partners' sexual needs as a social and religious obligation; and the key role husbands play as a source of sexual information for their wives. Despite these pivotal roles, men are largely off stage in menopause research, invoked in interviews with women as either a help, or more commonly, a hindrance in their coming to terms with the physical, psychological and sexual aspects of the experience (see, for example, Fenercioglu, 2017).

The few studies from the region examining how men perceive menopause do not bode well for women. Research to date reveals a well of male ignorance around the basic biology of the process, an assumption of diminished sexual interest on the part of their wives post-menopause and a firm focus on the impact on their own sexual satisfaction rather than their partners' sexual well-being (Hidiroğlu et al, 2014), along with a sense of female anxiety at changes in husbands' feelings post-menopause (Alzein et al, 2021).

Despite the culturally conditioned tendency to silence over their husbands' sexual dysfunction, the limited body of qualitative research with women in the region clearly shows the adverse impact of male sexual problems on their own sexual satisfaction (see, for example, Azar et al, 2021). While there is a growing body of research on andropause in MENA, it would benefit from a greater consideration of the impact of men's sexual function on that of their female partners (El-Sakka, 2020).

The few studies of sexuality in the wider region that include both older husbands and wives show a clear connection between the sexual satisfaction of men with erectile dysfunction and women's post-menopausal sexual function (Khalesi et al, 2020). Much more research is needed to illuminate the other side of the story: that is, the impact of older men's sexual challenges on their older female partners' intimate lives. Evidence clearly shows gaps in communication between older husbands and wives, leading to 'sexual disharmonies' and women's mistaken notions of how their husbands may be viewing their changing bodies – perceptions far off the mark, as shown in couples research (Ghazanfarpour et al, 2018).

In addition to its positive impact on marital relations, greater engagement of men on these issues is essential, given patriarchal cultures across the region and the key role men play in many communities as guardians and gatekeepers for their female relatives' access to the wider world (including healthcare). So, there is an urgent need for greater education of and better communication with and support (as opposed to control) by men when it comes to women's sexual needs pre- and post-menopause (El Feki and Barker, 2020).

Experience from Iran shows the value of proactively engaging men in their wives' climacteric transition, with education sessions on menopausal health and symptomatic management for men yielding positive results in terms of less severe physical and psychological symptoms among their partners as well as men's own sexual and marital satisfaction (for example, see Bahri et al, 2016; Yarelahi et al, 2021). Couples counselling with menopausal women and their husbands, grounded in cognitive-behavioural therapy with a focus on understanding and addressing physical and emotional changes in sexual response, has shown considerable success in improving communication skills of both men and women, leading to improved marital and sexual satisfaction for both partners (Rouhbakhsh et al, 2019).

Our understanding of menopause and sexuality in MENA mirrors the landscape itself – concentrations of data and knowledge on certain topics in certain countries surrounded by vast tracts of empty space, like oases in the desert. The majority of information to date is focused on heterosexual women – diversity, such as it is, in the research base is limited to variations in location (urban vs rural), education, employment, marital status and occasionally ethnicity (see, for example, Jamali et al, 2016). Much more research is needed with other groups (LGBTQ individuals, migrants and refugees, ethnic, racial and religious minorities) – to provide a more rounded picture and better tailored responses to the needs of increasingly diverse populations.

This need for greater intersectionality applies to the big picture as well. Given the extraordinary upheavals in MENA over the past decade – popular uprisings, autocratic clampdowns, wars, economic crises – there is little examination of how these overarching political, economic and social conditions are affecting older populations in general, and older women's intimate lives in particular. While there is an emerging body of literature connecting the personal to the political on some dimensions of SRHR – among them abortion, virginity and LGBTQ experiences – these dots have yet to be connected in the case of women's experiences of sexuality and intimacy in later life The exception is, again, Iran, where qualitative research is increasingly framing women's anger at double standards over men's and women's ageing as a critique of the regimen's policing of gender and sexuality (Amini and McCormack, 2019).

MENA's medicalisation of menopause and sexuality, with its emphasis on sexual function (or rather, dysfunction) and performance is ill-suited to the more nuanced approach that is needed to illuminate both the fine details and the broad strokes of intimacy in later life. To put it bluntly, more social, less medical, science is needed to reframe 'age of despair' from time of life to prime of life for women across MENA.

Notes

[1] Throughout this chapter, Arabic to English transliterations follow the *International Journal of Middle East Studies* (IJMES) guide. For more information, see https://ijmes.uark.edu/author-resources/

[2] For the purposes of this chapter, MENA is comprised of the 18 states that make up the United Nations Economic and Social Commission for Western Asia (ESCWA), from Morocco in the west to Iraq in the east. Given the relative abundance of research on menopause and sexuality in Turkey and Iran, these two countries beyond the conventional borders of MENA have also been included for consideration.

[3] Arabic dialects across MENA are full of alternative expressions for menopause, few of them flattering: *hīya kibrit*, 'she got old' (Egypt); *ma bqāt ṣālḥa*, 'she has expired' or *'yāt*, 'she became tired' (Morocco); such euphemisms serve as cover for taboo topics where explicit naming can compound embarrassment with the condition itself (Ghounane, 2017). On a rare positive note, menopause is referred to as *sinn al-'amal* 'age of hope' in Jerusalem (Hammoudeh et al, 2017), and *thəddnāt* 'she calmed down' is used in some parts of Morocco to describe a woman going through the transition (Ritt-Benmimoun and Procházka, 2009).

[4] Arabic is gendered, with different adjectival forms referring to male and female subjects or objects; for simplicity's sake, male forms are presented here. See Amer 2012 for more on the naming (and reclaiming) of female homosexuality in Arabic.

[5] *Sexual health* refers to 'a state of physical, emotional, mental and social well-being in relation to sexuality; it is not merely the absence of disease, dysfunction or infirmity. Sexual health requires a positive and respectful approach to sexuality and sexual relationships, as well as the possibility of having pleasurable and safe sexual experiences, free of coercion, discrimination and violence. For sexual health to be attained and maintained, the sexual rights of all persons must be respected, protected and fulfilled' (World Health Organization, 2006).

References

Abdelmoez, J.W. (2021) 'Deviants, Queers, or Scissoring Sisters of Men? Translating and Locating Queer and Trans Feminisms in the Contemporary Arabic-Speaking World', in T. Rosenberg, S. D'Urso, and A.R. Winget (eds) *The Palgrave Handbook of Queer and Trans Feminisms in Contemporary Performance*, Cham: Palgrave Macmillan, pp 283–302.

Abdelmonem, A. (2015) 'Reconceptualizing Sexual Harassment in Egypt: A Longitudinal Assessment of el-Taharrush el-Ginsy in Arabic Online Forums and Anti-Sexual Harassment Activism', *Kohl: A Journal for Body and Gender Research*. https://kohljournal.press/reconceptualizing-sexual-harassment-in-egypt

Abuidhail, J., Abujilban, S., and Mrayan, L. (2021) 'Arab Women's Health Care: Issues and Preventive Care', in I. Laher (ed) *Handbook of Healthcare in the Arab World*, Cham: Springer, pp 41–54.

Abyad, A., and Hammami, S.O. (2021) 'Geriatric Medicine in the Arab World', in I. Laher (ed) *Handbook of Healthcare in the Arab World*, Cham: Springer, pp 2149–76.

Aksu, H., Sevinçok, L., Kücük, M., Sezer, S.D., and Ogurlu, N. (2011) 'The Attitudes of Menopausal Women and their Spouses towards Menopause', *Clinical and Experimental Obstetrics and Gynecology,* 38(3): 251–5.

AlQuaiz, J.M., Siddiqui, A., Tayel, S., and Habib, F. (2013) 'Determinants of Severity of Menopausal Symptoms among Saudi Women in Riyadh City', *Climacteric,* 16: 1–8.

Alzein, H.J., Habasheh, S., Al Khatib, H., and Allari, R.S. (2021) 'Perceptions and Attitudes of Men towards their Wives' Menopausal Transition Period', *Medico-Legal Update,* 21(2): 554–62.

Amer, S. (2012) 'Naming to Empower: Lesbianism in the Arab Islamicate World Today', *Journal of Lesbian Studies,* 16(4): 381–97.

Amini, E., and McCormack, M. (2019) 'Medicalization, Menopausal Time and Narratives of Loss: Iranian Muslim Women Negotiating Gender, Sexuality and Menopause in Tehran and Karaj', *Women's Studies International Forum,* 76. https://doi.org/10.1016/j.wsif.2019.102277

Aslan, E., Beji, N.K., Gungor, I., Kadioglu, A., and Dikencik, B.K. (2008) 'Prevalence and Risk Factors for Low Sexual Function in Women: A Study of 1009 Women in an Outpatient Clinic of a University Hospital in Istanbul', *Journal of Sexual Medicine,* 5: 2044–52.

Ati, N., Elati, Z., Manitta, M., Mnasser, A., Zakhama, W., and Binous, M.Y. (2018) 'Sexual Dysfunction among Postmenopausal Tunisian Women', *The Journal of Sexual Medicine,* 15(7:3): S305–S306.

Ayranci, U., Orsal, O., Orsal. O., Arslan. G., and Emeksiz. D.F. (2010). 'Menopause Status and Attitudes in a Turkish Midlife Female Population: An Epidemiological Study', *BMC Women's Health,* 10(1). https://doi.org/10.1186/1472-6874-10-1

Azar, M., Kroll, T., and Bradbury-Jones, C. (2016) 'Lebanese Women and Sexuality: A Qualitative Inquiry', *Sexual & Reproductive Healthcare,* 8: 13–18.

Azar, M., Bradbury-Jones, C., and Kroll, T. (2021) 'Middle-aged Lebanese Women's Interpretation of Sexual Difficulties: A Qualitative Inquiry', *BMC Women's Health,* 21: 203–14.

Azar, M., Kroll, T., and Bradbury-Jones, C. (2022) 'How Do Nurses and Midwives Perceive Their Role in Sexual Healthcare?', *BMC Women's Health,* 22: 330–41.

Baber, R.J. (2014) 'East Is East and West Is West: Perspectives on the Menopause in Asia and The West', *Climacteric,* 17: 23–8.

Bahri, N., Yoshany, N., Morowatisharifabad, M.A., Noghabi, A.D., and Sajjadi, M. (2016) 'The Effects of Menopausal Health Training for Spouses on Women's Quality of Life During Menopause Transitional Period', *Menopause,* 23(2): 183–8.

Bahri, N., Roudsari, R.L., and Hashemi, M.A. (2017) '"Adopting Self-Sacrifice": How Iranian Women Cope with the Sexual Problems During the Menopausal Transition? An Exploratory Qualitative Study', *Journal of Psychosomatic Obstetrics and Gynecology,* 38(3): 180–8.

Benzineb, S., Fakhfakh, R., Bellalouna, S., Ringa, V., and Hajri, S (2013) 'Psychometric Properties of the Women's Health Questionnaire', *Climacteric,* 16(4): 460–8.

Biri, A., Korucuoglum, U., Ilhan, M., Bingol, B., Yilmaz, E., and Biri, H. (2007) 'Turkish Women's Level of Knowledge on and Attitude toward Sexual Health', *Maturitas,* 8: 236–40.

Bülbül, T., Mucuk, S., Dolanbay, M., and Turhan, I. (2021) 'Do Complaints Related to Menopause Affect Sexuality and Marital Adjustment?', *Sexual and Relationship Therapy,* 36(4): 465–79.

Busami, M., Matalka, K.Z., Elyyan, Y., Hussein, N., Hussein, N., Abu Safieh, N., Thekrallah, F., Mallah, E., Abu-Qatouseh, L., and Arafat, T. (2021) 'Age of Natural Menopause among Jordanian Women and Factors Related to Premature and Early Menopause', *Risk Management and Healthcare Policy,* 14: 199–207.

Ceylan, B., and Özerdogan, N. (2015) 'Factors Affecting Age of Onset of Menopause and Determination of Quality of Life in Menopause', *Turkish Journal of Obstetrics and Gynecology,* 12(1): 43–9.

Delanoë, D., Hajri, S., Bachelot, A., Draoui, D.M., Hassoun, D., Marsicano, E., and Ringa, V. (2012) 'Class, Gender and Culture in the Experience of Menopause: A Comparative Survey in Tunisia and France', *Social Science & Medicine,* 75(2): 401–9.

Dogan, S., Demir, B., Eker, E., and Karim, S. (2008) 'Knowledge and Attitudes of Doctors toward the Sexuality of Older People in Turkey', *International Psychogeriatrics,* 20(5): 1019–27.

Eich, T. (2010) 'A Tiny Membrane Defending "Us" Against "Them": Arabic Internet Debate about Hymenorraphy in Sunni Islamic Law', *Culture, Health & Sexuality,* 12(7): 755–69.

Eiz-Elregal, F.A., Abd El Haleem, S.A., and Bosilah, A.H.B. (2019) 'Health Awareness Program towards Minimise Symptoms of Menopause Women' [*sic*], *Egyptian Journal of Health Care,* 10(1): 286–96.

El Chaer, N. (2021) 'Learn the Story Behind Changing the Term Age of Despair to Age of Renewal', *Vogue Arabia,* 8 September 2021 [in Arabic].

El Feki, S. (2014a) *Sex and the Citadel: Intimate Life in a Changing Arab World,* Vintage: London.

El Feki, S. (2014b) 'Come the Revolution: Sex, Faith and Politics in Turbulent Times', in K. Forde, H. Beddard, and K. Angel (eds) *The Institute of Sexology.* London: Wellcome Trust.

El Feki, S. (2015) 'The Arab Bed Spring? Sexual Rights in Troubled Times across the Middle East and North Africa', *Reproductive Health Matters,* 23(46): 38–44.

El Feki, S., and Barker, G. (2020) 'Men, Masculinities and Gender Relations', in J.M. Ryan and H. Rizzo (eds) *Gender in the Middle East and North Africa: Contemporary Issues and Challenges,* London: Lynne Rienner, pp 13–30.

El Feki, S., Aghazarian, E., and Sarras, A. (2014) 'Love Is Culture: Al-Hubb Thaqafa and the New Frontiers of Sexual Expression in Arabic Social Media', *Anthropology of the Middle East,* 9(2): 1–18.

Elkazeh, E.A.E.E., and El-Zeftawy, A.M.A. (2015) 'Knowledge of Women in the Reproductive Age about Menopausal Problems and Preventive Health Behaviors in Tanta City, Al-Gharbiya Governorate, Egypt', *Journal of Nursing and Health Science,* 4(3): 51–63.

El-Sakka, A.I. (2020) 'Middle East Cultural Challenges and the Treatment of Sexual Problems in Men', in L. Rowland and E.A. Jannini (eds) *Cultural Differences and the Practice of Sexual Medicine,* Cham: Springer, pp 135–48.

Erbil, N., and Gümüsay, M. (2018) 'Relationship between Perceived Social Support and Attitudes Towards Menopause among Women and Affecting Factors', *Middle Black Sea Journal of Health Science,* 4(2): 7–18.

Erol, M. (2014) 'From Opportunity to Obligation: Medicalization of Post-Menopausal Sexuality in Turkey', *Sexualities,* 17(1/2): 43–62.

ESCWA (United Nations Economic and Social Commission for Western Asia) (2019) *The Arab Gender Gap Report 2020: Gender Equality and the Sustainable Development Goals,* Beirut: ESCWA.

Fenercioglu, N.D. (2017) *A Feminist Study on Social and Subjective Meanings of Women's Experiences in Menopause.* MSc Thesis. Middle East Technical University.

Ferrand, F., Hajri, S., Benzinem, S., Draoui, D.M., Hassoun, D., Delanoë, D., Zins, M., and Ringa, V. (2013) 'Comparative Study of the Quality of Life Associated with Menopause in Tunisia and France', *Menopause,* 20(6): 609–22.

Gharibi, T., Gharibi, T., and Ravanipour, M. (2019) 'Facilitators and Barriers Affecting Sexual Desire in Elderly Iranian Women: A Qualitative Study', *Sexual and Relationship Therapy,* 34(2): 228–41.

Ghazanfarpour, M., Khadivzadeh, T., Roudsari, R.L., and Hazavehei, S.M.M. (2017) 'Obstacles to the Discussion of Sexual Problems in Menopausal Women: A Qualitative Study of Healthcare Providers', *Journal of Obstetrics and Gynaecology,* 37(5): 660–6.

Ghazanfarpour, M., Khadivzadeh, T., and Roudsari, R.L. (2018) 'Sexual Disharmony in Menopausal Women and Their Husbands: A Qualitative Study of Reasons, Strategies, and Ramifications', *Journal of Menopausal Medicine,* 24: 41–9.

Ghounane, N. (2017) 'Aspects of Taboos Surrounding Algerian Females' Daily Issues and Language', *Arab World English Journal*, 8(2): 398–414.

Gozuyesil, E., Surucu, S.G., and Alan, S. (2018) 'Sexual Function and Quality-of-Life-Related Problems during the Menopausal Period', *Journal of Health Psychology*, 23(14): 1769–80.

Greer, W., Sandridge, A., Chehabeddine, R.S. (2003) 'The Frequency Distribution of Age at Natural Menopause among Saudi Arabian Women', *Maturitas*, 46(4): 263–72.

Hakimi, S., Simbar, M., Tehrani, F.R., Zaiery, F., and Khatami, S. (2016) 'Women's Perspectives toward Menopause: A Phenomenological Study in Iran', *Journal of Women & Aging*, 28(1): 80–9.

Hammoudeh, D., Coast, E., Lewis, D., van der Meulen, Y., Leone, T., and Giacaman, R. (2017) 'Age of Despair or Age of Hope? Palestinian Women's Perspectives on Midlife Health', *Social Science & Medicine*, 184: 108–15.

Hashemiparast, M., Naderi, B., Chattu, B.K., and Allahverdipour, H. (2022) 'Perceived Barriers of Expression of Sexual Desires among Older Adults: A Qualitative Study', *Sexual and Relationship Therapy*, DOI: 10.1080/14681994.2022.2056590

Heidari, M., Ghodusi, M., Rezaei, P., Abyaneh, S.K., Sureshjani, E.H., and Sheikhi, R.A. (2019) 'Sexual Function and Factors Affecting Menopause: A Systematic Review', *Journal of Menopausal Medicine*, 25: 15–27.

Hidiroğlu, S., Tanriover, O., Ay, P., and Karavus, M. (2014) 'A Qualitative Study on Menopause Described from the Man's Perspective', *Journal of Pakistan Medical Association*, 64(9): 1031–6.

Hinchliff, S., Gott, M., and Ingleton, C. (2010) 'Sex, Menopause and Social Context: A Qualitative Study with Heterosexual Women', *Journal of Health Psychology*, 15(5): 724–33.

Jamali, S., Javadpour, S., Mosalanejad, L., and Parnian, R. (2016) 'Attitudes about Sexual Activity among Postmenopausal Women in Different Ethnic Groups: A Cross-sectional Study in Jahrom, Iran', *Journal of Reproduction & Infertility*, 17(1): 47–55.

Javadivala, Z., Merghati-Khoei, E., Underwood, C., Mirghafourvand, M., and Allahverdipour, H. (2018) 'Sexual Motivations during the Menopausal Transition among Iranian Women: A Qualitative Inquiry', *BMC Women's Health*, 18: 191–201.

Khadivzadeh, T., Ghazanfarpour, M., and Roudsari, R.L. (2018) 'Cultural Barriers Influencing Midwives' Sexual Conversation with Menopausal Women', *Journal of Menopausal Medicine*, 24: 210–16.

Khalesi, Z.B., Jafarzadeh-Kenarsari, F., Mobarrez, Y.D., and Abedinzade, M. (2020) 'The Impact of Menopause on Sexual Function in Women and their Spouses', *African Health Sciences*, 20(4): 1979–84.

Khoshbooii, R., Hassan, S.A., Deylami, N., Muhamad, R., Engku Kamarudin, E.M., and Alareqe, N.A. (2021) 'Effects of Group and Individual Culturally Adapted Cognitive Behavioral Therapy on Depression and Sexual Satisfaction among Perimenopausal Women', *International Journal of Environmental Research and Public Health,* 18: 7711–20.

Kisa, S., Zeyneloglu, S., and Ozdemir, N. (2012) 'Examination of Midlife Women's Attitudes toward Menopause in Turkey', *Nursing and Health Sciences,* 14: 148–55.

Mâalej, M., Ben Thabet, J., Charfi, N., Ellouze, S., Omri, S., Zouari, N., Zouari, L., and Mâalej, M. (2018) 'Medical Trainees' Readiness for the Promotion of Sexual Health in Tunisia: A Cross Sectional Study', *Sexuality & Culture,* 22: 437–44.

Makara-Studzinska, M.T., Krys-Noszczyk, K.M., and Jakiel, G. (2014) 'Epidemiology of the Symptoms of Menopause: An Intercontinental Review', *Przeglad Menopauzalny,* 13(3): 203–11.

Müller, C., Oosterhoff, P., and Chakkalackal, M. (2017) 'Digital Pathways to Sex Education', *IDS Bulletin,* 48(1): 61–80.

Myrne, P. (2019) *Female Sexuality in the Early Medieval Islamic World: Gender and Sex in Arabic Literature*, London: Bloomsbury.

Namazi, M., Sadeghi, R., and Moghadem, Z.B. (2019) 'Social Determinants of Health in Menopause: An Integrative Review', *International Journal of Women's Health*, 11: 637–47.

Naz, M.S.G., Sayehmiri, F., Kiani, F., and Ozgoli, G. (2019) 'A Systematic Review and Meta-analysis on the Average Age of Menopause among Iranian Women', *Evidence Based Care Journal,* 8(4): 26–34.

Oksuz, E., and Malhan, S. (2006) 'Prevalence and Risk Factors for Female Sexual Dysfunction in Turkish Women', *Journal of Urology,* 175: 654–8.

Pitkin, J. (2010) 'Cultural Issues and the Menopause', *Menopause International,* 16: 156–61.

Raifman, S., Hajri, S., Gerdts, C., and Foster, D. (2018) 'Dualities Between Tunisian Provider Beliefs and Actions in Abortion Care', *Reproductive Health Matters,* 26(52): 47–57.

Rashad, H., Shawky, S., Khadr, Z., Sahbani, S., and Afifi, M. (2021) 'Achieving Sexual and Reproductive Health in the Arab Region: A New Role for the Health Sector', in I. Laher (ed) *Handbook of Healthcare in the Arab World*, Cham: Springer, pp 151–76.

Ravanipour, M., Gharibi, T., and Gharibi, T. (2013) 'Elderly Women's Views About Sexual Desire During Old Age: A Qualitative Study', *Sex and Disability,* 31: 179–88.

Reffat, L. (2022) 'The Woman Behind MENA's First Arabic Menopause Page', *AWIM News*, 9 September 2022. https://awimnews.com/the-woman-behind-menas-first-arabic-menopause-page/

Reyhan, F.A., Dagli, N., and Ozerdogan, N. (2022) 'Evaluation of Midwifery and Nursing Students' Knowledge and Attitudes toward Sexuality in the Elderly', *International Journal of Caring Sciences,* 15(2): 941–52.

Reynolds, R.F., and Obermeyer, C.M. (2003) 'Correlates of the Age at Natural Menopause in Morocco', *Annals of Human Biology,* 30(1): 97–108.

Reynolds, R.F., and Obermeyer, C.M. (2001) 'Age at Natural Menopause in Beirut, Lebanon: The Role of Reproductive and Lifestyle Factors', *Annals of Human Biology,* 28(1): 21–9.

Ritt-Benmimoun, V., and Procházka, S. (2009) 'Female Issues in Arabic Dialects: Words and Expressions Related to the Female Body and Reproduction', *Estudios de Dialectología Norteafricana y Andalusí,* (13): 31–92.

Rouhbakhsh, M., Kermansaravi, F., Shakiba, M., and Navidian, A. (2019) 'The Effect of Couples Education on Marital Satisfaction in Menopausal Women', *Journal of Women & Aging,* 31(5): 432–45.

Semerene, G. (2019) 'Mithliyy, Mithlak: Language and LGBTQ Activism in Lebanon and Palestine', in J.D. Luther and J.U. Loh (eds) *Queer Asia: Decolonising and Reimagining Sexuality and Gender,* London: Bloomsbury, pp 85–108.

Saïd, E. (1995) *Orientalism: Western Conceptions of the Orient,* London: Penguin.

Sallam, H., Galal, A.F., and Rashed, A. (2006) 'Menopause in Egypt: Past and Present Perspectives', *Climacteric,* 9(6): 421–9.

Siala, K., Mejdoub, Y., Zouari, L., Mâalej, M., Damak, J., and Mâalej, M. (2019) *Menopause and Sexuality,* 27th European Congress of Psychiatry, Warsaw, Poland, 5–8 April 2019.

Shaw, S.H., and Silverio, S.A. (2021) 'Transcending Shame through Rebellion: The Modern Arab Woman, Sexual Suppression, and the Will to Break Free', in C.H. Mayer, E. Vanderheiden, and P.T.P. Wong (eds) *Shame 4.0.: Investigating an Emotion in Digital Worlds and the Fourth Industrial Revolution,* Cham: Springer, pp 475–94.

Tabahi, S. (2020) 'The Construction and Reconstruction of Sexuality in the Arab World: An Examination of Sexual Discourse, Women's Writing and Reproductive Justice', *Sexuality & Culture,* 24: 1720–37.

Taylor, A., and Gosney, M.A. (2011) 'Sexuality in Older Age: Essential Considerations for Healthcare Professionals', *Age and Ageing,* 40(5): 538–43.

Tayyem, E.A.I., Labib, A.T., Ebrahim, R.M., and Yousif, A.M. (2022) 'Coping Strategies with Menopausal Symptom among Palestinian Women' [*sic*], *Egyptian Journal of Health Care,* 13(4): 697–710.

TENA (2021a) '#DespairNoMore'. https://www.tena-me.com/en/women/age-of-despair

TENA (2021b) 'TENA Supports Women's Ask for New and More Positive Phrase Instead of Age of Despair'. www.zawya.com/en/press-release/tena-supports-womens-ask-for-new-and-more-positive-phrase-instead-of-age-of-despair-trjhjic0

UNFPA (2022) 'United Nations Population Fund and TENA Bring Empowering Theme of "Age of Renewal" to EXPO 2020'. https://arabstates.unfpa.org/en/news/united-nations-population-fund-and-tena-bring-empowering-theme-%E2%80%98age-renewal%E2%80%99-expo-2020

Verit, F.F., Verit, A., and Billurcu, N. (2009) 'Low Sexual Function and its Associated Risk Factors in Pre- and Postmenopausal Women without Clinically Significant Depression', *Maturitas,* 64: 38–42.

Walsh-Haines, G. (2012) 'The Egyptian Blogosphere', *Journal of Middle East Women's Studies,* 8(3): 41–62.

Winterich, J. (2003) 'Sex, Menopause, and Culture: Sexual Orientation and the Meaning of Menopause for Women's Sex Lives', *Gender & Society,* 17(4): 627–42.

World Health Organization (2006) *Defining Sexual Health – Report of a Technical Consultation on Sexual Health, 28–31 January 2002,* Geneva: World Health Organization.

World Health Organization (2022) *Menopause.* www.who.int/news-room/fact-sheets/detail/menopause#:~:text=Most%20women%20experience%20menopause%20between,changes%20in%20the%20menstrual%20cycle

Wynn, L.L., Foster, A.M., and Trussell, J. (2009) '"Can I Get Pregnant from Oral Sex"? Sexual Health Misconceptions in E-mails to a Reproductive Health Website', *Contraception,* 79(2): 91–7.

Yağmur, Y. and Orhan, İ. (2019) 'Examining Sexual Functions of Women before and after Menopause in Turkey', *African Health Sciences,* 19(2): 1881–87.

Yangin, H.B., Kukulu, K., and Sözer, G.A. (2010) 'The Perception of Menopause among Turkish Women', *Journal of Women & Aging,* 22(4): 290–305.

Yanikkerem, E., Kolan, S.O., Tamay, A.G., and Dikayak, S. (2012) 'Relationship between Women's Attitude towards Menopause and Quality of Life', *Climacteric,* 15(6): 552–62.

Yanikkerem, E., Göker, A., Çakir, Ö., and Esmeray, N. (2017) 'Effects of Physical and Depressive Symptoms on the Sexual Life of Turkish Women in the Climacteric Period', *Climacteric,* 21(2): 160–6.

Yarelahi, M., Karimi, M., Nazarifar, E., Rezaian, E., Ghaedi, M., and Asadollahi, A. (2021) 'Can Menopausal Education Enhance Marital Satisfaction of Middle-aged Men?', *Journal of Health Sciences & Surveillance System,* 9(4): 272–7.

Yisma, E., and Ly, S. (2018) 'Menopause: A Contextualised Experience across Social Structures', in S. Choudhury, K.T. Eruasquin, and M. Withers (eds) *Global Perspectives on Women's Sexual and Reproductive Health across the Lifecourse,* Cham: Springer, pp 391–409.

Yücel, C., and Eroglu, K. (2013) 'Sexual Problems in Postmenopausal Women and Coping Methods', *Sexuality and Disability,* 31: 217–28.

7

Lost voices of Partition: carrying gender, nation and femininity across the life course

Nafhesa Ali

As the child survivors of Partition[1] have aged, contemporary social science literature has barely acknowledged the long-lasting effect of Partition and the impact of how the sexualisation of women and girls, of all ages, has influenced age(ing). Moreover, there remains a fissure in the narratives from those who 'lived' Partition and are now in later life. In Holocaust studies, child survivors have only recently come to the fore as having experiences that were distinct from those of adult survivors (Krell, 1993, p 384). Therefore, to appreciate the ways in which South Asian migrant[2] (SAm) women claim (de)sexualised later life positions, it is useful to examine how the interconnections of socio-historic events, such as Partition, magnified the sexualisation of the female body – to make it sexual or viewed in a sexual way – and trace the way in which early life course socialisations of gender and femininity continue to shape intersectional, ethno-religious cultural sexualities and identities.

For older migrants who have aged in their place of migration and settlement, inclusive insights in ageing studies can only occur when we extend discussions from post-migration experiences that are situated solely in the United Kingdom (UK) and begin to include pre-migration experiences. By taking a step back and looking at the whole life course, this chapter ameliorates understanding of the intersections and complexities of gender, age, sexuality and nation; lived across transnational histories and geographies.

By adopting a long view that includes a historical review of Partition, sociocultural ideals, practices and then later life, this chapter draws on Partition and social science literature, as well as selected quotes from empirical research conducted as part of my PhD research.[3] It aims to interrogate the sexualisation of older SAm women through a decolonial lens (see Lugones, 2010, 2020) and invite discussion around ways of seeing[4] gender and sexuality in later life. On the one hand, I wish to avoid homogenising the experiences of older SAm women and recognise the individual experiences of women in this chapter (in addition to the complexity of the term 'South Asian'; for a full critique see Puwar and Raghuram, 2020) and the diversity in which this term is situated in relation to national identity, variety of religions, class structures and sociocultural conditions of caste (society divided by social class and privilege). On the other hand, there is not enough space to address these discussions in more detail. The chapter, therefore, aims to contribute to knowledge in the field of ageing and Partition studies by connecting early life course socialisations and the intersecting politics of nation, gender, age and sexuality to this cohort of older women in later life – the child survivors of Partition (see Ali, 2006; Virdee, 2013; Butalia, 2017; Chattha, 2018; Gupta, 2019).

This chapter is based on an empirical study, titled 'Older South Asian migrant (SAm) women's experiences of old age and ageing in the United Kingdom (UK)'.[5] The research used life course methods, underpinned by a Black Feminist lens. Data included ten multi-sited ethnographic observations and 16 in-depth interviews with older SAm women aged between 60 and 87 years of age (see Table 7.1 in the Appendix). Interviews were organised in a Yorkshire town where a significant population of first-generation South Asian, Pakistani Muslim and Indian Sikhs have lived, harmoniously, since first migration from the late 1950s (see also Jamal, 2019). Participants shared both pre- and post-Partition heritage from similar areas in the Punjab. Some of the women I interviewed have passed away, creating a sense of urgency for more research and time to be given to the voices of older SAm women who came to the UK as a 'first generation' of South Asian migrants.

The chapter comprises three sections. First, it considers how the Partition of India, and postcolonial conflicts sexualise women's bodies through sites of ethno-religious, cultural and nationalist violence, which intensified ways of seeing[6] women of all ages. Second, it examines the ways in which the patriarchal positioning of the nation and its protection of 'vulnerable' sexualities locate gender and women's bodies as sites of '*izzat*' (honour/shame/respect). Here, the intersecting politics of race, religion, gender, femininity, family and nation are discussed in terms of societal change and the protection of women's sexuality through specific sociocultural recommendations. The third section looks at how older SAm women carry honour across the life course, and into later life, where the desexualisation of the ageing body and bodily desires create space for agency and autonomy. This also has intergenerational implications, where older women continue to transmit and transfer their own gendered expectations on to younger family and kin in the UK that are rooted in the foundations of their own socialisations of honour, gender and sexuality.

Women's sexuality as a site for the nation

To fully appreciate older SAm women's past and present sexualities, and how (de)sexualisation is approached in later life, it is useful to include

SAm women's histories and movements which have contributed to the construction of meaning (see Basu, 2012). As older women have aged in post-Partition and postcolonial times, the gendered aspects of the British Raj require attention due to the Empire's influence on the intersecting politics of race, religion, gender and sexuality. This section, therefore, aims to 'lift the curtain' (Basu, 2012) on how the event of Partition shaped the politics of gender, sexuality and South Asian women's bodies as a site for nation.

Indian independence and the creation of the new state of Pakistan[7] took place on 14–15 August 1947 (see Krishan, 1983; Talbot and Singh, 2009; Frischmann, 2010; Ansari, 2017). With the weakening and then dissolution of the British Raj, the British Indian Empire officially partitioned into two dominions – Hindu-dominated India and Muslim-majority Pakistan. The event resulted in the largest migration in the twentieth century, displacing around 15 million people, during which between one and two million were killed and 750,000 women were raped and abducted[8] (Saeed, 2012; Roy, 2019; Sobti and Kumar, 2022). Some note that the numbers of the actual tragedies were higher but were under-recorded to make them more palatable (Khan, 2017). Additionally, in the lead-up to this fateful set of events the information people received about Partition was patchy. The imminent Partition of India was publicised through word-of-mouth, newspapers or the radio, and 'government pamphlets' (Khan, 2017, p 1), but many did not hear of the event until it was too late. Khan (2017, p 1) adds that the 'population of almost four hundred million' lived and worked in rural areas and it was not until 'the butchery and forced relocation of the summer months of 1947' that most found out about the division and the creation of the two new states.

From this 'moment of rupture' (Zamindar, 2007, p 4) attention drawn to the experiences of women who lived and experienced Partition has remained modest (see Didur, 2000; Bhardwaj, 2004, 2021; Frischmann, 2010), despite the specific gendered element of the violence. Chattha (2018, p 273) writes that due to 'harrowing' content even the material in his paper documenting the experiences of women, children and those injured in the events that occurred immediately after Partition was 'sanitised' for readers. Yet, India and Pakistan are frequently depicted as fully formed (Chatta, 2018) – suppressing any conflict, displacement or resettlement (to name a few issues) which followed. This disregard for how Partition came at a great cost, where gendered violence included forced conversions, rapes, marriages and the honour killings of masses of women remains problematic (Saeed, 2012).

The attempts through state-sanctioned operations to bind citizens to either of the two new nations created further tensions that continue to be felt today (see Frischmann, 2010; Sobti and Kumar, 2022). Yet, Partition played a key role in illuminating the politics of gender and the sexualisation of women (see Basu, 2012), where people had to fend for themselves as the British left the newly formed states without governmental rule (see also Saeed, 2012). During this time of significant political unrest, women were targeted, cast 'as symbols of community honour' (Ansari, 2017, np) and typified as the 'sustainers' of family reputation (Bhardwaj, 2004, p. 5). Frischmann notes (2010, p 8) that 'the foundations of the new states of India and Pakistan were built on the bodies of its women'.

The tensions in which 'the new states were built' should not be understated, as they reveal how the sexualisation of women's bodies was infused with, and sometimes physically inscribed by, the paradigms of gender and nation (Chattha, 2018). The violence against women was not new in war, or during times of unrest, but Partition came to signal patriarchal hostilities in which the violence against women heralded an attack on male honour and the honour of the state (see also Saeed, 2012). Consequently, honour/respect (*izzat*) and shame (*sharam*) became symbolic in the preservation and protection of the vulnerability of women's physical bodies. The defiling of the sexual purity of its women became the easiest way to assault a community (Bagchi et al, 2003). The sexual appropriation of women was further enacted by men on both sides, constructing a retaliatory measure used to assert identity and humiliate the enemy through violence (Menon and Bhasin, 2011). The worth given to women's bodies was accorded legitimacy, as the property of the patriarch, through these violent acts and additionally complicated through state-sanctioned operations (Didur, 2000; Frischmann, 2010).

Approximately 100,000 women were abducted during Partition (Menon and Bhasin, 1993; Frischmann, 2010; Ansari, 2017) and only 10 per cent of these women were ever found (Frischmann, 2010). India and Pakistan's state political 'Recovery Operation (1947–1955)' sought to return Indian and Pakistani women, believed to be on the 'wrong' side of the border, back to the 'right' side so 'they could live the rest of their lives with izzat [honour]' (Didur, 2000, p 53). All through the Recovery Operation, women's own choice of return was unheeded. This persisted despite implications of disownment, and in worst cases murder, due to allegations around shame because of the loss of virginity or 'purity' (Das, 1991; Didur, 2000; Frischmann, 2010). Values assigned to '"legitimate" family and community "honour"' became negotiated through the 'regulation of women's sexuality' (Menon and Bhasin, 2011, p 120). Dishonour presented further complications. Women were removed, sometimes forcibly, from children, husbands and homes acquired in the places they were abducted to. The reasoning behind this was that the perceived benefits for sending women back to their original nations weighed higher than the cost of their return by the state (Didur, 2000; Frischmann, 2010; Ansari, 2017). Again, such reasoning mobilised women's bodies as a tool for political gain by the newly formed post-Partition nations.

Women of all ages and backgrounds became targets of violence (Chakraborty, 2014). Those who were destitute also became exposed to risks and upheaval during 'the dark side of freedom' (Menon and Bhasin, 2011, p 120). Boundaries of shame motivated attacks on women, and women's sexuality, which was targeted in such a way that 'rape was not "about" sex' but '*instead* an assault: an act of violence', substantiating the intersecting politics of nation, gender and sexuality as a 'weapon of war' (Unlu, 2018, p 23). The suffering women and girls faced created a 'master-narrative of sacrifice for the nation' (Chattha, 2018, p 282). This period was noted as a 'shameful chapter' in both the countries' histories, where 'dishonour' took precedent over the lives of women (Menon and Bhasin, 2011, p 125).

Furthermore, behaviours were situated as 'cultural responses to the traumatic effects' of that time (Kleinman et al, 1997, p x). Pregnant women were also under immense pressure where babies were forcibly 'dropped', aborted or miscarried or they 'were born dead or had been left behind as not likely to live' (Chattha, 2018, p 283). Likewise, the suffering of children was similarly downplayed, possibly because the 'history of children is hard to deal with' (Butalia, 2017, p 197). There were others who moved to safety and remained 'unaffected', as well as those in the midst of the tragedies (Chanana, 1993). There is insufficient space to cover all the experiences of women or the types of violence that occurred, but gender pathology remained at the centre of these experiences, where 'women were the victims' and purity was the main target (Mookerjea-Leonard, 2010, p 38).

The long-lasting consequences of how women's bodies became a space in which the 'competitive games of men are played' (Das, 1991, p 69), and the sexual history of Partition, have never fully been explored (see Vinay, 2022). The historically sanctioned 'silence' of South Asian women's trauma and survival dates to Partition (see Das, 1991; Bhari, 1999; Yusin, 2009), where the interconnections of colonialism, gender and sexuality in the global South, and women's bodies, identities and spaces remain riven with contradictions and tensions (Puri, 1999). Moreover, this narrative is reiterated by 'the generation of middle-class women who came to age amid tensions of postcolonial Indian nationalism' (Puri, 1999, p x), who have embodied the silences of Partition and continue to do so as they have aged.

The epoch of postcolonial India and Pakistan is indicative of the way in which gendered expectations for women signal femininity and how 'protecting our reputations and chastity was constantly emphasised' (Puri, 1999, p x). Controlling threats on 'bodies and sexualities' extended onto 'containing' 'sexual impulses' as 'femininity and sexual respectability were not negotiable' but were also linked to the 'pitfalls of modernity and westernization' (Puri, 1999, p x). Consequently, women's experiences became shrouded in silences, resulting in the ability to conceal experiences and/or information or even cast a new light on what occurred (Das, 1991). The impact of this enforced national and psychological amnesia of the Partition in 1947 (Sanghera, 2021; Sobti and Kumar, 2022) and its 'unanalysed silence' (Nair, 2004, pp 3–4) remains resounding. Moreover, older women in later life continue to situate these narratives. An interview with Nargis a Pakistani Muslim woman aged 87 at the time of interview, now deceased, shared her memory and silences of Partition:

Interviewer: Can you tell me about your experiences of Partition?
Nargis: You do not want to talk about that.
Interviewer: Why not?
Nargis: We were young. There were dead bodies everywhere […] Even in the holes in the walls walking around… [long pause] you don't want to talk about that.

Passing over memories of the past, in the present, highlights how girls learned to 'hide things' (Das, 1991, p 7) where 'you don't … talk' became a common reaction to experiences of Partition. The suppression of memories reiterates the politicisation of trauma through the silences shared by the women who lived through it (Sobti and Kumar, 2022). Hence Trouillot's question (1995, p 73): 'If some events cannot be accepted even as they occur, how can they be assessed later?'

This meaning-making, in which memories of the past are recalled (or not) in the present, and the weight of Trouillot's question echo Nargis' avoidance of talking about the events of Partition any further than the memory she authorises. The difficulty with Partition memories is that they were 'bodily memories', where 'bodies became important sites of memory in the aftermaths of Partition' (Sobti and Kumar, 2022, p 732).

Situating the body and mobilising *izzat* (honour)

For centuries, the South Asian woman and her body has been constructed in various ways. Pre-Partition *ayahs* (nannies) viewed as 'sexually empowered' were sought by 'many wooers' (Sobti and Kumar, 2022, p 734). In Partition literature, women's position reflects a focus on 'desire and pity' and how they were considered 'secondary' to men (Sharma and Velath, 2021, p 97). Also, Western-centric discourse referring to South Asian women has repeatedly reduced them to stereotypes of the 'passive, silent Asian female victim' or 'clichéd symbols of the Orient: sensual, erotic' (Holt and Turney, 2006, p 332). The construction of these images creates women's bodies, again, as a site for the performance of gender and cultural symbolism (see also Brah, 1987, 2005; DasGupta, 1989; Mirza, 2009, 2020; Frischmann, 2010). Yet, Vinay (2022, p 178) critiques these images at the intersections of sexuality and political rule by arguing that the effects of colonialism and the cause of sexual repression in South Asia are a consequence of British rule and its categorisation of its subjects as 'desexualised or hypersexualized compared to normalized pre-colonial attitudes towards sexuality'.

Moreover, sociocultural scripts position South Asian women with expectations of the proprietors of religion, where the safeguarding of 'purity and integrity of the community' is rooted in the cultural and religious politics of South Asia (Basu, 2012, p 3). Third space understandings – unconscious, unspoken knowledge shared by individuals, communities and societies (see Bhabha, 1990) – that centre around *ways of seeing* (Berger, 1972), construct the South Asian woman and her body with powerful cultural, political and national meaning (see Silverio, 2019). Mohanram (2019) posits that this link between sexuality and women's embodiment becomes shared within a nation. Besides, distinct social recommendations for honour, which also existed before Partition were amplified to foster 'a heightened value on tradition, conformity, and security values' (Sharma and Velath, 2021, p 96). Consequently, the externally induced changes in society caused by the event had a direct impact on how family and societal strategies around protecting vulnerabilities functioned.

One sociocultural practice that has been pivotal is '*izzat*' (honour). *Izzat* is the performance of the public part of the self (Alvi, 2001), which shapes subjective behaviours, but is also an important indicator of collective honour (Cihangir, 2013). The use of *izzat* as a sociological construct was widespread in social science literature in the late 1990s and 2000s in its examination of the intersections of South Asian women and diasporic identities (Dwyer, 1999, 2000; Werbner, 2005; Wilson, 2006). Research on *izzat* has since included intergenerational negotiations in the UK (Werbner, 2005), honour killings and domestic violence (Khan and Lowe, 2019; Hadi, 2020; Bhanbhro, 2021), parenthood (Matoo, 2022), masculinity and caring roles within families (Gill, 2020), sexuality (Jaspal, 2019; Roshanravan, 2019), sexual abuse (Jassal, 2020; Begum and Gill, 2022), and the shame in using mental health services (Sangar and Howe, 2021; Prajapati and Liebling, 2022), to name a few. Whether the term is outdated in the context of diasporic lives is a question we must consider, but for this cohort of older women in later life, *izzat* remains relevant as many continue to carry it across the life course (see the later section on Desexualisation and carrying honour (*izzat*) in later life).

During Partition and immediately afterwards, *izzat* was negotiated with both positive and negative political gains, where it was either performed with the 'need to guard female sexuality' (Werbner, 2005, p 27) or to dishonour the nation through the torture, rape and/or slaughter of women (Sobti and Kumar, 2022). The protection and preservation of the female body was a significant characteristic for how *izzat* was socially constructed and mobilised to promote moral behaviours, responsibilities, practices and expectations. Its value is situated in its pursuit of preserving and concealing sexuality, sexual intimacy and sexual maturity; habitually achieved within the social sphere (family, community and nation) (Werbner, 2005; Cihangir, 2013). Furthermore, *izzat* it is not momentary but moves across the girl/woman's life. The preservation and protection of *izzat*, however, vary across cultural and religious interpretations, but notably share connections with their subjective reward (that is, heightened honour, respect and increased reputation). Here, '*purdah*' (covering/seclusion) can strengthen *izzat* by increasing spaces for mobility for women and girls within the home, education and spaces of employment (see Werbner, 2005; Roomi and Harrison, 2010). After Partition, *purdah* was employed by both sides to protect women's vulnerabilities (Chattha, 2018).

Another sociocultural construct is early marriage. In this instance, this refers to examples where marriage occurs under the age of 16. For older SAm women, now in later life, early marriage was common (see Dwyer, 2000; Jones, 2020) and in parts of South Asia the practice, marked by puberty, still continues (UNICEF, 2015). The premature sexualisation of women and girls through marriage was challenged by Gandhi, when he drew attention to Hindu practices that encultured this practice:

> I passionately desire the utmost freedom for our women. I detest child-marriages. I shudder to see a child widow, and shiver with rage when a husband just widowed with brutal indifference contracts another marriage. I deplore the criminal indifference of parents who keep their daughters utterly ignorant and illiterate and bring them up only for the purpose of marrying them off to some young men of means. Notwithstanding all this grief and rage, I realize the difficulty of the problem. (Gandhi, 1999, pp 468–9, cited in Mookerjea-Leonard, 2010, p 9)

The constraints of child marriages highlight the premature sexualisation of girls but also as a form of gender socialisation. Consequently, these practices are not isolated and still occur across areas in South Asia and the sub-Saharan continent (UNICEF, 2015). Early marriage, built on the foundations of *izzat,* aimed to ensure sexual activity took place within ethno-religious and cultural conventions. Moreover, sociocultural recommendations for South Asian women – daughters, wives, sisters and nieces – is characterised by sexuality (see Wilson, 2006). These ideals encourage girls to internalise perceptions of women's sexuality as dangerous with a need for regulation and control. Moreover, women's sexuality as 'patriarchal property' (Wilson, 2006, p 13) reifies typifications of male policing of gender that focuses exclusively on sexual transgression.

It must also be noted that positive aspects of *izzat*, defined within the context of respectful behaviours, are often overlooked. Shaw (2000, p 37) asks: 'Why should they risk izzat (honour, respect) by exposing their wives and daughters to the influences of a society which does not value purdah and female modesty?'

Western-centric opinion around the cultural ideals of honour and the value attached to modesty when sociocultural and ethno-religious ideals of *izzat* and *purdah* can serve cultural needs, has been problematised by Shaw (2000), and particularly those which underlie South Asian honour codes (Cihangir, 2013). Both constructs of *izzat* and *purdah* are internalised principles embedded within the complex sociocultural understandings older SAm women, families, communities and homeland nations place on preserving and sustaining *izzat*. Equally, fear plays a significant role in the internalisation of behaviours where punishment, guilt and consequence (for example, on the family, social sphere, afterlife) impact on subjective behaviours to adhere to honourable forms of conduct. Reputation and dishonour similarly belong to *izzat*, and again structure *izzat* around the social group or network it is attached to (Fuchs, 2001). Wilson (2006) adds that (dis)honour is not isolated to South Asia but has commonly shared interpretations across the globe. Such 'codes' (Cihangir, 2013, p 2) allow homeland identities to be sustained through shared practices and ideologies in the place of migration and settlement.

Desexualisation and carrying honour (*izzat*) in later life

The desexualisation of the ageing body, for many older SAm women, acts as a form of resistance in the way it sanctions space to move away from previously exposed and hazardous gendered positions that were subsequently claimed by family, society and nation. Later life and the move towards desexualised positions allow older women to signal autonomy and agency by (re)claiming the body as their own. Not all South Asian women in later life claim desexualised positions but, interestingly and representative of this generational cohort, all the older women in my study had been married. Some were still married, others were now widowed but most shared how they negotiate the move towards desexualised positions in later life; as discussed later in this section.

In the West, desexualisation and stereotypes of the non-sexual older person are commonly thought to go hand-in-hand (see Simpson et al, 2021a), where ageing and later life typify the older person as sexually unattractive, unappealing and undesirable (see also, Simpson et al, 2021b). Yet, to fully comprehend the diversity of experience (de)sexualisation should not be seen in isolation but with the complex political meanings that individuals, groups and societies attach to it. Silverio (2019, p 149) posits that women in the West are frequently positioned as 'passive, sexualised, and objectified; without the opportunity to subvert the shame they are forced to withstand'. This shame is consequential to being 'gazed upon' and in 'patriarchal and phallogocentric societies' contempt is created through 'unconscious biases toward women's bodies' (Silvero, 2019, p 149). Not all older SAm women experienced constraints and some had enjoyed freedoms such as education, in daily interactions and home visits. But sociocultural practices structured around socio-historic events resulted in tensions, where education for girls was often affected and renegotiated within the domestic space. Nargis notes how she was not allowed "to anyone's house" and Aisha shared that "there was a fear you would be taken". As discussed in the previous section (Situating the body and mobilising *izzat* (honour)), older women did experience early marriage: "[T]hey used to say the sooner the girls get married and go to their own house the better. It was the thinking of the older people" (Satnam).

The justifications for girls 'to get married and go to their own homes' created paternal homes and parental responsibilities of *izzat* (the honour of the girl/woman) as temporary, which were then conceded into the marital home and onto the husband and in-laws. Nargis, Satnam and Mandeep were all young when their marriages took place:

> 'I didn't see him! That's the story that I'm telling you that it shouldn't even be that much.' (Mandeep, age 76, Indian Sikh)

> 'I got married when I was 15 … it was an arranged marriage. My parents did it.' (Satnam, age 72, Indian Sikh)

> 'I was young. I was sleeping and they did the marriage ceremony (*nikkah*). … It was my brother's word. … I was about 12 years old. … Then we got the burdens.' (Nargis)

Early experiences of marriage frequently occurred without women being present or even knowing that their marriage had taken place. This then created new and additional roles and responsibilities from a young age, which Nargis terms 'burdens' that were often a consequence of multiple pregnancies, adolescent fertility and/or complications with pregnancy (for example, stillbirths, miscarriages and so on) (see also Ahmed et al, 2014). Noor, aged 78, but 18 at the time of marriage, adds: "I would say to my parents I can't give him milk, it tickles me, take him away", adding, "you didn't know how to look after a child". Some older women did express some knowledge of their marriage but, while still marrying young, negotiations were habitually made in terms of the delay of moving into the marital home. Shankar et al (2013) describe these instantiations of gender thus:

> Men are the providers and protectors of the family; ... a girl is a transient family member as she moves to her husband family after marriage; ... a woman who does not give birth to a son has no status and can be divorced; women must suffer in silence for the sake of the family; if a family breakdown occurs it is the mother who is to be blamed; girls must be socialized to sacrifice their autonomy and freedom for the husband and his family; ... woman is the holder of the family honour or 'izzat'; a girl is a moral responsibility; if she is not a virgin at the time of marriage it is shameful for her parents ...; parents must regulate the sexuality of their daughters because their actions represent the family's honor; ... women are men's property. (Indian Women's Cultural Association (2010), quoted in Shankar et al, 2013, p 249)

For Shankar et al, gendered roles are affirmed by strong sociocultural recommendations attached to gendered responsibilities and sexual behaviour, such as, 'If she is not a virgin at the time of marriage' this is considered 'shameful for her parents'. These prescriptions of gender, sexual behaviours and implications for honour and shame ramify across the life course, and particularly in later life, where older women marshal gender and sexuality onto others by encouraging appropriate ways in which sexual intimacy and behaviour should be enacted. This was particularly relevant for study participants' children and kin:

> '[I]t's a good thing that they get a good relationship for marriage, in the parent's lifetime, that is a good thing. Then the children's life is set.' (Riffat, aged 70)

> 'She is not married ... she is forty years old ... that girl is so busy, I said to her that your whole life will pass you by like that.' (Hafza, aged 80)

These 'rules of the game' (Kandiyoti, 1988, p 274) construct ways in which older women, such as Riffat and Hafza, can exert agency through recommendations for marriage. This occurs within the domestic sphere and the hierarchical system (Kandiyoti, 1988; Choudhry, 2001), which allows women to regulate the sexual behaviour of others through subtle values attached to sociocultural ideals. 'Appropriate' sexualities include suggestions of heteronormative relationships (Jaspal, 2019; Roshanravan, 2019) and ethno-religious and cultural ideals of marriage and relationships before sexual intimacy/activity (see Ali et al, 2020; Phillips et al, 2020,

2021). Often, the reasoning for this is to move into desexualised life course positions where they can complete their sense of 'duty' and obligation to others (Satnam).

The rights of older South Asian family managing intergenerational behaviours and controls around sexuality, sexual activity and reproductive powers are not new (see Werbner, 2005). The politics of embodiment are part of a more complex cultural system that has been aided by international migration (Werbner, 2005). 'Appropriate' femininities and 'behaviours' (Dwyer, 1999, p 140) are often shared in older women's negotiations of their own gendered behaviours where their sexuality was veiled from others, often men and strangers, in their early years:

> 'You weren't allowed to go (out), the lifestyle was like that. … If you got married and you went out, then you would go with *purdah* (covering).' (Nazia, aged 64)

> '[I]f anyone said something here or there, then that would be an insult (dishonour) to us. So, we would keep covered with our scarves.' (Mandeep)

The wearing of a head covering signals respect within this honour and shame symbolic complex. It is a sign of sexual modesty and cannot be understood apart from it (Werbner, 2005, p 2). *Izzat*, *purdah* and dishonour are then seen as clear negotiations in terms of appropriate femininities and the veiling of sexualities to avoid dishonour. Like the veil itself, these politics are embedded in customary notions of honour and shame, which surround the right to control the sexuality and reproductive powers of young people. The 'veil', as a form of sociocultural practice, therefore aims to reduce the way in which the body was a target of gendered violence. The transmission of these practices and the added value for them are reiterated as the women have aged, creating tensions between young and older generations on the policing and management of sexualities.

The bargaining power of desexualisation in old age can signal women's autonomy and agency within and across the family structure to situate authority and have agency over others through 'non-threatening' gendered positions that are imbued with reverence and wisdom. Desexualised positions and meaning are created through a higher calling of 'good works', rather than bodily acts of marriage and the veiling of sexuality, which Satnam highlights: "If a person has done good works, then you will get its rewards ahead. That's if you are in this world and don't do bad things."

Later life provides opportunities for older SAm women to reconfigure and reclaim agency and autonomy by moving away from the once perilous, sexualised positions of the female body. These later life positions may be culturally and religiously affirmative, but this 'refashioning the self' (Mukherjee, 1992, p 11), and recovery, (re)constructs the body from being a quarry for the other to mine into a space cultivated by the older woman as her own. Here, autonomy and agency are (re)claimed through desexualised positions – not as an object of desire but revered as the matriarchal elder – the highest point of the familial hierarchy, where filial piety and reverence is a moral obligation from kin (see Choudhry, 2001).

Furthermore, agency and autonomy are negotiated when women feel they have 'done their duty' to others, often promoted after the marriage of (all) their children (Satnam), when 'life has passed' (Mandeep) or when there is a repositioning of faith and affirmation of impending death, where the "delicate body, one that has laid on flowers, one day it will lay on a pillow of stones" (Nargis). Silverio (2019, p 149) argues that the body itself becomes 'a form of language' in its own right. Older women visibly use detachment from the body as crucial in their move into desexualised positions and moving away from the body and bodily desires: "When you leave the world, there is some sort of recollection waiting for you. You will take some other rebirth, because your own body is left behind, but your soul it will fly to some place or another" (Satnam).

It is also noteworthy that the experiences of Partition have not left older women. Indeed, Sobti and Kumar (2022, p 732) argue that they are 'still unhealed' and held 'in the recesses of their heart' where the drawing of the borders between India and Pakistan affected women most severely. (De)sexualisation as an active form of resistance, particularly in old age, constructs the body as a 'project of the self' (Holmes, 2022, p 119) and is a consequence of historical events and third space socialisations (see Bhabha, 2003); complicated through the experience of migration and transnational loyalties. The politics of gender, sexuality and nation construct the body as a site of 'cultural symbolism' (Bhabha, 2003) in which previously 'eroticised female bodily norms' (Holmes, 2022, p 118) are (re)negotiated consciously to set aside earlier life course vulnerabilities. The poignant affirmation by Przybylo (2021, p 181) that, with age, 'sexy expires', allows older SAm women to move towards desexualised positions that involve 'removal of body-specific shame', where the body can be 'sexual without having to be sexualised' (Silverio, 2019, p 149).

Conclusion

Some older SAm women featured in this chapter, who grew up and grew older in the UK, were child survivors of Partition. Many have now passed away, but a few still remain. Other women were born during or shortly after Partition and their gendered socialisation was deeply affected by one of the largest socio-historic Imperial atrocities where South Asian women's bodies were targeted as an act of war and violence.

This chapter has provided a long view of (de)sexualisation for older SAm women by tracing how the intersections of gender, sexuality and age, situated within ethno-religious and cultural politics because of this momentous socio-historic event, have impacted on the sexualisation of South Asian women and girls. It is difficult, in a short space, to highlight the multiple intersections at play and to fully appreciate, and acknowledge, the ways in sexuality and femininity built on the foundations of political unrest have continued to shape migrant sexualities and (de)sexualisation across transnational contexts, and as diasporic identities in the UK. This is even more challenging given the lack of research in this area (see Vinay, 2022).

It is also crucial to note the diversity of experiences where some Partition survivors express that they did not see any violence or that they do not remember the event due to their young age(s), and yet others have vivid memories of the event (The 1947 Partition Archive; Virdee, 2013; Chawla, 2014; Gupta, 2019). This was a time when the reverberations of post-Partition life were still felt with varying levels of intensity across the two nation/s and which has continued for many years after (see Saeed, 2012; Sobita and Kumar, 2022). Therefore, even those who did not directly experience Partition and the violence that followed have been, were, and continue to be enmeshed in the politics of social expectations and sociocultural negotiations of gendered practices and sociocultural ideals of the sexualisation of the gendered body that have followed.

However, older Indian women can, and do, (re)claim agency and autonomy by moving towards new ways of being where intersectional sexualities, gender and femininity are (re)constructed in ways that conform to the notion of 'sexy expires' (Przybylo, 2021, p 181). It must be noted that not all older SAm women encompass desexualised positions in later life but, where they do, desexualisation has (inter)generational implications, whereby moving into the revered elder position, they are able to impose sexual and sociocultural recommendations on others. Here, older women transmit and transfer their own gendered expectations onto younger generations in the UK that are rooted in the same foundations of their own socialisation of honour, gender and sexuality, and frequently framed within heteronormative practices.

This chapter has also drawn attention to the child survivors of Partition and the pressing need to include the impact of socio-historic events across transnational lives, and more specifically, the impact this has had on later life. I have tried to capture the complexity and diversity of the experiences here but I am aware that I have only scratched the surface. I therefore make recommendations for further research to examine the history of sexuality from the event of Partition and the impact on later life sexualities for older transnational migrants who have aged in the West.

Appendix

Table 7.1: Older South Asian Migrant (SAm) women included in this chapter, elicited from the author's PhD research

Name	Age	Place of birth	Ethnicity and religion
Aisha	60	Pakistan	Pakistani Muslim
Satnam	72	India	Indian Sikh
Noor	78	India	Pakistani Muslim
Nargis	87	India	Pakistani Muslim
Nazia	64	Pakistan	Pakistani
Mandeep	76	India	Indian Sikh
Riffat	70	Pakistan	Pakistani
Hafza	80	India	Pakistani Muslim

Notes

[1] It is important to note that some of the women referred to in the chapter as the 'children of Partition' or 'child survivors of Partition' have aged and/or passed away, which adds to tensions around the lost voices of Partition memories from those who were children at the time. This is an area that remains under-researched.

[2] This chapter refers to the experiences of older South Asian women aged 60 years and over, particularly those previously termed as 'first-generation' migrants who came to the United Kingdom (UK) from Pakistan and/or India in the 1960s and early 1970s. This cohort of women, often termed as 'followers' came, sometimes with young children, to join their husbands (see Rodger and Herbert, 2008), acknowledged by Ahmed (2016) as women who became pioneer migrants. It is recognised that South Asian migration to the UK pre-dates this period, however, a large influx of South Asians migrated during this period as labour migrants and to work in the industries. The large numbers resulted in the reference of migrants to be constructed as a 'first generation'. I am aware the term generation is contentious (see Wray and Ali, 2014) and that this cohort of women are not a homogeneous group.

[3] Research ethics for the PhD research (2011–2015) was submitted and approved by the host institution's School Research Ethics Panel (SREP) in 2012.

[4] *Ways of Seeing* is a seminal book by John Berger (1972, p 5) in which he states, 'It is the seeing which comes before words'. In this chapter, this relates to how the woman's/girl's body is seen as sexualised before determining any other aspect of who she is.

[5] See also Ali (2024).

[6] See endnote 4.

[7] Prior to 1947 there was no *State* of Pakistan. After 1947 the *Dominion* of Pakistan was created with territories west and east of India (which are now the Islamic Republic of Pakistan and the People's Republic of Bangladesh). The Indian Independence Act, passed by the British Parliament on 18 July 1947, provided the foundation to the setting up of the independent dominions of India (predominantly Hindu) and Pakistan (predominantly Muslim) from 15 August 1947. At the exact stroke of midnight on 14 August 1947, Britain formally transferred its power to the two newly formed dominions of India and Pakistan (see The Parliament of the Commonwealth of Australia, 1999).

[8] See endnotes 1 and 7.

References

Ahmed, N. (2016). *Family, Citizenship and Islam: The Changing Experiences of Migrant Women Ageing in London*. UK: Routledge.

Ahmed, S., Khan, A.K.S. and Noushad, S. (2014). 'Early Marriage: A Root of Current Physiological and Psychosocial Health Burdens', *International Journal of Endorsing Health Science Research*, 2(1): 50–3.

Ali, N. (2006). 'Imperial Implosions: Postcoloniality and the Oribits of Migration', in Ali, N., Kerla, V.S. and Sayyid, S. (eds) *A Postcolonial People: South Asians in Britain*. London: Hurst: pp 158–67.

Ali, N. (2024). *Older Migrant Women's Experiences of Age and Ageing in the UK: Intersectional Feminist Perspectives*. New York: Palgrave Macmillan.

Ali, N., Phillips, R., Chambers, C., Narkowicz, K., Hopkins, P. and Pande, R. (2020). 'Halal Dating: Changing Relationship Attitudes and Experiences among young British Muslims', *Sexualities*, 23(5–6): 775–92.

Alvi, A. (2001). 'The Category of the Person in Rural Punjab', *Social Anthropology*, 9(1): 45–63.

Ansari, S. (2017). 'How the Partition of India Happened – And Why its Effects Are Still Felt Today'. *The Conversation* [online], https://theconversation.com/how-the-Partition-of-india-happened-and-why-its-effects-are-still-felt-today-81766

Bagchi, J., Dasgupta, S. and Ghosh, S. (eds) (2003). *The Trauma and the Triumph: Gender and Partition in Eastern India*. London: Virago Press.

Bhardwaj, D.A. (2021). 'Nation and its "Other" Women: Muslim Subjectivity and Gendered Agency in Delhi', *South Asia: Journal of South Asian Studies*, 44(2): 380–97.

Basu, A. (2012). 'Appropriating Gender', in Jeffery, P. and Basu, A. (eds) *Appropriating Gender: Women's Activism and Politicized Religion in South Asia*. New York: Routledge: pp 3–14.

Begum, H. and Gill, A.K. (2022) 'Understanding the Experiences of British South Asian Male Survivors of Child Sexual Abuse', in Gill, A.K. and Begum, H. (eds) *Child Sexual Abuse in Black and Minoritised Communities: Improving Legal, Policy and Practical Responses*. Cham: Palgrave Macmillan: pp 59–113.

Berger, J. (1972). *Ways of Seeing*. London: Penguin.

Bhabha, H. (1990). 'The Third Space: Interview with Homi Bhabha', in Rutherford, J. (ed) *Identity, Community, Culture, Difference*. London: Lawrence & Wishart: pp 207–21.

Bhabha, H. (2003). *The Other Question: Difference, Discrimination and the Discourse of Colonialism*. New York: Routledge.

Bhanbhro, S. (2021). 'Brothers Who Kill: Murders of Sisters for the Sake of Family Honour in Pakistan', in Buchanan, A. and Rotkirch, A. (eds) '*Brothers and Sisters: Sibling Relationships across the Life Course*. London: Palgrave Macmillan: pp 297–312.

Bhardwaj, A. (2004). 'Partition of India and Women's Experiences: A Study of Women as Sustainers of their Families in Post-Partition Delhi', *Social Scientist*, 32(5–6): 69–88.

Bhari, D. (1999). 'Telling Tales: Interventions', *International Journal of Post Colonial Studies*, 1(2): 217–34.

Brah, A. (1987). 'Women of South Asian Origin in Britain: Issues and Concerns', *South Asia Research*, 7(1): 39–54.

Brah, A. (2005). *Cartographies of Diaspora: Contesting Identities*. London/New York: Routledge.

Butalia, U. (2017). *The Other Side of Silence: Voices from the Partition of India*. London: Penguin.

Chakraborty, C. (2014). 'Mapping South Asian Masculinities: Men and Political Crises', *South Asian History and Culture*, 5(4): 411–20.

Chanana, K. (1993). 'Partition and Family Strategies: Gender-Education Linkages among Punjabi Women in Delhi', *Economic and Political Weekly*, WS25–WS34.

Chattha, I. (2018). 'After the Massacres: Nursing Survivors of Partition Violence in Pakistan Punjab Camps', *Journal of the Royal Asiatic Society*, 28(2): 273–93.

Chawla, D. (2014). *Home, Uprooted: Oral Histories of India's Partition*. New York: Fordham University Press.

Choudhry, U.K. (2001). 'Uprooting and Resettlement Experiences of South Asian Immigrant Women', *Western Journal of Nursing Research*, 23(4): 376–93.

Cihangir, S. (2013). 'Gender Specific Honor Codes and Cultural Change', *Group Processes and Intergroup Relations*, 16(3): 319–33.

Das, V. (1991). 'Composition of the Personal Voice: Violence and Migration', *Studies in History*, 7(1): 65–77.

DasGupta, S.D. (1989). *A Patchwork Shawl: Chronicles of South Asian Women in America*. New Brunswick, NJ: Rutgers University Press.

Didur, J. (2000). 'At a Loss for Words: Reading the Silence in South Asian Women's Partition Narratives', *TOPIA: Canadian Journal of Cultural Studies*, 4: 53–71.

Dwyer, C. (1999). 'Negotiations of Femininity and Identity for Young British Muslim Women', in Laurie, N., Dwyer, C., Holloway, S. and Smith, F. (eds) *Geographies of New Femininities*. London: Longman, pp 135–52.

Dwyer, C. (2000). 'Negotiating Diasporic Identities: Young British South Asian Muslim Women', *Women's Studies International Forum*, 23(4): 475–86.

Frischmann, N.E. (2010). 'Silence Revealed: Women's Experiences during the Partition of India' [online], www.academia.edu/611322/Silence_Revealed_Womens_Experiences_during_the_Partition_of_India.

Fuchs, S. (2001). 'Beyond Agency', *Sociological Theory*, 19(1): 24–40.

Gandhi, M.K. (1999). *Collected Works of Mahatma Gandhi, Volumes 1–100*. New Delhi: Government of India, Publications Division.

Gill, S.S. (2020). '"I Need To Be There": British South Asian Men's Experiences of Care and Caring', *Community, Work and Family*, 23(3): 270–85.

Gupta, R. (2019). 'Memories of Women Who Lived through Partition and Independence', *She the People: The Women's Movement*, www.shethepeople.tv/home-top-video/memories-of-women-who-lived-through-partition-and-independence/

Hadi, A. (2020). '"Honor" Killings in Misogynistic Society: A Feminist Perspective', *Academic Journal of Interdisciplinary Studies*, 9(3): 29.

Holmes, H. (2022). 'The Body in Personal Life', in May, V. and Nordqvist, P. (eds) *Sociology of Personal Life* (second edition). London: Bloomsbury Publishing: pp 117–39.

Holt, J. and Turney, L. (2006). 'The Singular Journey: South Asian Visual Art in Britain', in Ali, N., Karla, V.S. and Sayyid, S. (eds) *A Postcolonial People: South Asians in Britain*. London: Hurst & Company: pp 329–39.

Jamal, F. (2019). *A New Life in Huddersfield: The Memories of Partition and Migration. What is the Legacy of Partition in the Diaspora Community in the UK?* (Doctoral Dissertation, University of Huddersfield).

Jaspal, R. (2019). 'Honour Beliefs and Identity among British South Asian Gay Men', in Idriss, M.M. (ed) *Men, Masculinities and Honour-Based Abuse*. London: Routledge: pp 114–27.

Jassal, V. (2020). 'Sexual Abuse of South Asian Children: What Social Workers Need To Know', *Community Care Internet*, University of Kent repository, https://kar.kent.ac.uk/83327/1/Sexual%20abuse%20of%20South%20Asian%20children%20-%20community%20care%20article.pdf

Jones, G.W. (2020). 'New Patterns of Female Migration in South Asia', *Asian Population Studies*, 16(1): 1–4.

Kandiyoti, D. (1988). 'Bargaining with Patriarchy', *Gender and Society*, 2(3): 274–90.

Khan, R. and Lowe, M. (2019). 'Homophobic "Honour" Abuse Experienced by South Asian Gay Men in England', in Idriss, M.M. (ed) *Men, Masculinities and Honour-Based Abuse*. London: Routledge: pp 95–113.

Khan, Y. (2017). *The Great Partition: The Making of India and Pakistan*. New Haven, CT: Yale University Press.Kleinman, A., Das, V., Lock, M. and Lock, M.M. (eds) (1997). *Social Suffering*. Oakland, CA: University of California Press.

Krell, R. (1993). 'Child Survivors of the Holocaust: Strategies of Adaptation', *The Canadian Journal of Psychiatry*, 38(6): 384–9.

Krishan, Y. (1983). 'Mountbatten and the Partition of India', *History*, 68(222): 22–38.

Lugones, M. (2010). 'Toward a Decolonial Feminism', *Hypatia*, 25(4): 742–59.

Lugones, M. (2020). 'Gender and Universality in Colonial Methodology', *Critical Philosophy of Race*, 8(1–2): 25–47.

Matoo, G. (2022). 'Othered Subjects: Marginalised Voices of Black and South Asian Mothers', *Critical and Radical Social Work*, 10(1): 109–26.

Menon, R. and Bhasin, K. (1993). 'Recovery, Rupture, Resistance: Indian State and Abduction of Women during Partition', *Economic and Political Weekly*, WS2–WS11.

Menon, R. and Bhasin, K. (eds) (2011). *Borders and Boundaries: Women in India's Partition*. New Brunswick, NJ: Rutgers University Press.

Mirza, H.S. (2009). 'Plotting a History: Black and Postcolonial Feminisms in "New Times"', *Race, Ethnicity and Education*, 12(1): 1–10.

Mirza, N. (2020). *Navigating the Everyday as Middle-Class British-Pakistani Women: Ethnicity, Identity and Belonging*. London: Palgrave Macmillan.

Mohanram, R. (2019). 'Sexuality after Partition', in Mohanram, R. and Raychaudhuri, A. (eds) *Partitions and Their Afterlives: Violence, Memories, Living*. London and New York: Rowman and Littlefield: pp 49–82.

Mookerjea-Leonard, D. (2010). 'To Be Pure Or Not To Be: Gandhi, Women, and the Partition of India', *Feminist Review*, 94(1): 38–54.

Mukherjee, B. (1992). 'Refashioning the Self: Immigrant Women's New World', *Studies in Short Fiction*, 29(1): 11–17.

Nair, N. (2004). '"We Left Our Keys with Our Neighbours": Memory and the Search for Meaning in Post-Partitioned India', https://dspace.mit.edu/handle/1721.1/97627

Phillips, R., Chambers, C., Ali, N., Pande, R. and Hopkins, P. (2020). 'Mobilizing Pakistani Heritage, Approaching Marriage', *Ethnic and Racial Studies*, 43(16): 1–19.

Phillips, R., Chambers, C., Ali, N., Karmakar, I. and Diprose, K. (2021). *Storying Relationships: Young British Muslims Speak and Write about Sex and Love*. London: Bloomsbury Publishing.

Prajapati, R. and Liebling, H. (2022). 'Accessing Mental Health Services: A Systematic Review and Meta-Ethnography of the Experiences of South Asian Service Users in the UK', *Journal of Racial and Ethnic Health Disparities*, 9(2): 598–619.

Przybylo, E. (2021). 'Ageing Asexually: Exploring Desexualisation and Ageing Intimacies', in Hafford-Letchfield, T., Simpson, P. and Reynolds, P. (eds) *Sex and Diversity in Later Life*. Bristol: Policy Press: pp 181–98.

Puri, J. (1999). *Woman, Body, Desire in Post-Colonial India: Narratives of Gender and Sexuality*. New York: Routledge.

Puwar, N. and Raghuram, P. (eds) (2020). *South Asian Women in the Diaspora*. London: Routledge.Rodger, R. and Herbert, J. (2008). 'Narratives of South Asian Women in Leicester 1964–2004', *Oral History*, 36(2): 554–63.

Roomi, M.A. and Harrison, P. (2010). 'Behind the Veil: Women-Only Entrepreneurship Training in Pakistan', *International Journal of Gender and Entrepreneurship*, 2(2): 150–72. Doi:10.1108/17566261011051017

Roshanravan, S. (2019). 'Witnessing Faithfully and the Intimate Politics of Queer South Asian Praxis', in Lugones, M., *Carnal Disruptions: Mariana Ortega interviews María Lugones. Speaking Face-to-face: the Visionary Philosophy of María Lugones*. Albany, NY: New York State University Press: pp 103–22.

Roy, A.G. (2019). *Memories and Postmemories of the Partition of India*. London: Routledge.

Saeed, H.Z. (2012). *Persisting Partition: Gender, Memory and Trauma in Women's Narratives of Pakistan* (PhD thesis, University of Manchester).

Sangar, M. and Howe, J. (2021). 'How Discourses of Sharam (Shame) and Mental Health Influence the Help-Seeking Behaviours of British-Born Girls of South Asian Heritage', *Educational Psychology in Practice*, 37(4): 343–61.

Sanghera, S. (2021). *Empireland: How Imperialism Has Shaped Modern Britain*. London: Penguin.

Shankar, J., Das, G. and Atwal, S. (2013). 'Challenging Cultural Discourses and Beliefs that Perpetuate Domestic Violence in South Asian Communities: A Discourse Analysis', *Journal of International Women's Studies*, 14(1): 248–62.

Sharma, R. and Velath, P.M. (2021). 'Encountering "Identity": Refugee Women and the Partition of the Subcontinent', *Journal of Migration Affairs*, 4(1): 95–109.

Shaw, A. (2000). *Kinship and Continuity: Pakistani Families in Britain*. Oxon and New York: Routledge.

Silverio, S.A. (2019). 'Reconstructing Gender to Transcend Shame: Embracing Human Functionality to Enable Agentic and Desexualised Bodies', in Mayer, C.H. and Vanderheiden, E. (eds) *The Bright Side of Shame*. Cambridge: Springer: pp 149–65.

Simpson, P., Reynolds, P. and Hafford-Letchfield, T. (eds) (2021a). *Desexualisation in Later Life: The Limits of Sex and Intimacy*. Bristol: Policy Press.

Simpson, P., Reynolds, P. and Hafford-Letchfield, T. (2021b). 'Introduction to Volume Two: Themes, Issues and Chapter Synopses', in Simpson, P., Reynolds, P. and Hafford-Letchfield, T. (eds) *Desexualisation in Later Life: The Limits of Sex and Intimacy*. Bristol: Policy Press: pp 1–16.

Sobti, P. and Kumar, D. (2022). 'Partition as Memory: Construing Women Narratives', *Journal of Positive School Psychology*, 6(9): 731–8.

Talbot, I. and Singh, G. (2009). *The Partition of India*. Cambridge: Cambridge University Press.

The 1947 Partition Archive (nd). 'Women During Partition: Courage, Compassion, Survival'. The 1947 Partition Archive, https://artsandculture.google.com/story/women-during-partition-courage-compassion-survival-1947-partition-archive/zQVh0uAuub4HLw?hl=en

The Parliament of the Commonwealth of Australia. (1999). 'India and Pakistan: The New Dominions'. In *The 1998 Indian and Pakistani Nuclear Tests: Report of the Senate Foreign Affairs, Defence and Trade References Committee*, June 1999, Canberra: pp 3–14.

Trouillot, M.-R. (1995). *Silencing the Past: Power and the Production of History*. London: Beacon Press.

UNICEF. (2015). 'Early marriage: A traditional harmful practice – a statistical exploration'. UNICEF Data, https://data.unicef.org/resources/early-marriage-a-traditional-harmful-practice-a-statistical-exploration/

Unlu, M.D. (2018). 'Rape as a Political Tool and as a Weapon of War', *International Journal on Rule of Law, Transitional Justice and Human Rights*, 9(9): 23–34.

Vinay, V. (2022). 'The (Colonial) History of Sexuality: The Colonial Categorization of Sexuality in Colonized India', *MUNDI*, 2(1): 177–98.

Virdee, P. (2013). 'Remembering Partition: Women, Oral Histories and the Partition of 1947', *Oral History*, 41(2): 49–62.

Werbner, P. (2005). 'Honor, Shame and the Politics of Sexual Embodiment among South Asian Muslims in Britain and Beyond: An Analysis of Debates in the Public Sphere', *International Social Science Review*, 6(1): 25–47.

Wilson, A. (2006). *Dreams, Questions, Struggles: South Asian Women in Britain*. London and Ann Arbor, MI: Pluto Press.

Wray, S. and Ali, N. (2014). 'Understanding Generation through the Lens of Ethnic and Cultural Diversity', *Families, Relationships and Societies*, 3(3): 469–73.

Yusin, J. (2009). 'The Silence of Partition: Borders, Trauma, and Partition History', *Social Semiotics*, 19(4): 453–68.

Zamindar, V.F.Y. (2007). *The Long Partition and the Making of Modern South Asia: Refugees, Boundaries, Histories*. New York: Columbia University Press.

PART III

Agency through fantasy, erotic tales and pleasure

8

Sexual fantasies and older, Indigenous Purépecha women: sociocultural constraints and possibilities

Cuauhtémoc Sanchez Vega

The lives and sociocultural structure of Indigenous communities in Mexico have been extensively documented, as evidenced in the documentary heritage of the National Commission for the Development of Indigenous People. While little attention has been paid to native people's sexuality, on rare occasions when the erotic lives of Indigenous people have been addressed, the focus has been placed mainly on teenage pregnancies, early marriages, ignorance of the body and sexually transmitted infections. Consequently, the experience of pleasure is neglected and emphasis placed on the reproductive age population, erasing from the erotic panorama the sexual and post-reproductive lives of older Indigenous people.

In light of the concerns just described, this chapter explores the sociocultural phenomena that enable, nurture or condition expressions of sexual fantasies of Purépecha women aged 50 years and above, inhabitants of Purépecha Indigenous communities in the state of Michoacán, in north-western Mexico. The first part of this chapter sets the historic-cultural and political contexts for subsequent examination of the empirical materials co-generated with older Purépecha women study participants. The first part of my analysis, then, refers to information contained in the oldest source of the pre-Hispanic history of the state of Michoacán, Mexico: the sixteenth-century codex (collection of old manuscripts) called 'Relación de las ceremonias y ritos y población y gobernación de los Indios de la Provincia de Michoacán' ['Relation of the ceremonies and rites and population and government of the Indians of the Province of Michoacán'; hereafter 'La Relación'] (Miranda and Le Clezio, 1980; Amezcua and Sánchez Díaz, 2015). This source is recognised as the most authoritative by the scholarly community for its knowledge of the ways of life and sociocultural organisation of the population settled in the Michoacán territory before, during and after it was conquered by the Spanish Crown in the sixteenth century (Amezcua and Sánchez Díaz, 2015).

From the codex, we gain insight into components of social and cultural organisation which, as Weeks (1986), Rubin cited in Lamas (2000) and

Foucault (2007a, 2007b) would argue, regulate erotic activity. With such considerations in mind, this chapter answers several key questions: (1) what concrete and symbolic sociocultural references persist, which make possible or impossible the experience of pleasure, sexual desire and loving for Purépecha women? (2) What concrete and symbolic factors shape the sexual fantasies of these women? (3) What novel factors of reported experience reveal the content of sexual fantasies of Purépecha women who question women's duty in that particular cultural social context?

The method of data analysis underpinning this chapter consists of a content review from a critical feminist perspective through the proposals of Esteban Galarza (2011), Hierro (2014), Mogrovejo (2016), Pessah (2016) and Rosso (2016). This method is applied to narratives about sexual fantasies co-generated via in-depth interviews which form the basis of later discussion, reflecting on possible sociocultural influences that persist or represent reconfigured thinking about Purépecha women, the latter suggesting new ethics of pleasure, itself pointing towards a more convivial model of sexual morality that positively acknowledges (Purépecha) women's pleasure.

The puzzle: the origins of practices associated with Purépecha sexuality

This section provides insight into aspects of history, culture and politics that have, inevitably, shaped Purépecha life and sexuality. The codex already referred to – 'La Relación' (1988) – contains invaluable information on the sociocultural life of the inhabitants of Michoacán before Mexico's conquest. However, it lacks elements that give a clear account of the practices and sexual life of men and women from Michoacán. Authors such as Dávalos López (1998), López Austin (2010) and Jacinto Zavala (1980) have examined the content of the codex and have identified three salient themes: (1) marriage, endogamy and polygamy; (2) adultery/infidelity and traits of morality before marriage (one of the most frequently recurring themes in the codex); and (3) the political relevance of kinship and its possibilities. In turn, such factors represent key sociocultural influences on the sexual and erotic lives of Purépecha people in pre-Hispanic times.

Marriage, inbreeding and polygamy

The structure of Purépecha society attracted the curiosity of religious people and largely because this structure involved 'marriage within the neighborhood' or endogamy (Dávalos López, 1998):

> Others married for love without informing their parents and arranged among themselves. Others from very young were appointed to marry

them. Others first took the mother-in-law when the daughter was little, and after the girl was old, they left the mother-in-law and they took the daughter, whom they married. ('La Relación', p 53)

The codex also reveals that marriages across status/caste: between lords, *caciques* (community leader/s) and common people were not allowed: 'When people were to marry, relatives of the woman came down and they agreed with each other and the priests withheld their blessings' or they lacked status (section *De la manera en que se casaba la gente vaja* [On the way in which those people accorded low status got married], p 53). Indeed, marriage within the culture signified as an act of prestige, particularly for the ruling elite, for whom it was important who they became related to: an inappropriate choice could mean social repudiation:

> I who am your Father did not walk in this way that you walk, you have done me a great affront, throwing the earth in my eyes; I wanted to say I will not dare to appear among the people nor will I have eyes to look at them because everyone will tell me to my face and they will affront me for what you have done, he said more to his daughter. ('La Relación'; section *Los señores entre sí se casaba de esta manera* [Gentlemen married each other this way], p 55)

Moreover, according to Dávalos López (1998), the *cazonci* (community ruler) maintained polygamous relationships for the political reasons, as this practice helped ensure sufficient alliances to maintain a certain degree of trust, solidarity and mutual aid with other community members. Above all, this arrangement helped secure a sense of communal belonging and identity. By marrying the daughters or sisters of lords, his offspring were related to other lords or *caciques* [chiefs], guaranteeing the continuity of his lineage and domain: 'many ladies, daughters of principals. ... In these the *cazonci* [sovereign/ruler] had many children and ... later some of these ladies married men of status' ('La Relación', p 236; in Dávalos López, 1998, p 82).

Adultery, infidelity and morality in marriage

As already mentioned in 'La Relación' (1988), it is made clear that marital ties play a central role in Purépecha people's lives, since throughout the text there are references associated with the political, social, religious and ontological importance of being Purépecha. Jacinto Zavala (1980) has observed the establishment of a divine connection between man and nature, and, therefore, the actions of man/humankind are intimately related to divinity (*curicaueri*). Indeed, any affront to marriage was to be regarded as an affront to divinity itself.

Further, among the religious beliefs of the ancient inhabitants of Michoacán, it was considered that inappropriate behaviour of the offspring directly affected the entire family, so another of the recommendations that the religious gave to newlyweds was: '[B]e well married; look, don't get killed for adultery or lust' (Dávalos López, 1998, p 151).

Indeed, the codex indicates that adultery was one of the most commonly observed of Purépecha sexual behaviours, and it was sanctioned in different ways. Although descriptions of the way in which they were punished change according to the documents consulted, one significant point is that women were more severely sanctioned or even warned against such behaviour; the married woman who committed adultery was punished, but not the single man who committed adultery with a married woman. According to evidence in texts, only the woman who dared to break the marriage vow of fidelity was punished.

Political relevance of kinship and its possibilities

> After a few days, the lord of Curinguaro called his sons and asked them, 'What will we do? Look, what do you think? Say it and I will listen to you. … Wouldn't it be good if you took your sister to him [Tariacuri]?' And the sons said, 'You have spoken well, sir. What should we say? Your opinion is great and it is good', and they agreed to give her to Tariacuri as a wife. ('La Relación', pp 191–92)

From the previous sections, and especially from the quote just referred to, we can see that pre-Hispanic Purépecha society was based on the exchange of women (Rubin, 2000). This practice signified as a form of commitment and reciprocity that reinforced the structures of social bonding and was thought to enrich social relationships and key social structures, from the family unit to the organisation of government.

Indeed, according to Rubin (2000, p 53): 'Kinship is organisation, and organisation gives power. But who do they organise or what do they organise? To whom and over what do they give power?'. For Rubin, most tribal societies were characterised by maintaining a social system of great men, in which the exchange of women meant not only a simple gift, but the greatest of gifts and the means of organisation that guaranteed social peace through alliances between groups of great men. Rubin's thinking here appears reflected in the narration of the much-discussed origin of the appropriate adjective to name the native habitants from the Michoacán region: Purépecha or Tarasco:

> A little while ago, three Spaniards arrived at the city of Mechuacan on horseback. … And the cazonci treated the Spaniards in the same way

as they treated their gods, with gold garlands and put gold roundels around their necks, and to each one of them placed his offering of wine in front of him in large cups, and offerings of bread and fruits ... and before they left, the Spaniards asked the cazonci for two of their female relatives and they took two Indian women with them, and along the way they got together with them and they called the Indians who went with the Spaniards tarascue, which means sons-in-law in their language, and from there they later began to give the Indians this name and instead of calling them tarascue, they called them tarascos. ('La Relación', pp 91–2)

This story shows both the instrumental and concrete structure of the power of great men through gifts and reception of the first Spaniards in Michoque land, similar to the way in which the Purépecha people treated their gods, including the delivery of the female relatives of the *cazonci*. It represented the meeting of two cultures, modifying the language, relationships and social structure of those involved, such that even today the denomination Tarasco versus Purépecha is still not entirely clear (Franco Mendoza, 2007).

In line with Rubin's approach (2000): 'The exchange of women concretely is the establishment of political positions, preservation of a lineage and wealth, but also freedoms, possibilities and rights; rights that in exchange system, men have over their female relatives, but that women do not have over their male relatives.' Hence, rights and freedoms were exclusive to men before and after the conquest of Purépecha people, and men held power through family organisation and the specific form of kinship, since consistently in 'La Relación', throughout this, it is men who choose women or who give women to other men.

Strictly speaking, the kinship system that works through the exchange of women establishes certain basic processes: obligatory heterosexuality and the asymmetrical division of sex-gender; the first one described thus: 'Furthermore, in clandestine marriages, the male partner would speak in the promissory future tense: "I will marry you", as the present tense was used to signal a desire for sex' ('La Relación', p 57).

Given the foregoing discussion, it may come as no surprise that women in Mesoamerican towns did not have access to formal political power. For Purépecha women, such a possibility was apparently forbidden, and, similarly, they could not choose their partners and most of their social activities were centred on the care of offspring. Gendered power asymmetries were not just manifest in the organisation and distribution of formal power but also influenced the experience of pleasure, and emotions involved in desire, liking and feeling.

Arguably, the lack of erotic representations and writings on the pre-Hispanic period would not seem strange, due in part, to the very probable censorship initiated with the conquest and followed by the sexual conceptions of the native people. According to López Austin (2010), Fray Bartolomé de las Casas affirmed that sexual transgression was the most significant form of sin: 'When they referred to sin, without addition, they meant the sin of the flesh, and that of fornication mostly' (p 33).

In 'La Relación' (pp 243–4), an episode is described, unique of its kind for making direct mention of the expression of a woman's desire:

> Tariacuri tells his nephews, that a daughter of Zurunban named Mauina asked that a tent or pavilion (called xupaquata) be made for her in the market with a chamber made of dyed blankets, and there, sitting on many blankets as they used to put the goddess Xaratanga, she sent for the beautiful young men who passed through the market and all day she got together with them saying: 'If I were a man, wouldn't I get together with a woman?'

Tariacuri's express request was that, because of her statement, the brothers should throw their sister into the river; in addition to the specific assertion that none of the brothers would become lord of Tararán because not only had they not sacrificed their sister, they had also tolerated her behaviour, which tells us about desire and pleasure of this woman on a physical level, which relates to a fantasy that transgressed the moral strictures that allowed the exchange of women: the sexual/carnal desire of men.

Other pre-Hispanic cultures, such as Nahuas societies, refer to women's sexual potency, as described by Dávalos López (1998), López Austin (2010), and Jacinto Zavala (1980). We find something similar with Otomi (Indigenous) women, as described by Dávalos López, concerning how they dressed. In 'La Relación' we cannot find any narrative that even makes a reference to erotic elements or dressing of Purépecha women.

Sexual fantasies: key elements of experience

Cultures furnish various resources that are manifested in all domains of life through specific practices and that establish the meanings of sex, sexuality and eroticism, though there is some scope for nuance and adaptation through creativity. However, sexuality has been constituted for thousands of years as a form of power and control (Foucault, 2005, 2007a, 2007b).

Plummer (in Weeks, 1986, p 31) informs us that each society and culture establishes restrictions on sexual and erotic expression, for example, by age, sex, gender, sexual preference, ethnicity, and so on, which prescribes who can engage or not in certain sexual activities and who may or may not marry, express/manifest their desire or flirt. But, another set of restrictions tells people how to perform or 'do' sex, where, when and how often. Such restrictions ordain which orifices or body parts to stimulate, highlight or not, or even make in/visible. Such restrictions are generally regulated in legal systems or backed by a well-known moral structure grounded in society and culture. Given the historical, political and social influences already explained, both kinds of regulation appear integral to Purépecha culture.

The restrictions that Plummer establishes (in Weeks, 1986, p 31) focus their attention on both concrete and practical aspects of regulation. However, there is another element that is essential to address the central theme of this chapter, which concerns restrictions that society and culture establish for imaginative activity (Vigotsky, 2015). In this category of restrictions, we find reproductive and productive ones. The imaginative reproductive restrictions allude to those elements that, as individuals, we are able to produce freely, countless times; those that are not necessarily valued, validated or recognised by society, but, nevertheless, are very much integral to our social and cultural experience. For this type of imaginative restrictions, collective creativity is fundamental, since its raw material is what is already known, whether through personal experience or that of others; it is what we would call crystallised imagination.

Productive imaginative restrictions refer to those elements that, as individuals, we are also able to produce freely, but the difference is that they are nourished both by elements of the crystallised imagination and by new elements that come from the creative activity and dynamics of experimentation in spaces, backgrounds and with unknown people, of questioning what is already given and established. Language, for example, is a clear product, tool and technique for enabling such creativity.

For Vigotsky (2015), human creativity is always accompanied, promoted, stimulated or manipulated, punished, or sanctioned by culture, that silent and sometimes thunderous structure, that interferes in lives of human beings even before birth through its laws, norms, concessions, myths, taboos, language, institutions and restrictions. For Ribot (cited in Vigotsky, 2015, p 37): 'No matter how individual it may seem, every creation always includes a social coefficient. In this sense, no invention will be individual in the strict sense of the word, it will always be a secret and unknown collaboration.' Indeed, it is very difficult accurately to trace and even give a conscious account of the origin of what we think, imagine or do. Hence, what we understand as an autonomous creation is actually a product of our experience in the material and historical reality that conditions our psychic reality (Aguinis, 1999).

Psychic life is practically nourished by fantasy (Aguinis, 1999), without this implying a tacit separation from material and historical reality. Rather, it is nourished and is dynamic thanks to the influences of material and historical reality, which serve to update, rearrange, modify and even eliminate experiences and symbolic content and, consciously or unconsciously, to reduce displeasure. The influences of material and historical reality (social and individual) constitute a common thread that nurtures everything accumulated through experience and the senses (Lizarraga-Cruchaga, 2016) in memory (Shaie and Willis, 2003), nourishing fantasies, which are promoted by desire.

Furthermore, psychoanalytic literature refers to fantasies or daydreams, which are narrations of the erotic content of the waking subject, and which make up the story and representation of the intimate and sometimes 'shameful' content of that psychic life to which the person has access in a conscious state (Aguinis, 1999). For Sanz (1999), sexual fantasy is a faculty and resource of the human being to mentally eroticise himself, which emerges from a desire or allows its formation; fantasy is constituted as a mental process of thoughts and images that derive in physical sensations that can be experienced in a pleasant way. For Moyano and Sierra (2014), sexual fantasies reflect the direct relation with erotic and pleasurable stories and, consequently, sexual satisfaction, which also highlight the social influences on their content, at least at the level of gender.

Research design

Participants: 20 Indigenous women participated in the study, all of them speakers of the Purépecha language, five of them monolingual, the rest bilingual (Purépecha and Spanish), their native tongue being Purépecha. One participant took part in the workshop as a translator, from Spanish to Purépecha and from Purépecha to Spanish. She was also one of those interviewed as a key informant. The women participating in this study spanned 50–82 years of age. Originally from the communities of Erongarícuaro and Turícuaro, both are communities that belong to the municipal region of San Andrés Tziróndaro in the state of Michoacán, Mexico.

Process: Reports of sexual fantasies were obtained at the end of a three-hour discussion workshop about topics associated with sexuality in old age and ageing. At the end of the workshop, participants were asked to write a sexual fantasy and specify their name and age. Participants were asked to let us know if they wanted to share their fantasy (for research purposes) – eight of them agreed to the request.

Data collection technique: documentary analysis and content; focused interviews with key informants (Valles, 2007; Rapley, 2014).

Sample: a purposive sampling strategy was deployed by criteria: Indigenous Purépecha women, aged over 50 years, monolingual speakers of Purépecha language and bilingual speakers of Purépecha and Spanish (Izcara, 2014). For ethical purposes, participants are disguised by use of an initial not connected to their actual names.

Inclusion criteria for sexual fantasies: the narratives of those who at that time were over 50 years old, comprising at least half a page and no more than a page and a half, regardless of their content, were selected for reasons of data manageability.

Analysis and codification: copies of the fantasies articulated were taken (the participants decided to keep the originals), then they were printed to allow work on the content, making side notes. Five focused interviews were transcribed textually, lasting between 20 and 35 minutes each, with a total recording of 105 minutes.

For the content analysis and data reduction of sexual fantasies, keywords and narrative topics were identified, reviewing word by word and line by line, in an inductive way. Peripheral categories associated with the following themes were obtained: (1) respectful and affectionate treatment by partners; (2) sensations and emotions; (3) setting and scenarios; (4) partner's sexual characteristics; (5) active (sexual) participation; (6) protected sex; (7) fidelity; and (8) desires.

Data analysis of the focused interviews with five key informants consisted of a critical feminist content analysis, from the perspective of '*amor y contramor*' (love and against love) (Herrera, 2011; Mogrovejo, 2016), which was carried out word by word, identifying thematic and discursive axes associated with the sociocultural background of participants. From both the content analysis of the sexual fantasies and focused interviews, three central categories were obtained: (1) influence of culture on the sexual/erotic life of women; (2) influences on their lives associated with romantic love; and (3) personal agency with respect to erotic life. The discursive content of the fantasies and the focused interview materials describe in the participant's voices elements of discourse that favour, enrich, delimit and condition the erotic life of Purépecha women.

Analysis of results

The content analysis of sexual fantasies reveals interesting aspects of reported experience that are correlated at the content level, and which can be analysed from a critical feminist perspective: (1) influence of culture on the sexual/erotic life of women; (2) elements associated with romantic love; and (3) personal agency regarding erotic life. The analysis to be developed intersects with feminist thinking (Esteban Galarza, 2011; Mogrovejo, 2016).

Influence of culture on the sex-erotic life of women

> 'For me and for Purépecha culture it is very difficult to think about these things. It is not discussed. It is not said here. ... But, well, I barely, after 50 that was not bad ... for you to have sex, you have to be married to the law, to God, to society, to all, and then you can do whatever you want with your husband.' (E, 50)

I have already observed how society and culture have a determining influence on the regulation of erotic life, of sexual practices and expression. However, these regulations do not work in the same way for men as for women; female oppression is evident in some backgrounds when women have to assume obligatory reproduction, be in charge of domestic services without any remuneration, and show fidelity:

> '[A]nd well I never complained to him, actually for me it was better that he was away [referring to the husband's infidelity]. … They told me you have to have sexual relations, you have to find a partner because otherwise you'll harm yourself and I mean it's not something that was in my head, and nothing happened. I didn't have and, well, finally, sometimes I had but I didn't enjoy it. … When my husband came and wanted to have sex I couldn't, I just couldn't. So, I forgot because I was married. I couldn't fail and say I'm going to find someone else. I think it was like a brake and I denied myself.' (E, 50)

It is assumed as a social and cultural mandate that pleasure is linked to reproduction, which is only valid within marriage: marriage and reproduction that women do not necessarily want or enjoy, but the ultimate goal of which is to preserve family (Rosso, 2016):

> 'In the beginning when you are young and when you get married you know you are going to have sex and you don't know how or anything and you don't enjoy it, because you are afraid, because you are young, because you don't want to have children yet because you have other goals in life and that, personally, did not allow me to feel. I was kind of restricted, like I had my children without feeling, like I was pregnant and that's it. … I had to have them and I've always been responsible, because I suffered a lot. I didn't like it. I always said I didn't want to have children and yet they are there but I have been very responsible.' (E, 50)

It seems that the only event that can dissolve the mandate of imposed monogamy on women is the death of the spouse; which opens up a small possibility of recuperating desire and erotic experience.

> '[B]ecause at the beginning I was closed off and I was married for many years and I closed, that is, I didn't pay attention, here … and that's how my culture works and how they told me and only death can separate us. I mean, it's something so stuck in our heads that it was like that until he died or I died.' (E, 50)

Society and culture become so determining and totalising that even after the relationship ends due to the death of the spouse, for women social surveillance endures:

'My late husband's relatives still say after his death: "It's not right for you to leave your children to follow another man." ... The culture here is very macho. It hits you in many ways, people whether, women are tearing down, they are dead in life, they have no enjoyment, they have no life.' (E, 50)

However, the psychological consequences for women of the internalisation of a social order that represents monogamy and fidelity in marriage can be devastating. Even after the relationship ends or the partner dies, as expressed in the following narrative segment:

'Even with that person I was living in secret. It was hidden. Because of education, I didn't want anyone to find out here. I left where we were going and I felt that everyone was looking at me and you feel everybody was staring everywhere and that's how you were left feeling, the sorrow, the shame, the culture. You feel like a whore, you are a whore and a prostitute if you leave, if you mess with a person. I really felt that way and sometimes the moment comes when you say, "I'm a whore, I'm a whore" and it's not true. I mean, no, no.' (E, 50)

Accounts of romantic love

For most of history, it was inconceivable that people would choose their partners based on something as fragile and irrational as love and then concentrate all their sexual, intimate and altruistic desires on the marriage that resulted from that choice (Coontz, 2005, cited in Rosso, 2016, p 73).

Rosso (2016) affirms that marriage for love is a modern invention, which updates the structure of marriage – which, in principle, was intended to provide stability and social recognition – now adding the obligation to sustain and provide emotional satisfaction and psychological well-being. Because of discourses and practices associated with romantic love that are established in the collective imagination of the monogamous couple, it is not surprising that parts of the content of women's sexual fantasies make reference to this factor. Such thought and practice have been 'sold' for more than a century – that people are involved in a tireless search for the 'other half' that embodies true love and will know how to satisfy each other's needs, including sexual ones, and therefore will make us complete, happy beings:

'I allowed myself just now because I always said when I was a widow, I was about to look for someone, I'm not going to die without having loved. I'm still fine and I'm going to look for someone.' (E, 50)

> 'With the person you love, kisses of the person you love makes you feel appreciated and trusted.' (M, 62)
>
> 'Looking at each other like it was the first day, like saying love at first sight.' (E, 60)
>
> 'I would like to live it [life] with my only partner because he is the only person with whom I want to end my days.' (N, 66)
>
> 'Sexual relations help you to have a stable emotion to feel safe with your partner.' (M, 62)
>
> 'That they treat me well, with respect and not violence.' (M, 52)
>
> 'He tells me nice things in my ear.' (M, 56)
>
> '… performs the sexual act with respect and love.' (E, 60)
>
> 'With affection, with tenderness, with passion and if we come to a sexual relationship, that it is willingly.' (M, 52)
>
> 'We have the right to be. The only thing I would recommend is that if they look for their permanent partner, fine for now, that would be very good if they did it, with respect for themselves of their person.' (E, 50)

The discourse and practices of romantic love linked to monogamy specifically for women legitimise a system of oppression, of their relationships, bodies, desires and lives; since romantic love includes by definition monogamous fidelity, and this, also introduces a series of demands such as: (a) exclusivity in its different manifestations (emotional, affective, sexual, relational); and (b) possession/property, which naturally brings with it the idea that this 'all of mine' concretely and symbolically represents possession of affections, of the body, desires and pleasures and even of the life of the partner. It should be made clear that all these factors invariably apply to women, though it works the same way for men, at least in a symbolic way.

Personal agency regarding erotic life

> '[B]ecause now one chooses better, because at the beginning it is how you fall in love, you have to get married, you have to have children, that is the culture. … Now, on this second occasion, and in these five decades, one says, "I am going to choose well. I'm going to look. I'm going to see." I was open, I stayed like that for many years, five years,

a widow and later, I said "I'm going to give myself a chance but if the person you want comes, you do, and if not, then you don't leave, your freedom remains".' (E, 50)

Societies controlled by powerful men are, obviously, heteropatriarchal. In terms of Purépecha society, Segato (2018) observes that native people had completely differentiated practices for men and women, which constitutes of itself (viewed through Western eyes) a pre-Hispanic sex-gender system that mandates a dimorphic or binary masculinity and femininity. Segato (2018) has referred to this as a low-intensity patriarchy that was later reconfigured with the conquest, with that high-intensity patriarchy, and when they combined, it reached such extreme forms of violence (Segato, 2018).

In this section, I refer to that low-intensity patriarchy (Segato, 2018) to explain those practices that do not denote extreme violence against women but that, undoubtedly, have a profound impact on their lives. Put more simply, we could frame this issue as Pessah (2016) does, in terms of 'bad education' in that education, both formal and informal, that persists today in the daily life of women, is reminiscent (or not) of that low-intensity patriarchy, where the exchange of women as a basis of society and culture is nourished by monogamy, fidelity, sexual exclusivity and a sense of ownership of women.

'Bad education' for Pessah (2016) concerns ways of transmitting knowledge-culture, as invaluable knowledge that has to be apprehended, introjected, assimilated and put into practice by women for them to be recognised as women. In the field of women's sexual life, it seems that a requirement to start building personal agency and freeing oneself from that bad education requires questioning of the culture; as reflected by one of the key informants:

> 'I don't know. Maybe I left, what's it called, I put "culture" aside? Maybe I disobeyed something that wasn't present? But all your life educates you … sex is bad. Sex is the Devil's thing. Sex is where if a man takes you, he doesn't want you for good. It means you don't give to a person what you are worth. For you to have sex, you have to be married to the law, to God, to society, to everything, and then you can do whatever you want with your husband.' (E, 50)

As stated, 'bad education' has generated a sexual morality based on patriarchy, creating the power-knowledge-pleasure triad, a triad to which women have restricted or no access (through men's eyes and practices). Therefore, when women question that sexual morality, either from experience or reflection, they become open to the possibility of building a sexual morality or ethics of pleasure (Hierro, 2014), a path towards autonomy and discovery of potential of women's own erotic lifestyle. Thus, the sexual morality of women could be represented through a triad: appropriation of the body; choices around desire; and on its intensity, as reflected in the following quotes that represent the elements of the triad:

> '[W]hen he had already left, I had desires and searched and wanted and … it was until then, not even before, I said what a wonderful life, I said, "That's why there are women so happy because they have what I had in a very short period of time".' (E, 50)

> 'That he participated with me, I also caress him, love him, kiss him, hug him.' (M, 52)

> 'I touch him with my hands just out of the shower.' (E, 60)

> 'We kiss, we touch our bodies, we feel our breath, we feel our bodies, the smell of each other. For the first time, I want to make love on the couch. … "Let's do it once", then he gives me oral sex, I'll give it to him. … Then I'll ask him to take a bath and make love in that tub. Let's do it, then I look at myself in the mirror in the room and I tell myself, "It's really you".' (V, 59)

> 'Safer sex using a female or male condom to avoid sexually transmitted infections.' (M, 52)

> 'By the way, we are using strawberry condoms for oral sex.' (V, 59)

Personal agency effectively requires questioning what is supposedly already given, but also personal work that allows us to deal with guilt, shame or the sorrow of having transgressed what is already established (Pick and Rirkin, 2010). It also involves learning to question pariah status, which entails exclusion from social experiences that at some point offer support and sustenance, but with a new knowledge about oneself that enables people to continue living their lives:

> '[We]ll, if I'm free, yes, it's like I don't care now what people say, now my coworkers tell me here, "Teacher, you're foul-mouthed, you this, etc. …". And I say, "Yes, so what? Yes someone sees it badly. I'm very sorry, actually, you have to come with me to teach you, you who are alone, then find someone, I am totally fulfilled in my thoughts, in my actions and feelings".' (E, 50)

Discussion and conclusion

Analysis of the sexual fantasies from the focused interviews with Purépecha women reflects key elements of Purépecha society and culture, such as obligatory monogamy, with which they reaffirm concepts such as conjugal exclusivity and the sense of ownership of women. This analysis has also highlighted the varying expressions of romantic love that, according to Mogrovejo (2016) and Esteban Galarza (2011), as well as being a contemporary manifestation of patriarchy as per family structure, limit Purépecha women's autonomy. Romantic love underpins the domination and control of women, their bodies and sexual, reproductive and erotic resources. Yet another factor that consolidates these constraints concerns issues associated with the inalienable acceptance of motherhood and compliance with sexual fidelity.

However, the content of sexual fantasies reveals possible processes of reconfiguration of the desires and pleasures of Purépecha women. Discursive elements, such as those contained in the peripheral categories discussed earlier, are indicative of a more active participation in sexual activity, where women are placed as sexual actors and authors of their own fantasy with autonomy and capacity to act and decide on their own pleasure. This suggests some escape from the supposedly 'natural' status of being the object of desire to materialise, participate and act on their desire. This repositioning may be the prelude to a change in the mentalities and specific practices of women to the extent that the process of 'Westernisation' of the same also brings benefits to the communities that still retain features of the social and cultural organisation of the original towns.

However, this process requires profound reflection on the possibilities that exist or not in the societies and cultures of Purépecha people for the construction of an ethic associated with pleasure, an ethic to be and live as a Purépecha woman, a mestizo woman. This would also constitute an ethic that enables women with social, symbolic and personal tools to live their sexuality, desire and love more outside the old structures of patriarchy.

Finally, I consider it important to highlight the vision of Esteban Galarza (2011, p 191), as a civilising project of sexual morality associated with women's pleasure:

> [T]o maintain that it is essential to think and develop beyond dichotomous forms of relationships and opting for open, alternative relationships; daring to build our own creative way of relating as we go, trying out new ways that also lead us to generate social transformations that lead to horizontal collectivities.

In order to achieve this aim, it is essential to 'question the family/marriage/monogamy/coexistence quartet, as well as the deconstruction of love, desire, sexuality, intimacy'.

Acknowledgement

The author extends sincere thanks to Karina G. López Rodríguez for translation from Spanish into English.

References

Aguinis, M. (1999) 'Una Magistral Iluminación [A Masterful Enlightening]', in Person, E.S., Fonagy, P. and Figueira, S.A. (eds) *En Torno a Freud: El Poeta y los Sueños Diurnos. Serie Freud en la Actualidad: Temas Críticos y Nuevas Orientaciones* [*On Freud: The Poet and Daydreams. Freud Today Series: Critical Issues and New Orientations*]. Spain: Asociación Psicoanalítica Internacional, Biblioteca Nueva.

Amezcua, L.J. and Sánchez Díaz, G. (2015) *Pueblos Indígenas de México en el Siglo XXI. Volumen 3. Purhépecha* [*Indigenous People from the 21st Century in Mexico. Vol 3. Purépecha*]. Edited by V. Rojo Leyva. Mexico: Comisión Nacional para el Desarrollo de los Pueblos Indígenas (CDI).

Dávalos López, E. (1998) 'La Sexualidad en los Pueblos Mesoamericanos Prehispánicos: Un Panorama General [Sexuality in Pre-Hispanic Mesoamerican People: A General View]', in Szasz, I. and Lerner, S. (eds) *Sexualidades en México: Algunas Aproximaciones desde la Perspectiva de las Ciencias Sociales* [*Sexualities in Mexico: Some Approximations from a Social Science Perspective*]. Mexico: Colegio de México.

de Alcalá, J. (credited to) (1988) *La Relación de Michoacán* [*Michoacan Relations*]. Edited by Francisco Miranda. Mexico: Secretaria de Educación Pública.

Esteban Galarza, M.L. (2011) *Crítica del Pensamiento Amoroso* [*Critics of Romantic Thinking*]. Barcelona: Bellaterra.

Foucault, M. (2005) *Historia de la Sexualidad* [*History of Sexuality*] (16th edition). Mexico: Siglo XXI.

Foucault, M. (2007a) *Historia de la Sexualidad: la Voluntad de Saber* [*History of Sexuality: The Will to Knowledge*] (31st edition). Mexico: Siglo XXI.

Foucault, M. (2007b) *Historia de la Sexualidad: la Inquietud de Sí* [*History of Sexuality: The Care of the Self*] (15th edition). Mexico: Siglo XXI.

Franco Mendoza, M. (2007) 'La Lengua de Michoacán (Purépecha o tarasca?) [Michoacan Language (Purépecha or tarasca?)]', in Márquez Joaquín, P. (ed) *¿Tarascos o Purépecha? Voces sobre Antiguas y Nuevas Discusiones en Torno al Gentilicio Michoacano* [*Tarasco or Purépecha? Voices on Old and New Discussions on the Michoacan's Demonym*]. Morelia, Mexico: Universidad Michoacana de San Nicolás de Hidalgo, Instituto de Investigaciones Históricas, El colegio de Michoacán, pp 173–178.

Hierro, G. (2014) *La Ética del Placer* [*Pleasure's Ethics*] (2nd edition). Mexico: UNAM-PUEG.

Izcara Palacios, S. (2014) *Manual de Investigación Cualitativa* [*Qualitative Research Manual*] (1st edition). Mexico: Fontamara.

Jacinto Zavala, A. (1980) 'La Visión del Mundo y la Vida entre los Purépecha [World's Vision and Life among Purépecha People]', in Miranda, F. (ed) *La Cultura Purhé: II Coloquio de Antropología e Historia Regionales* [*Purhe Culture: Colloquium of Regional Anthropology and History*]. Fuentes e Historia, pp 143–158. 14–16 August 1980. Zamora, Michoacán. Colegio de Michoacán. Fondo para Actividades Sociales y Culturales de Michoacán (FONAPAS Michoacán).

Lizarraga-Cruchaga, X. (2016) *El Comportamiento a través de Alicia: Propuesta Teórico Metodológica de la Antropología del Comportamiento* [*Behaviour across Alicia: Theoretical Methodological Proposal in the Anthropology of Behaviour*] (1st edition). Mexico: Instituto Nacional de Antropología e Historia.

López Austin, A. (2010) 'La Sexualidad en la Tradición Mesoamericana [Sexuality in Mesoamerican Tradition]', *Arqueología Mexicana* [*Mexican Archaeology*] XVIII(104), pp 28–35.

Miranda, F. and Le Clezio, J. (1980) '*La Relación de Michoacán y Otras Fuentes para la Historia Prehispánica de la Cultura Purhépecha* [*Michoacan Relations and Other Sources for Prehispanic Purépecha History*]', in Miranda, F. (ed) *La Cultura Purhé: II Coloquio de Antropología e Historia Regionales* [*Purhe Culture: Colloquium of Regional Anthropology and History*]. Fuentes e Historia, pp 31–45. 14–16 August 1980. Zamora, Michoacán. Colegio de Michoacán. Fondo para Actividades Sociales y Culturales de Michoacán (FONAPAS Michoacán).

Mogrovejo, N. (ed) (2016) *Contra-amor, Poliamor, Relaciones Abiertas y Sexo Casual: Reflexiones de Lesbianas del AbyaYala* [*Counter-love, Polyamory, Open Relationships and Casual Sex: Reflections of Lesbians from AbyaYala*]. Colombia: Desde Abajo.

Moyano, N. and Sierra, J.C. (2014) 'Fantasías y Pensamientos Sexuales: Revisión Conceptual y Relación con la Salud Sexual [Sexual Fantasies and Thinking: Concept Review and Its Relationship with Sexual Health]', *Revista Puertorriqueña de Psicología* 25(2): 376–93.

Pessah, M. (2016) 'Pasajera en Tránsito [Passenger in Transit]', in Mogrovejo, N., (ed) *Contra-amor, Poliamor, Relaciones Abiertas y Sexo Casual: Reflexiones de Lesbianas del AbyaYala* [*Counter-love, Polyamory, Open Relationships and Casual Sex: Reflections of Lesbians from AbyaYala*] (1st edition). Colombia: Desde Abajo, pp 57–60.

Pick, S. and Rirkin, J. (2010) *Pobreza: Cómo Romper el Ciclo a Partir del Desarrollo Humano* [*Poverty: How to Break the Cycle since Human Development*] (1st edition). Mexico: Limusa.

Rapley, T. (2014) *Los Análisis de la Conversación, del Discurso y de Documentos en Investigación Cualitativa* [*Analysis of Conversation, Discourse and Documents in Qualitative Research*] (1st edition). Mexico: Morata.

Rosso, N. (2016) 'El Cuerpo Lesbiano y la Propuesta Política Contra-amorosa [The Lesbian Body and Political Proposals Against Love]', in Mogrovejo, N. (ed) *Contra-amor, Poliamor, Relaciones Abiertas y Sexo Casual: Reflexiones de Lesbianas del AbyaYala* [*Counter-love, Polyamory, Open Relationships and Casual Sex: Reflections of Lesbians from AbyaYala*] (1st edition). Colombia: Desde Abajo, pp 67–80.

Rubin, G. (2000) 'El Tráfico de Mujeres: Notas sobre una Economía Política [The Traffic in Women: Notes on a Political Economy]', in Lamas, M. (ed) *El Género: la Construcción Cultural de la Diferencias Sexual* [*Gender: The Cultural Construction of Sexual Differences*]. Mexico: Miguel Ángel Porrúa. Programa Universitario de Estudios de Género, pp 35–96.

Sanz, F. (1999) *Psicoerotismo Femenino y Masculino: Para unas Relaciones Placenteras, Autónomas y Justas* [*Feminine and Masculine Psychoeroticism: for Pleasurable, Autonomous and Fair Relationships*] (4th edition). Barcelona: Kairós.

Segato, R.L. (2018) *Contra-pedagogías de la Crueldad* [*Counter-pedagogies of Cruelty*]. Buenos Aires: Prometeo Libros.

Shaie, W. and Willis, S. (2003) *Psicología de la Edad Adulta y la Vejez* [*Psychology of Ageing and Old Aage*] (5th edition). Madrid: Pearson.

Valles, M. (2007) *Técnicas Cualitativas de Investigación Social: Reflexiónmetodológica y Prácticaprofesional* [*Qualitative Techniques of Social Research: Methodological Reflection and Professional Practice*] (4th edition). Spain: Editorial Síntesis.

Vigotsky, L. (2015) *La Imaginación y el Arte en la Infancia: Ensayopsicológico* [*Imagination and Children's Art: A Psychological Essay*] (10th edition). Mexico: Coyoacán.

Weeks, J. (1986) *Sexualidad* [*Sexuality*] (1st edition). Mexico: Paidós/UNAM.

9

Indigenous elders as sexual agents through storytelling as a queer and decolonial practice in 'Canada'

Madeline Burns

Introduction

This chapter argues that Indigenous elders 'in' so-called 'Canada' have much to teach us about sexuality (and by extension relationality and kinship ethics) through storytelling as a queer and decolonial practice. 'Elder' as a term in Indigenous communities refers to someone with immense knowledge and trusted insight; someone with a plethora of lived experiences and valuable understandings. As a trusted source of knowledge, elders are often who we (as Indigenous peoples) turn to for our (hi)stories (Adese, 2014), which can include multi-species, 'dirty' and erotic (hi)stories.

As a result of the positionality of elders in our communities, I argue that elders are critical to sexuality as keepers of our intimate (hi)stories and as active agents of sexuality and/or intimacy themselves. To accomplish this, I demonstrate the ways storytelling and eco-erotic Indigenous (hi)stories (wherein folks engage in intimate/sexual relations with more-than-human beings) trouble settler colonial and heteronormative imposed ideas of intimacy, time, age and 'acceptable' relationalities.

'More-than-human-beings' refer to lands, waters, elements, spiritual beings, tricksters, plant and animal nations. More-than-human-beings are animate beings with personality, sovereignty, relationships, joys and responsibilities. The term 'trickster' refers to beings that exist across many Indigenous communities and (hi)stories. They are ambiguous and fluid beings, constant and fleeting disruptors, who are constantly breaking boundaries (Nelson, 2017). Are tricksters neither good nor evil, or maybe, they are both good and evil? That is tricksters' power and beauty. They are fluid beings who work outside of, and operate as disruptors to, 'Judeo-Christian' constructions/binaries such as 'good and evil', while offering us teachings about the world (King, 1993, cited in Nelson, 2017, p 240).

For those who are first interacting with the term 'more-than-human-beings' as a lens through which to view the world and our environment, this will be a crucial underpinning to the chapter ahead, and the worldview of sexuality, relationality and kinship ethics it will speak to. These multi-species relations, wherein one engages in intimate and sexual relations with more-than-human-beings is represented within 'eco-erotics'.

This analysis is framed around eco-erotic (hi)stories such as 'Why Ravens Smile to Little Old Ladies as they Walk By …', shared by Richard Van Camp (2002) and 'The Woman Who Married the Beaver', shared by Melissa Nelson (2017). Furthermore, as this chapter largely discusses Indigenous elders who are women and femmes and their queer and decolonial role in sexuality/intimacy through storytelling, it is also important to note the role femininity and sexuality play in many Indigenous communities.

Indigenous women, two-spirit, femmes, and gender and/or sexually diverse people are valued within and across many Indigenous communities. Women are highly respected across many Indigenous communities as they have frequently held, and continue to hold, valuable positions and responsibilities (Bourgeois, 2018). Within my discussion of Indigenous women, trans women are fundamentally within my discussion, and this is important to note from the outset, that when I speak to the value of women in my community, I am speaking to the value of all women. However, this is not to wash over the distinct experiences of being Indigenous and trans in the world, which cisgender individuals do not experience and may not understand.

'Two-spirit' as a title and descriptor was asserted in 1990 at a gathering of two-spirit and LGBTQIA+ Indigenous folks, in order to better discuss sexuality and gender within Indigenous contexts (Driskill, 2004, p 52; Wilson 2018, p 168). 'Two-spirit' is a versatile term referring to folks who have existed across many Indigenous communities and continue to do so. For some, two-spirit is understood as 'queer and Indigenous' (Fayant-McLeod, quoted in Tyndall (2013), cited in Wilson, 2018, p 168) or 'a balance of masculinity and femininity', or an overall acceptance of one's gender and sexual variety and diversity (Wilson, 2018, p 168).

There is not a stable or fixed definition of two-spirit as it is dependent on which community you claim and are claimed by, the (hi)stories and experiences of your ancestors (Fayant-McLeod, quoted in Tyndall (2013), cited in Wilson, 2018), as well as the language you and/or your ancestors are gifted with. Not all Indigenous folks use this language of 'two-spirit', and not all sexually and/or gender diverse Indigenous folks are two-spirit (Trans Care BC, 2022). Understandings of sexuality and gender are both community contextual and up to the individual to connect with. Fellow valued community members are transgender, gay, non-binary, lesbian, bisexual, unlabelled, pansexual, indigiqueer, intersex, and so on, as these descriptors are the most applicable, comfortable and right for themselves.

Furthermore, I recognise femininity and femme expression to be separate from gender identity. Thus, I utilise the term 'femme' to describe those who are femme-presenting, those who frequently express their femininity, or folks who are frequently read as bearing femme characteristics or expressions, across gender and sexual diversities. This distinction is important, as being femme (as a way of being in the world) is seen as a significant strength across many Indigenous communities, and due to this recognised strength, femininity (in all its constructions) is also frequently targeted by colonisation due to the threat we pose to settler colonialism and patriarchy (Simpson, 2016). Thus, I find 'femme' to be the best language I can employ in this current context to speak to a shared experience of strength and joy in femme expression across genders and sexualities, and, simultaneously, a characteristic or quality that is frequently violently targeted.

Many Indigenous communities have held, and continue to hold, understandings of sexuality and gender that may not be fully captured within colonial contexts, as these contexts and languages rely on an introduction of strict gender and sexual regimes (Driskill, 2004). However, the reason I have directed attention to these insights is to demonstrate that irrespective of which labels (or the absence of labels) we utilise, our communities are filled with powerful folks across genders and sexualities who are culturally and traditionally valuable previously, presently and in our futures.

In the sections ahead, I begin by offering a self-location, placing myself and my accountability into the telling of this story. I offer theoretical understandings at the foundation of this discussion and share examples of two eco-erotic (hi)stories. By sharing this theoretical background and eco-erotic (hi)stories, I identify the ways elders disrupt and resist settler colonialism and heteronormativity, both within eco-erotic (hi)stories and in the act of telling eco-erotic (hi)stories. Ultimately, I propose elders are sexual agents through storytelling as a queer and decolonial practice, as the (hi)stories shared and the practice of telling them troubles settler colonial imposed logics regarding age, intimacy, time and relationality.

Self-location

Self-locating grants space to name who and what I am accountable to and share the ways they influence me and the research at hand (Kovach, 2009). As I share my accountability to my community, lived experiences and the relations which shape me, self-locating is also a recognition of subjectivity in research (Kovach, 2009). Subjectivity is critical to research as 'neutrality and objectivity do not exist in research, since all research is conducted and observed through human epistemological lenses' (Absolon and Willet, 2005, p 97, as cited in Burns, 2020, p 30).

When I write, I continually follow the path carved out by storyteller Shawn Wilson (2008) and consider this chapter to be a story and position myself as its storyteller. When positioning myself as a storyteller, a relation, and therefore an accountability, is formed between myself and this research, and between you as the recipient of this story, and me as the one sharing it (Wilson, 2008). As a story it should be absorbed with an 'open heart and open mind', and situated into 'relational contexts' (Wilson, 2008, p 126).

As a result of this 'relational accountability' to each other (Wilson, 2008, p 22), we will both locate ourselves in this section. As I share my positionality with you, I ask that you also consider the lived experiences and identities that you bring with you while receiving it, and I ask that you honour the land your body is currently grounded upon, whether it is your community's land or someone else's.

I share this chapter as a Métis community member with cultural, political and land ties to Red River and homelands across the prairies on my mother's side, and as a person with Scottish roots on my father's side. I view myself and my responsibilities through a temporal lens of being an 'elder in the making' (Whitehead, 2022, p 178) and a future ancestor. I am currently writing to you as an uninvited guest on Lək̓ʷəŋən (Songhees and Esquimalt) and W̱SÁNEĆ (SṮÁ,UTW̱, W̱JOŁEŁP, BOḰEĆEN, and W̱SÍḴEM) lands (Native Students Union, 2021), and I come to these territories after being born on q̓ic̓əy̓ (Katzie), q̓ʷɑ:n̓ƛ̓ən̓ (Kwantlen), Semiahma (Semiahmoo) and Matsqui lands.

I am an urban Indigenous, sexually fluid, femme-presenting, white-bodied, middle-class, able-bodied, younger person. It is due to these aspects of my being that I understand settler colonialism to be an intersection at which I am simultaneously oppressed, privileged and engaged in resistance. Settler colonialism has intentionally dislocated me from my homelands, creating a loss of language, knowledge and kinship relations, and estrangement of my understandings of relationality, sexuality, gender, time and age. Meanwhile, settler colonialism also privileges me as a middle-class, white and able-bodied person.

It is at this lived intersection that I find myself to reside in the tension of being created through the process of colonisation and experience its privileges due to the structures that maintain and uphold it. Simultaneously, I act as a conflicting force to those structures by living every day as an act of protest to the settler colonial state project of elimination (Wolfe, 2006), as I continue to live, breathe and disrupt as an Indigenous person, actively engaging in resistance to our attempted elimination.

Since there are a range of theories, thoughts and worldviews across Indigenous communities, the theoretical and practical teachings I pull from elder erotic (hi)stories in this chapter should not be taken as the opinion, thought or experience of all Indigenous peoples. These are my understandings and reflections as one community member, as one Métis person, and someone who comes to this discussion of elders as eco-erotic storytellers with my own lived experiences, just as you do. Thus, this chapter speaks to a deeply intimate and subjective process of resistance by decolonising and queering intimacy, age, relationality and time.

Theoretical framework and underpinnings

In this section, I offer a brief overview of the theoretical perspective and concepts this chapter is speaking to and informed by. I accept the understanding of heteronormativity as deeply distinctive from heterosexuality, instead, it is as a culture (Berlant and Warner, 1998). Heteronormativity as a culture produces heterosexuality as the coherent, default and privileged mode of being, however that is not to suggest that all heterosexual relations are heteronormative (Berlant and Warner, 1998). In other words, sexuality is regulated by how the rest of culture is organised through heteronormativity; sexuality is not simply the force governing heteronormativity (Berlant and Warner, 1998).

Thus, heteronormative culture shows up beyond the confines of sex and sexuality, it is not unitary or singular, it consists of institutions, practices, habits and the ways our material world is organised (Berlant and Warner, 1998). Due to these characteristics of heteronormative culture, heteronormativity is 'always-already bound up in racialising and imperial projects' as it holds 'kinship, residency, and land tenure' at its core (Rifkin, 2010, p 6). In turn, heteronormativity cannot be conceptualised as distinct from settler colonialism (just as neither can be understood as distinct from capitalism and white supremacy); they exist within a shared and overlapping culture (Driskill, 2010).

Furthermore, to define settler colonialism, I turn to Patrick Wolfe. Wolfe suggests settler colonialism bears a 'logic of elimination', which may be expressed through genocide, though it expresses itself in numerous ways, always operating with goals of eliminating Indigenous folks, so settler society may try to replace us in our territories (Wolfe, 2006, pp 387–8). In turn, settler colonialism is a 'structure' that is continual and ongoing, 'rather than a one-off (and super-superseded) occurrence' (Wolfe, 2006, p 388).

This attempted elimination (by settler colonialism overlapping with heteronormativity) is also a targeted practice. Moreover, 'Canada' attempts to assert itself as sovereign by proclaiming that its self-constructed foundations of whiteness, heteronormativity and therefore patriarchy, are innately valuable, valid and inevitable (Simpson, 2016). As a result of these foundations, the state 'seeks to destroy what it is not' and 'disappear' those who are antithetical to its self-proclaimed 'legitimacy' and validity (Simpson, 2016, para 3).

Thus, the state targets Indigenous women, girls (Bourgeois, 2018), two-spirit, femmes and sexually and/or gender diverse folks (Wilson, 2018), whose existence, influence in Indigenous political orders, and value is directly oppositional to the state's character and foundational values, exposing its self-proclaimed sovereignty as invalid (Simpson, 2016). This targeted 'logic of elimination' (Wolfe, 2006, p 387) results in a 'death drive' of the state, which is continually present and demonstrated by the horrifying rate of murdered and missing Indigenous girls, women (Simpson, 2016, para 1; Bourgeois, 2018), femmes, two-spirit and sexually and/or gender diverse peoples 'in' so-called 'Canada' (Wilson, 2018).

This process of settler colonialism also carries temporal elements, which impose Western versions of time and history (Rifkin, 2017; Smith, 2021). Settler colonialism has asserted a temporal structure along a 'singular axis', a linear view of time that is interconnected with capitalism (Rifkin, 2017, p 2; Smith, 2021). History became regarded as more 'scientific', 'measurable' and valued as written during 'The Enlightenment' or so-called 'Age of Reason' (Smith, 2021, p 62). These notions of time create perceptions and dualisms of history and progress, wherein progress is quantified 'in terms of technological advancement and spiritual salvation' (Smith, 2021, p 63). Linear notions of time and history are not passive or neutral constructions. They have been built through settler colonialism, at odds with Indigenous cosmologies and ways of being, in order to inflict a self-proclaimed authority through oppression (Rifkin, 2017; Smith, 2021).

Linear time, in this sense, is a settler colonial construct which obscures Indigenous relations with 'temporalties', understandings of plural and living (hi)stories (Rifkin, 2017, pp 2–10; Smith, 2021). If life-course is viewed in these terms of a comprehensive 'single axis' (Rifkin, 2017, p 2), and progress is viewed in terms of capitalist work (Smith, 2021), it is no wonder people fear ageing. Ageing becomes a 'coming to an end' rather than being continuously in cycle or seeing 'progress' through a lens of successful reciprocal knowledge gifting and relation building.

Since settler colonialism is an ongoing structure (Wolfe, 2006), and as decolonisation is a disruption to that structure, it must be an active and ongoing process as well. Moreover, decolonisation consists of dynamic and continual practices and processes that are a part of everyday relations and 'inherently connected to the lands, lives, histories, and futures of the Indigenous peoples of Turtle Island' (Hunt and Holmes, 2015, p 157).

Further, just as decolonisation is a disrupting practice to settler colonialism, 'queer' can be understood as an actively disrupting practice to heteronormativity, outside of it being conceptualised as an identity. Moreover, both decolonisation and queer can be understood as deeply interconnected verbs, which describe actively '[unsettling] power relations' (Hunt and Holmes, 2015, p 156). Queer and decolonisation can be viewed as fleeting and mobile disruptions, processes and practices that are lived. In turn, I suggest both queer and decolonisation are not entirely 'about a way of "being," and more about "doing"' (Hunt and Holmes, 2015, p 156).

Elders as eco-erotic storytellers and sexual beings

The (hi)stories shared in this section have been published by Indigenous folks. (Hi)stories that have not already been published by community members or were privately shared with me will not be distributed here. It should be noted, however, that even sharing (hi)stories as literature (which have been published already) can and should be considered 'contradictory, at best' (Nelson, 2017, p 240). There is a politics to sharing (hi)stories and tension when working to decolonise academia through Indigenous knowledge sharing.

Storytelling is meant to be oral; it is with the introduction of settler colonialism that the written word becomes celebrated as the valued mode of knowledge sharing, with the delineation of what is supposedly 'fact' versus 'folklore' (Absolon and Willet, 2005, p 8). Academia is built of this colonial structure and has an ongoing history of extractive research and discourse production about Indigenous peoples globally (Absolon and Willet, 2005). Through oral knowledge production there is more agency to decide who to share knowledge with 'in a way that is not possible once my words are written down' (Wilson, 2008, p 126).

I continue to live in the tension of sharing through academia as I understand it to also be a re-worlding endeavour, by '*re*writing and *re*righting' the ways we have been discursively produced, by sharing knowledge for our own purposes (Smith, 2021, p 31). In this way, research is consciousness raising, it is storying with a (cautious) trust in the recipient, and a recognition that Indigenous peoples have engaged in research and theorising about the world since time immemorial and we continue to (Wilson, 2008; Smith, 2021).

However, by sharing knowledge in Western academia there is a continual danger of reproducing the same harms, and once oral stories are shared it leaves the door open for folks to re-share them with their own insights (as I am doing as well). Thus, there is a contradictory element that must be noted. Due to this contradiction, I urge you to also read the (hi)stories cited in the context the authors wrote them in, outside of the way I understand them.

In my third year of my Bachelor of Arts degree, I was fortunate to have a (hi)story read to me by Dr waaseyaa'sin Christine Sy. They read, 'Why Ravens Smile to Little Old Ladies as They Walk by…' of Dogrib Nation, published by Richard Van Camp in *Angel Wing Splash Pattern* (2002). 'Why Ravens Smile to Little Old Ladies as They Walk by …' tells the story of raven, whose tongue deeply pleasures the 'sunshine spot' of a powerful, blind, old medicine woman (Van Camp, 2002, p 22). To summarise, after raven pulls yet another trick on the Dogrib Nation, his beak is taken and given to a blind elder who was a medicine woman, in order to conceal it. The elder hides his lengthy beak up her dress, and raven's tongue, longing for a mouth begins squirming around, extending deep inside her.

The elder barely leaves the house from this day forward. Her daughters visit her thinking she must be ill, yet the elder and the tongue were both as happy as ever with their pleasurable relation. The elder spends her days writhing and squirming, while raven on the other hand, angrily returned to the Dogrib community. While community members claimed to know nothing of the beak, raven listened in on the daughters worrying about their mother's well-being, suggesting she spends her days locked in the house 'moaning all hours of the night, sometimes crying out with a heavy voice' (Van Camp, 2002, p 22).

After hearing this, raven scurries to the elder's home and finds her in deep rhythmic pleasure on her hands and knees. The old woman jolts to her feet and quickly questions the intruder, but being the trickster he is, raven masks his voice and suggests it is her daughter. As the old woman asks her daughter to leave, raven lifts up the elder's dress to see his hard beak exposed and he begins pulling on it, but his tongue holds on for dear life to his new friend.

Raven uses all his strength until, finally, his tongue relaxes, and he is able to leave with his beak positioned back on his mouth. However, he stops in his tracks to taste the liquid remaining in his beak. The elder, being a powerful medicine person, continues to feel the pleasure of his tongue deep within. The two exchange smiles and raven goes on his way, leaving satisfied and ready to play yet another trick on the community.

Therefore, 'that's why, even to this day when you see a raven open its mouth towards you, you will see a flaming red tongue and a beautiful pink pussy inside. And this too is why we ravens smile to little old ladies as they walk by' (Van Camp, 2002, p 23). 'Why Ravens Smile to Little Old Ladies as They Walk by …' demonstrates Indigenous elders as sexual agents, with insight and experience engaging in meaningful relations with the world around them. Moreover, raven and the elder engage in a reciprocal and mutually pleasurable sexual relation, resulting in the powerful medicine woman receiving an intimate understanding of raven and raven receiving an intimate understanding of her.

Another (hi)story that stands out is 'The Woman Who Married the Beaver', shared by Melissa Nelson (2017). In this frequently shared Anishinaabeg (hi) story, a young woman marries a 'human-looking person' who she resides with for years and they end up producing four children together (Nelson, 2017, p 243). After time passes, she begins to notice something is different about her husband and comes to the understanding that she has married a beaver. After her children and husband would return from trips, they would bring home items that would all be used when one is consuming a beaver.

The woman recognised that they were leaving to meet with the humans, to be killed 'but not *really* killed', rather, they were exchanging furs for these human gifts (Nelson, 2017, p 243). Once her husband grew old and passed away, the now old woman returned to live with the humans, bringing with her the knowledge of beavers she gained while being in an intimate and sexual relation with one. She shared with the other humans that one must never speak badly or hold ill feelings towards a beaver, or they will never be able to kill one.

This story expresses the reciprocal and therefore respectful relation one must be in, in order to nourish oneself and community, as well as the agency more-than-human-beings bear in these relations with us (Nelson, 2017). The young woman in this (hi)story is an 'elder in the making' (Whitehead, 2022, p 178) and when she returns to her community in later life, she returns as an elder and her community benefits from her precious knowledge and lived experiences wherein she engaged in a sexual and intimate relation with her beaver husband (Nelson, 2017).

There is a wealth of (hi)stories, written short stories and poems shared by Indigenous folks that involve women and femmes gaining intimate knowledge of more-than-human-beings in this same erotic fashion (Akiwenzie-Damm, 2002; Nelson, 2017). As a result, women and femme elders (including two-spirit and gender/sexually diverse folks) can be seen continually represented within our communities as valuable and 'fluid boundary crossers' and knowledge keepers of our relations with more-than-human-beings (Nelson, 2017, p 244).

Decolonising and queering age and time

As our 'kihteyayak or lii viyeu ("the mature ones; the older people")' (National Aboriginal Health Organization, as quoted in Adese, 2014, p 50) are our knowledge keepers, they are deemed the best source for our (hi)stories (Adese, 2014), including those considered erotic or 'dirty'. Therefore, although frequently swept to the side in Western society, elders play a significant role in sexuality, not only within (hi)stories themselves, but through the act of storytelling. By way of erotic storytelling, elders are actively recentred as those with sexual/intimate knowledge and experience. This value placed on elders' sexuality conflicts and disrupts Western discourses that frame their sexuality as either non-existent, problematic, or at least unimportant when compared to other aspects of life such as health and care (Reynolds et al, 2021).

The stories recounted, then, offer an intersectional insight that disrupts settler colonial and heteronormative ideas about age and sexual desirability, activity, femininity and knowledge. Through constructions of femininity and age, older women are frequently represented as undesirable and categorised as people experiencing a decline in sexual desires and activity (McHugh and Interligi, 2015). In turn, they are cast as incapable of sex and/or uninterested in sexual activity, and if they do show interest, it is thought simply improper for someone of their age (McHugh and Interligi, 2015). Their sexuality is also regulated when it is 'too low', and defined as a 'sexual dysfunction' by the medical system (McHugh and Interligi, 2015, p 100). In turn, older people bearing femme qualities generally, and specifically older women are placed into these limited and regulated sexual scripts with little space for pleasure or, simply, agency (McHugh and Interligi, 2015).

Erotic (hi)stories have the ability to recentre older women and femmes as people with experience and knowledge, as well as assert them as sexual agents, people who are desirable and may bear desires themselves. This also speaks to the historical and ongoing value placed on women, femmes (Bourgeois, 2018), gender/sexually diverse, and two-spirit folks in our communities (Wilson, 2018) which deeply conflicts with cultures that only value bodies with the potential to reproduce, and as objects for cisgender and heterosexual men's sexual desires (McHugh and Interligi, 2015).

In turn, recentring Indigenous femmes and women as sexual agents disrupts negative stereotypes of older women and femmes that are frequent in 'Western' individualistic cultures, values which link youthfulness, femininity and desirability together (McHugh and Interligi, 2015). In disrupting these values, there is space for elders' agency, filled with sexual self-determination. Therefore, this discussion is also not meant to erase the spectrum of asexuality or further hyper-sexualise or essentialise Indigenous women and femmes. Instead, these (hi)stories can work to directly conflict with the violent and dehumanising sexual scripts Indigenous women, femmes, two-spirit and sexually and/or gender diverse folks are often relegated to (Burns, 2020) by offering a script of sovereignty, pleasure and agency, which can include the spectrum of asexuality rather than inflict a compulsory asexuality or hyper-sexuality.

Furthermore, as our ideas of age and the value we attach to this construct are also linked to notions of time, storytelling as a method of sharing sexuality also disrupts heteronormative and colonial ideas of time. As mentioned previously, linear time as a construct has been imposed and continually relied upon through settler colonialism and its capitalist ideas of progress (Rifkin, 2017; Smith, 2021). Storytelling as a practice disrupts this imposed vision of linear time, effectively queering and decolonising our ideas of time itself. Leanne Simpson (2017), in their retelling of 'Binoojiinh Makes a Lovely Discovery', offers an insight into how storytelling accomplishes this disruption, as they describe the ways this story of Binoojiinh (meaning child) is continually reproduced and in motion (Bao Nguyen – Grad. Admin Comparative Literature, 2019).

Moreover, in this (hi)story, Binoojiinh discovers maple sap by curiously nibbling on a branch after witnessing a squirrel do the same (Simpson, 2017, pp 145–7). In a public lecture, Simpson suggests, 'Binoojiinh's story isn't just from the past, every year in the spring the squirrels nibble on the twigs and drink the sap. It is a story that happens in various incarnations all over our territory every year in March when the Anishinaabe return to the sugar bush' (Bao Nguyen – Grad. Admin Comparative Literature, 2019). Similarly, (hi)stories shared in the previous section continue to occur while they are shared, they have already occurred, and they are continually reproduced. Thus, time can be recognised as 'plural' and multiple 'temporalities', which disrupts the settler colonial constructed 'singular axis' version of time (Rifkin, 2017, p 2).

Moreover, eco-erotic (hi)stories and sentiments continue to be enacted, retold, re-written and reproduced across communities. Stories and poems such as 'The Woman Who Married a Goose' by Ipellie, and 'The Woman Who Married a Bear' by Midge (Akiwenzie-Damm, 2002) once again present Indigenous women and femmes as engaging in intimate and sexual relations with more-than-human-beings. These eco-erotic, multi-species relations do not occur and are not retold in a vacuum, they are yet another reincarnation of our relations with more-than-human-beings.

Ultimately, just as the stories shared are histories, they are also constantly reoccurring and in motion. They are occurring right now as I share them with you and they are still in motion the next time you are on the land and realise you are amid a pleasurable and intimate relation, just as little old ladies are enjoying their sexual relations with ravens. The moment we recognise the ways we are in intimate and sexual relations with the land, tricksters, waters, elements, animal and plant nations, elder's (hi)stories continue to be cyclical and reoccurring through our relationships, which disrupts notions of linear time.

Decolonising and queering relationalities

This section explores how eco-erotic (hi)stories shared by elders disrupts understandings of relationality that are rooted in heteronormativity and settler colonialism, and, as a result of this disruption, they demonstrate relationalities that exist outside of these structures, rooted in a recognition of multi-species sex/eco-erotic relationality. As sex and intimacy continue to be scripted and regulated through the settler colonial, heteronormative gaze, a discursive veil is placed over alternative ways of relating (TallBear and Willey, 2019). Recognising elders as sexual agents and people with influence over our understandings of sexuality and intimacy through storytelling, confronts and calls into question these normative ways of relating by disrupting and expanding ideas of sex, intimacy and, therefore, relationality.

This does not solely involve pushing the boundaries of 'sex' beyond being seen as simply a penetrative penis-vagina practice (although they do accomplish that as well), but they demonstrate relationalities and kinship ethics that disrupt the process and culture of settler colonialism/heteronormativity. Notions of 'sex' itself through an eco-erotic lens can be understood as 'a symbol for intimate, visceral, embodied kinship relations with other species and with natural [phenomena]' (Nelson, 2017, p 252).

Eco-erotic (hi)stories shared by elders also offer the opportunity to look at the ways pleasure plays a key role in these multi-species relations. Experiencing pleasure with the land has been attempted to be estranged by settler colonialism which views lands, waters, plant and animal nations as 'natural resources' for humans (Kimmerer, 2013, p 17). Yet, despite this attempted estrangement, more-than-human-beings continue to gift us with pleasure every day, every time we '[breathe] in the scent of Mother Earth [it] stimulates the release of the hormone oxytocin, the same chemical that promotes bonding between mother and child, between lovers' (Kimmerer, 2013, p 236).

By sharing eco-erotic (hi)stories, elders' (hi)stories can also demonstrate the ways we always already have multiple partners. Since we are in constant relation with the land, waters, tricksters, elements, plant and animal nations, our relations cannot be contained to one person or being. Concurrently, however, many eco-erotic (hi)stories, such as 'The Woman Who Married the Beaver' (Nelson, 2017) involve a marriage or intimate relation between only two beings. Thus, eco-erotic (hi)stories shared by elders challenge ideas of monogamy versus non-monogamy, since eco-erotic relationships between two beings demonstrate the constant relationships we bear with all beings. There is a beautiful ambiguity here, a 'both/and logic' (Hunt and Holmes, 2015, p 159) that heteronormative and colonial binary logic cannot capture when it comes to relationality.

Additionally, tricksters (such as raven) are seen across communities and (hi)stories shared by elders. By sharing (hi)stories of our trickster companions, elders' storytelling frequently cross and destabilise imposed binaries (Nelson, 2017). In turn, there is once again, a 'both/and logic' (Hunt and Holmes, 2015, p 159) of 'disorder and order', nature and human, and sexual and gender fluidity (King, 1993, as cited in Nelson, 2017, p 240).

These multi-species relations demonstrate the ways our environments and all beings are inseparable from each other and ourselves (Nelson, 2017). Therefore, through these (hi)stories of intimacy, we can recognise our inseparable relationship with all beings as we extend beyond a 'contained being' (Nelson, 2017, p 230). When one thinks of bacteria, fungi and other micro-organisms, it is clear that 'other beings are always inside of us', we are always contingent on other beings (Nelson, 2017, p 232) and effectively outnumbered at all times (Haraway, 2008). Comparably, eco-erotic (hi)stories offer a lens that decentres human beings as the be-all-and-end-all, offering space to see the ways we are built through these relations with more-than-human-beings.

A Métis (and largely prairie Indigenous) concept, *wahkohtowin*, expresses this multi-species theory further as it describes an interrelationality (and intrarelationality) with all beings (Adese, 2014; Gaudry, 2014; Whitehead, 2022). Due to this expansive 'interrelatedness' (Gaudry, 2014, p 2), *wahkohtowin* describes a kinship ethic that extends and includes all beings and ecosystems we are a part of (Adese, 2014; Whitehead, 2022).

By looking through a lens of *wahkohtowin* coupled with eco-erotics, one can recognise that we are constantly in sexual and intimate relations with more-than-human-beings, in order to unpack how we are always already 'constituted in intra- and interaction' (Haraway, 2008, p 4), making the margins between us and more-than-human-beings blurry and indistinct. We can see the ways we are not enclosed, fixed, or beings with stable boundaries, as we sink into our surrounding environments, and they sink into us. Thus, it is in the act of intimate multi-species relations where uncertainty in our distinctions occurs, wherein we are liminal and simultaneously formed by our relations.

Engaging with sexy (hi)stories about multi-species relations shared by elders or about elders as sexual agents with their environments, breathes life into this concept of *wahkohtowin* for me. By looking through this lens of eco-erotic relationality, we can better recognise lands, animals, plants, tricksters and elements as conscious, living beings with agency, and therefore the sovereignty (Nelson, 2017) to choose to engage in relations with us.

Thus, eco-erotic (hi)stories shared by elders directly confront heteronormative colonial constructions such as notions of relationality and ethics of kinship that are narrowly reduced to nuclear families. Instead, relationality in this sense is the recognition that we are actively engaged in a network of radiating reciprocal relationships with embedded responsibilities (Nadasdy, 2007; Simpson, 2008; and Wilson, 2008, all cited in Manson, 2019). Furthermore, as our relations occur across imposed spatial, temporal and species boundaries so do our responsibilities (Rifkin 2011, cited in Manson, 2019).

With this knowledge we can actively live in ways that go beyond just understanding being interconnected and dependent on all beings; rather, we can see the responsibilities we bear when we recognise we are in dynamic intimate relations with all beings (Starblanket and Stark, 2019). Thus, in recognising these 'intra- and interaction[s]' (Haraway, 2008, p 4) as intimate relationships, we are better able to act on the responsibilities that emerge. Responsibilities such as consent, respect, mutual aid and reciprocity are embedded in the act of being in relation (Starblanket and Stark, 2019).

This understanding of relationality shatters notions of binary logic which are embedded within a hierarchical value system (Derrida, 2016), and deconstructs perceptions of subject formation that rely on fixed and whole subjects with borders and boundaries, while demonstrating kinship ethics that arise when we look through this eco-erotic, relational lens. These conceptualisations of relationality extending from elders as sexual agents via storytelling deeply trouble constructed binaries of human and nature, pushing ideas of kinship ethics and relationalities outside of the realm of heteronormative, settler colonial constructs. In doing so, elders' roles as knowledge keepers of our eco-erotic (hi)stories enable us to reconsider the ways we understand our relation to the world and the kinship ethics we must carry as a result.

Thus, consider the old woman who is being satisfied by the raven (Van Camp, 2002) the next time you breathe in the land and experience that same erotic, earthly and pleasurable bond. Think of the sensation and relation you bear with the more-than-human-beings the next time you consume ripe juicy berries on a sweaty summer day. Contemplate the intimate 'carnal knowledge' of a beaver the elder now holds (Nelson, 2017, p 243), the next time you practise this same knowledge of one's body when catching and gutting a fish. Are these not erotic practices, pleasures and relations? Will you pass on this intimate knowledge of the land when you are an elder? Are we really separate or distinct from the raven, beaver, berries or the fish when we are in an active relationship with them? How are you established in these relationships, and what responsibilities arise as a result?

When one thinks through this eco-erotic and disrupting lens that our elders' intimate knowledge and experience with more-than-human-beings can provide us, a powerful everyday relationality is enacted. 'Embracing our eco-erotic nature helps us recognise the generosity of creation, and our part in it, so we can truly embody an ethic of kinship' (Nelson, 2017, p 255). When gutting a fish, eating berries, or simply taking a walk and breathing in the land, all as sexual/intimate practices, reciprocity, relationality and an understanding of sovereignty, all become principal concepts in our relationships.

Conclusion

This chapter adds to the current state of knowledge, as Indigenous elder sexuality is rarely discussed, and Indigenous women, femmes, two-spirit and gender/sexually diverse people's sexual being is infrequently discussed outside of narratives of violence (Burns, 2020). This chapter fills a gap by honouring the sexual agency and value of women and femme elders, by explicitly demonstrating their fundamental influence and positionality in sexuality and intimacy.

This demonstration of their valuable positionality in intimacy and sexuality has been further achieved by exploring the ways Indigenous women and femme elders act as disruptors to imposed ideas of time and age, and the ways they do so through eco-erotic (hi)stories and storytelling. Further, this chapter illustrates how elders as sexual agents through eco-erotic storytelling ignite an understanding of sex and intimacy through multi-species relationalities.

In doing so, they provide an alternative lens of kinship and relationality practices through which to view and organise the world, by piercing the veil that has been placed over a diversity of ways of relating (TallBear and Willey, 2019). Moreover, elders' (hi)stories of sexuality and intimacy with more-than-human-beings, offer us space to reimagine and recreate our own relations by resisting settler colonial and heteronormative impositions, as a queer and decolonial practice.

It is through this exposed multi-species, relational lens, that we see the value and intelligence of all beings and environments, and recognise the knowledge, pleasure and care they share with us every day. In return, we can treat them with mutual care, bask in this joint pleasure, accept that we must also bear sovereignty in order to be in relation with them, and be thankful to elders for sharing this lens with us, so we may know this form of intimacy.

Acknowledgements

I would like to acknowledge Dr waaseyaa'sin Christine Sy, Morgan Mowatt, Dr Georgia Sitara, Dr Heather Tapley, Dr Mara Marin, Dr Feng Xu, Dr Laura Parisi and Julie Funk, who all influenced my thoughts, feelings and knowledge reflected in this chapter and introduced me to many of the medicine bundle of authors, theories and (hi)stories shared.

References

Absolon, K. and Willett, C. (2005). Aboriginal Research: Berry Picking and Hunting in the 21st Century, *First Peoples Child & Family Review: A Journal on Innovation and Best Practices in Aboriginal Child Welfare Administration, Research, Policy & Practice*, 1(1): 5–17.

Adese, J. (2014). Spirit Gifting: Ecological Knowing in Métis Life Narratives, *Decolonization: Indigeneity, Education & Society*, 3(3): 48–66.

Akiwenzie-Damm, K. (ed). (2002). *Without Reservation: Erotica Indigenous Style*, Ontario: Kegedonce Press.

Bao Nguyen – Grad. Admin Comparative Literature (2019). Leanne Simpson's public lecture: 'As We Have Always Done.' Available at www.youtube.com/watch?v=5P5l0vcGqKE&t=1801s

Berlant, L. and Warner, M. (1998). Sex in Public, *Critical Inquiry*, 24(2): 547–66.

Bourgeois, R. (2018). 'Generations of Genocide', in Anderson, K., Campbell, M. and Belcourt, C. (eds) *Keetsahnak: Our Missing and Murdered Indigenous Sisters*, Edmonton: The University of Alberta Press, pp 65–87.

Burns, M.M.L. (2020). Reclaiming Indigenous Sexual Being: Sovereignty and Decolonization through Sexuality, *Arbutus Review*, 11(1): 28–38.

Derrida, J. (2016). *Of Grammatology*, Baltimore, MD: Johns Hopkins University Press.

Driskill, Q. (2004). Stolen from Our Bodies: First Nations Two-Spirits/Queers and the Journey to a Sovereign Erotic, *Studies in American Indian Literatures*, 16(2): 50–64.

Driskill, Q. (2010). Doubleweaving Two-Spirit Critiques: Building Alliances between Native and Queer Studies, *Journal of Lesbian and Gay Studies*, 16(1–2): 69–92.

Gaudry, A. (2014). '*Kaa-tipeyimishoyaahk*' – '*We Are Those Who Own Ourselves*': *A Political History of Métis Self-Determination in the North-West, 1830–1870*, Victoria, BC: University of Victoria.

Haraway, D. (2008). *When Species Meet: Posthumanities Volume 3*, Minneapolis, MN: University of Minnesota Press.

Hunt, S. and Holmes, C. (2015). Everyday Decolonization: Living a Decolonizing Queer Politics, *Journal of Lesbian Studies*, 19(2): 154–72.

Kimmerer, R.W. (2013). *Braiding Sweetgrass: Indigenous Wisdom, Scientific Knowledge and the Teachings of Plants* (first edition), Minneapolis, MN: Milkweed Editions.

Kovach, M. (2009). 'Situating Self, Culture, and Purpose in Indigenous Inquiry', in *Indigenous Methodologies: Characteristics, Conversations, and Contexts*, Toronto: University of Toronto Press, pp 109–20.

Manson, J. (2019). Workmanship and Relationships: Indigenous Food Trading and Sharing Practices on Vancouver Island, *British Columbian Quarterly*, (200): 215–306.

McHugh, M.C. and Interligi, C. (2015). 'Sexuality and Older Women: Desirability and Desire', in Muhlbauer, V., Chrisler, J.C. and Denmark, F.L. (eds) *Women and Aging*, New York and Cham: Springer International Publishing, pp 89–116.

Native Students Union (2021). Territory Acknowledgments. Available at: www.uvicnsu.ca/about/lands

Nelson, M. (2017). 'Getting Dirty: The Eco-Eroticism of Women in Indigenous Oral Literatures', in Barker, J. (ed) *Critically Sovereign: Indigenous Gender, Sexuality, and Feminist Studies*, Albany: Duke University Press, pp 229–60.

Reynolds, P., Simpson, P. and Hafford-Letchfield, T. (eds) (2021). 'Series Editors' Introduction', in Hafford-Letchfield, T., Simpson, P. and Reynolds, P. (eds) *Sex and Diversity in Later Life: Critical Perspectives*, Bristol: Bristol University Press, pp xiv–xxiv.

Rifkin, M. (2010). *When Did Indians Become Straight? Kinship, the History of Sexuality and Native Sovereignty*, Oxford: Oxford University Press.

Rifkin, M. (2017). *Beyond Settler Time: Temporal Sovereignty and Indigenous Self-Determination*, Durham, NC: Duke University Press.

Simpson, A. (2016). The State is a Man: Theresa Spence, Loretta Saunders and the Gender of Settler Sovereignty, *Theory & Event*, 19(4).

Simpson, L. (2017). 'Land as Pedagogy', in Simpson, L. (ed) *As We Have Always Done*: *Indigenous Freedom, through Radical Resistance*, Minneapolis, MN: University of Minnesota Press, pp 145–73.

Smith, L.T. (2021). *Decolonizing Methodologies: Research and Indigenous Peoples*, London: Bloomsbury Publishing.

Starblanket, G. and Kiiwetinepinesiik Stark, H. (2019). 'Towards a Relational Paradigm – Four Points for Consideration: Knowledge, Gender, Land, and Modernity', in Asch, N., Borrows, J. and Tully, J. (eds) *Resurgence and Reconciliation*, Toronto: University of Toronto Press, pp 175–208.

TallBear, K. and Willey, A. (2019). Critical Relationality: Queer, Indigenous, and Multispecies Belonging beyond Settler Sex and Nature, *Imaginations: Journal of Cross-Cultural Image Studies*, 10(1): 5–15.

Trans Care BC (2022). Two-spirit, Provincial Health Services Authority. Available at: www.phsa.ca/transcarebc/gender-basics-education/terms-concepts/two-spirit

Van Camp, R. (2002). *Angel Wing Splash Pattern*, Wiarton, ON: Kegedonce Press.

Whitehead, J. (2022). *Making Love with the Land: Essays*, Toronto: Penguin Random House: Knopf.

Wilson, A. (2018). 'Skirting the Issues: Indigenous Myths, Misses, and Misogyny', in Anderson, K., Campbell, M. and Belcourt, C. (eds) *Keetsahnak: Our Missing and Murdered Indigenous Sisters*, Edmonton: The University of Alberta Press, pp 161–74.

Wilson, S. (2008). *Research Is Ceremony*, Winnipeg: Fernwood.

Wolfe, P. (2006). Settler Colonialism and the Elimination of the Native, *Journal of Genocide Research*, 8(4): 387–409.

10

Sex, intimacy and older life in Muslim contexts

Shanon Shah

Introduction: de-Orientalising 'older life'

Sex and gender remain contentious issues within many debates about the relationship between Islam and modernity (a term often used interchangeably with 'the West'). The influence of these geopolitical fault lines extends to trends in scholarly research on Islam and Muslims. For example, after the terrorist attacks of 9/11, academic publications on women and Islam, especially in Middle Eastern contexts, multiplied exponentially (Charrad, 2011). This was followed by a rise in interest in lesbian, gay, bisexual, trans and queer (LGBTQ) issues in Islam. Political controversies in the West involving Muslims, such as the recurring issue of women's dress, are often framed in the mass media as problems about what Islam supposedly says about women and LGBTQ people.

Since the 1990s, there has been a growing body of work by Muslim scholar-activists, especially Islamic feminists that employ 'multiple critique' to address these questions (cooke, 2001). These works challenge patriarchal, heteronormative interpretations of Islam while also deconstructing stereotypes about Islam and Muslim that have grown out of historical Eurocentric viewpoints that accompanied, or even justified, Western colonialism (a phenomenon often referred to as Orientalism). They show that sex and gender are not recent fault lines in contemporary ideological claims of a supposedly intractable clash of civilisations between Islam and the West. Joseph Massad (2007), for example, points out that while contemporary Western ideologues accuse Islam of being too sexually repressive and homophobic, early modern Orientalists were dismissing Islam as too sexually permissive and queer friendly.

Such dualistic conceptions of Islam are exacerbated by the religion's critics' *and* traditionalist defenders' tendencies to highlight the more controversial aspects of Islamic law – often styled 'Sharia' and loaded by ideological baggage that the traditional concept of *sharia*[1] did not carry – to support their positions. While legal texts are crucial sites for the construction of sex and gender in Muslim societies, these were not composed in isolation from their surrounding contexts or the influence of other texts. There are other sources that can illuminate lived experiences in different environments in different periods of history. These include texts on dream interpretation, medicine and healing, travel, poetry and the performing arts, and ethics and morality (Ze'evi, 2006). Attention to these sources can provide fresh avenues of inquiry about sex and intimacy in contemporary contexts, too. But identifying how the category of older/later life, or age more generally, fits into this corpus is less straightforward. In fact, the lack of attention to intersections of sex, intimacy and older age in the West (especially among women) is mirrored in many past and present Muslim contexts (for example, see Amini and McCormack, 2021).

Age *does* appear in many of the more recent works that look at this variety of Muslim texts, but usually to describe or analyse the age differences that characterised (and continue to characterise) various eroticised or sexualised relationships. The focus in these texts has mostly been on youth as a key factor that structures attraction and desire, whether in heteronormative or queer relationships (for example, see Najmabadi, 2005). Explicit mentions of older age, by comparison, are more central to polemical Islamophobic discourses, especially those that accuse the Prophet Muhammad of being a paedophile and a sexual pervert.

Herein lies the challenge of incorporating 'older life' as part of an analysis of sex and intimacy in Muslim contexts. It is not merely that this focus can unwittingly reproduce Orientalist and Islamophobic stereotypes. In the West, there is also a tendency to invoke religion as a cause of predatory sexual behaviour and paedophilia – just think of the perennial accusations of child sexual abuse in Roman Catholicism. While many of these accusations are based on fact, the relationship between religion and sex (and age) is far more complex than polemical debates allow for.

Against this background, this chapter gives an overview of the ways in which sex, intimacy and older life have been portrayed in a range of Muslim sources. It starts by highlighting some of the ways that older life, sex and/or intimacy intersect in Islam's primary sources about the life of the Prophet Muhammad. It then provides a summary of some other patterns in premodern scenarios in different Muslim cultures, as well as more recent patterns according to modern sources. The recurring assumptions and themes from these primary and secondary sources, both historical and contemporary, go on to inform a discussion of two pre-modern Muslim texts – *The Delight of Hearts* (from the 13th century CE) and *The Perfumed Garden of Sensual Delight* (from the 15th century CE).

The broad nature of this chapter does risk reifying an ahistorical, monolithic view of Islam. By selecting short excerpts from longer sources and/or juxtaposing primary and secondary sources within the space of a short chapter, I might be guilty of distortion or, at the very least, of downplaying or ignoring important nuances. But this is a perennial issue when particularistic, qualitative historical sources are used to derive more general insights about a specific phenomenon. Besides, the content of these texts could also be contradicted by other as-yet-unanalysed sources. Bearing these caveats in mind, this chapter refers to these textual excerpts to think through certain concepts and trends related to sex, intimacy and older life in Muslim contexts, and to suggest further areas of investigation.

The Prophet Muhammad's sexual and intimate life

Sex and intimacy are not and were never taboo topics in Islam, albeit within the rubric of lawful, heterosexual marriage. In conventional Islamic narratives, especially modern summaries of earlier sources, a crucial aspect of the Prophet Muhammad's biography is his different marriages, the nature of his relationships with his wives, and narrations about his married life. Some contemporary scholarly works that discuss sexuality and Islam have argued that the recorded traditions (*hadith*) of the Prophet Muhammad are evidence of a 'sexually enlightened religion', including teachings about the importance of joyful sexual union (Ze'evi, 2006). While some Islamic scholarship tends to stretch these examples for apologetic or even polemical purposes, their existence as part of the Islamic canon is undisputed.

The conventional biographical narrative of the Prophet's life contains explicit references to age, including as a marker of his marital relationships in his younger and later life. According to the many modern summaries, when Muhammad was 25, he married Khadija, a 40-year-old financially independent trader. In several Islamic commentaries, especially modern retellings, Khadija is portrayed as exercising agency in initiating contact with Muhammad as her prospective husband. And, after he received the first revelation of the Quran when he was 40, Khadija comforted Muhammad when he questioned his sanity. She bore him children, including Fatimah, the only one of their children to have survived him after his death. Khadija was also Muhammad's only wife until her death around 619 CE, when she was 65 and he was nearly 50, which triggered immense grief for him.

While there is plenty of biographical material about Muhammad, it is not easy to pin down the details of what 'exactly' happened during his lifetime. Moreover, specific details such as Khadija's age at marriage, 40, and Muhammad's age when he later received the Divine revelation, also 40, can usefully be treated as symbolic rather than literal facts (Ali, 2014). There probably was an age gap between Muhammad and Khadija, but the '40' used in Muslim reports to describe her age was likely meant to demonstrate a deeper spiritual significance. The audience who received this message would most likely have understood '40' symbolically, referring to a process of spiritual trial and maturation. This symbolism would not have been alien to this audience – the Hebrew Scriptures, for example, refer to the Israelites wandering in the desert for 40 years, the flood lasting 40 days, and the Gospel of Matthew refers to Jesus's retreat into the desert for 40 days and 40 nights before the devil tries to tempt him. The same logic applies to Muhammad's age when he first received the Divine message. This religious symbolism, however, does not erase the human aspects of the accounts contained in many Islamic narratives, including Muhammad's vulnerability at this first experience of revelation, or the mutual affection and respect between him and Khadija.

According to several narratives, the death of Khadija was part of a series of turning points in the development of Muhammad's mission. While she was alive, she was a source of moral, spiritual and economic support for him as his message gained ground among the marginalised sectors of Meccan society (Rahemtulla and Ababneh, 2021). This led to hostility and persecution of Muhammad's followers by the Meccan status quo. But it was after Khadija's death that Muhammad and his followers embarked on the migration, or *hijra*, to Medina in 622 CE.

It was during the post-*hijra* Medinan period that Muhammad and his followers developed their own form of political administration, and in which they embarked on defensive and offensive military campaigns to protect and consolidate their nascent religious community and polity. It is within this context that Muhammad contracted his plural marriages, including to Aisha, who according to some reports was six at the time of marriage and Muhammad in his mid-50s. Several sources say that the marriage was consummated when Aisha was nine, or even later, when she had passed puberty.

As with Khadija's age, there are disputes about the precision or exactness of the reports of Aisha's age. There is speculation that she could have been in her early or late teens at marriage, which would not have been unusual at the time. The reference to her being six was probably a legitimating strategy to highlight her youth and purity before marriage. This legitimating strategy can be understood considering the contentious references to Aisha in early Muslim reports. There was, (in)famously, Aisha's alleged infidelity, popularly known as 'the affair of the necklace' – which was refuted by a Quranic revelation, no less (Lings, 1991). There are also accounts of how she offended several of Muhammad's closest companions, including some of her co-wives. She was reportedly jealous of Khadija – she once insulted Khadija's memory, which hurt Muhammad deeply (Khalidi, 2009). After Muhammad's death, Aisha became an interested party in the early schism in Islam that led to the development of the Sunni sect which now constitutes between 85 and 90 per cent of all Muslims globally and the Shia sect which constitutes around 10 per cent of Muslims globally. Many Shia sources have not and still do not portray Aisha favourably, with some even reviling her openly. Against this background, insisting that Aisha was six (or seven) when Muhammad married her 'might prove her *religious* purity over and above concern with her sexual purity' (Ali, 2014).

The point remains, however, that just as there probably was an age gap between Muhammad and Khadija, there was undoubtedly an age gap between Muhammad and Aisha. Yet Aisha's age did not pose many problems for early Muslim commentators. Nor was it the focus of early Christian anti-Muslim polemics – for many centuries, marriage by adult men to girl children was also a common occurrence in many other contexts, including Christendom. Christian anti-Muslim polemicists instead targeted the fact that Muhammad had sex at all and engaged in plural marriages, evidence of his lustfulness or debauchery, which they contrasted with the purity of Jesus's celibacy (Ali, 2014). It was only in the era of modern colonialism in the late nineteenth and twentieth centuries that Aisha's age became weaponised by anti-Muslim ideologues *and* morally defended by traditional Islamic authorities (Ali, 2014).

The primary sources of early Islam are ripe for investigating the intersections of sex, intimacy and later life in relation to non-heteronormative intimacies, too. Intriguing accounts, for example, can be found in the wealth of reports about Muhammad's interactions with his followers at key moments, such as their preparations for battle. One account refers to the building of a trench around the city of Medina by Muhammad and his followers as a defensive tactic in anticipation of an attack by their Meccan opponents. Sources record the Battle of the Trench as occurring circa 626–27 CE when, according to the conventional Islamic timeline, Muhammad would have been in his late 50s. According to the sources, able bodied Muslim men worked for days digging this trench, 'stripped to the waist', including Muhammad (Lings, 1991). Years afterwards, one follower, Bara, recalled Muhammad's 'great beauty' as he dug the trench wearing a cloak, with his bare chest sprinkled with dust and his hair long enough to touch his shoulders. 'More beautiful than him I have not seen', said Bara. While it might be a stretch to read erotic or sexual subtext into this episode, at the very least this appears to be an example of homosocial bonding that was sensual and intimate.

There are two important caveats to bear in mind when exploring these possibilities for rethinking sex, intimacy and older life in the earliest Muslim sources. First, the abundance of detail in the biography of the Prophet's life means that these elements have been used to justify and endorse contradictory positions and factions throughout the history of Islam (Khalidi, 2009). Second, sex was not only legally allowed within heterosexual marriage, it was legally permissible for male slave owners to have sex with their female slaves. Islamic rulings also paid attention to the interplay of age and soundness of mind when adjudicating on lawful sexual relations (Omar, 2012). For example, the minor and/or 'insane' party within an illicit sexual encounter could not be regarded as a transgressor. He or she would not be punishable for acts that would be impermissible for free adult men or women of sound mind. Furthermore, the Islamic punishment for sexual transgressions applied only to Muslims. This is why, for instance, not all homosexual relations carried the same penalty according to classical *fiqh* (Islamic jurisprudence or the study and application of *sharia*). Homosexual relations between two married, Muslim, adult, free and sane men could potentially carry the death sentence in some schools of *fiqh*, while homosexual relations between two boys, or between two male slaves, or between two men who were considered not of sound mind, were usually not punishable.

Historical and cultural practices

The examples in Muhammad's biography discussed in the preceding section were summarised from details that can be found in different genres of Islamic sources. These include the text of the Quran, later commentaries on the Quran (*tafsir*), the recorded Traditions of the Prophet Muhammad (*hadith*), accounts of Muhammad's military expeditions (*maghazi*) and biographical material on his life (*sira*). The Quran and the *hadith* were and remain core sources of Islamic jurisprudence (*fiqh*) but, as mentioned above, there were other textual genres that served as sources of guidance and edification in Muslim contexts throughout history. The abundance of stories and even different versions of the same vignettes have led to varying interpretations and expressions of Islam in different historical periods and cultural environments. This is also partly why cultures and practices of sex and intimacy could flourish among Muslims in ways that seemed – to modern and/or Eurocentric sensibilities, at least – to subvert or contradict Islamic legal pronouncements. In turn, there have been different ways of explaining this supposed inconsistency in more recent studies of Islam and sexuality.

One theory is that 'Islamic homosexualities' flourished in contradistinction to Western 'modern homosexualities' (Roscoe and Murray, 1997). In the West, there was historically a 'gender-variant' model (where 'to be homosexual was to be a non-masculine man or a non-feminine woman') as well as a 'sexed-being' model, referring to people who were attracted to individuals of the same anatomical sex, regardless of their levels of masculinity and femininity. According to this theory, homosexuality in Muslim societies historically consisted of the gender-variant type – the sexed-being model was virtually absent (Roscoe and Murray, 1997). There is also an argument that Muslim civilisations inherited a status-differentiated or age-differentiated model of homosexuality based on Hellenistic pederasty, seen especially in mystical Sufi orders (Roscoe, 1997). Meanwhile, the gender-variant model has ostensibly given rise to 'third gender' cultures in many Muslim environments (Roscoe, 1997). These include Nigeria's *'yan daudu*, the Indian subcontinent's *hijra/khwajasara*, and notably the Malay Archipelago's *bissu*, *waria* and *mak nyah*, where there is evidence of historical social acceptance of 'gender pluralism' and 'heterogender' homosexuality (Peletz, 2011).

Proponents of the gender-variant and age-differentiated models have also made a key underlying assumption, in that 'Islamic homosexualities' could only flourish because of 'a common Islamic ethos of avoidance in acknowledging sex and sexualities' (Murray, 1997). This assumption is debatable.

The idea of wilful ignorance about sex and sexuality in Muslim societies belies the evidence of abundant accounts – some extremely explicit – about sexual and/or intimate relationships in different Muslim cultures throughout history. Perhaps, the argument goes, these accounts pertained to non-legal or 'folk' genres of oral or written texts or, conversely, they were reserved for a restricted, literary and elite audience. This, too, is debatable. For example, between approximately 1500 CE and 1800 CE in the Ottoman era, popular homoerotic poems were sometimes composed by senior Islamic scholars who *also* maintained the illegality of penetrative anal sex in their formal legal judgments (El-Rouayheb, 2009).

A more plausible explanation is that these authors saw a specific sexual act – penetrative anal sex, or *liwat* – very differently from romantic or even erotic (but non-penetrative) intimacy between an older man and a youth. Thus, while disapproval of *liwat* was nearly universal, other expressions of same-sex affection, for example, kissing, caressing, engaging in intercrural intercourse or simply just gazing at the object of one's affection, were considered less reprehensible or even tolerated to some extent (El-Rouayheb, 2009).

Furthermore, Islamic legal judgments about same-sex female relationships were often ambivalent or even non-existent – because these did not involve penile penetration. If anything, traditional Islamic rulings on sex and intimacy were phallocentric (Omar, 2012). So, as long as penile penetration (either vaginal or anal) was not at issue, there was a considerable degree of ambivalence or even tolerance of other expressions of non-marital intimacy and erotic behaviour, because these were not regarded as 'real' or 'proper' sex.

While this logic made sense from many Islamic legal perspectives, it scandalised many European visitors to Muslim environments, especially at the height of the colonial Victorian era. This is the basis for another level of criticism of the two-model explanation of 'Islamic homosexualities'. In the context of Qajar Iran, for example, the stigma that was introduced by the European gaze on local practices turned the *amrad* – the beardless youth who was pursued by adult male suitors – from an object of desire into one of shame and ridicule (Najmabadi, 2008). But even this process was complicated. The gradual disappearance of the *amrad* in Iranian cultural memory did not immediately translate into a blanket condemnation of 'homosexuality'. This is because the very concept of the *amrad* challenged the binary Victorian perception of gender, in which figures such as the *amrad* were understood as the feminised male partner in a homosexual dyad. Instead, according to native understandings, the position of the *amrad* was more intermediate – akin to someone who was not-a-woman and not-yet-bearded-man (Najmabadi, 2005). This characteristic of being not-yet-man is what made the *amrad* an acceptable object of adult male (and sometimes adult female) affection. But neither could *amrad* be classified as boys or children. Inferring from Qajar sources, it can be assumed that a typical *amrad* was a male adolescent, typically in his teens but who could even be in his early 20s, provided he had not yet grown a beard (Najmabadi, 2005). The *amrad*'s adult male suitors were usually in their mid-20s to mid-30s – but some were much older.

While the example of the *amrad* is specific to Qajar Iran, it provides important clues into the trajectories of modernisation in colonised and/or politically weakened Muslim regimes, especially regarding sex, intimacy and age. Against this backdrop, the road to full blown, anti-homosexual discourse and legislation in the modern Islamic Republic of Iran can be seen as an extension of the gendered culture wars that first erupted in the Qajar era. Yet such Islamicised and institutionalised expressions of homophobia can be found in many other Muslim political environments, too, often justified by anti-colonial and anti-Western logic. At the same time, the Iranian regime has been a pioneer of sorts in the recognition of transgender identities and rights, a trend that can also be seen in other Muslim-led states such as Pakistan and Bangladesh (Najmabadi, 2011).

Setting aside these interesting developments on 'third gender' rights for the moment, the strident anti-homosexual rhetoric of different Muslim regimes is now often accompanied by aggressive assertions of male-dominated heterosexuality. As Najmabadi (2005) points out, this dual position gives rise to new contradictions. The basis of these contradictions lies in the insistence of Islamic revivalists in different Muslim-majority contexts on strict gender segregation in accordance with their interpretations of Islam. Within this schema, opportunities for heterosexual social contact are severely limited. Sex and intimacy between heterosexuals are only permissible within marriage – all non-marital heterosexual relations carry severe punishments. Meanwhile, homosexual relations also carry stringent punishments amid the reality that public and private spaces are only conducive to homosocial or same-gender contact. Rather than following an 'Islamic ethos' that avoids acknowledging sex and sexuality, it appears that these regimes are hypervigilant.

We seem to have returned to the claim that sex is a fault line in the widespread assumption of an inherent clash of civilisations between Islam and the West. Is this really the case? The next section organises the insights gleaned from the discussion so far and incorporates the rubric of age to expand our understanding.

Recurring themes

So far, older life has appeared in different ways in this chapter's exploration of sex, intimacy and age in Muslim sources. First, in my summary of the intersections of sex, intimacy and older life in the founding narratives and textual sources in Islam, the rubric of age was a central part of the analysis. Second, age appeared more implicitly when I summarised the historical and cultural trajectories of sex and intimacy in Muslim contexts.

This section aims to consolidate these insights by looking specifically at types of sources or examples that contain references to older age. These will be organised according to two criteria – first, whether they focus on heterosexual intimacies or sexual relations and, second, whether they treat these relationships sympathetically. The combination of these two criteria produces four categories – sympathetic heterosexual examples, unsympathetic heterosexual examples, sympathetic queer examples and unsympathetic queer examples.

Sympathetic heterosexual examples

These are exemplified by the narratives of Muhammad's marriages to Khadija and Aisha in the primary sources. These narratives are now increasingly repurposed by modern Muslim writers to challenge violent or patriarchal interpretations of Islam as well as Orientalist or Islamophobic perspectives. In these works, the younger Muhammad's relationship with the older Khadija is often stressed as an example of a monogamous, companionate and mutually supportive marriage (Ali, 2014). At the same time, the controversial characterisations of Aisha in the earliest sources have also been appropriated by modern writers – including feminists – to turn her into a protagonist in a reimagining of early Islam (Ali, 2014).

The dynamics surrounding Aisha are instructive – namely springing from her legacy in Sunni–Shia relations and how she is remembered far less deferentially in Shia sources. But Aisha is not the only complex character in the Muslim sources. Tarif Khalidi (2009) argues that the earliest Muslim biographers of the Prophet would include everything – including contradictory or even unflattering – accounts about his own life in their reports. For them, thoroughness and inclusiveness were a hallmark of their devotion to the memory of the Prophet, which is why they were keen to include even unsavoury accounts – what Khalidi (2009) refers to as 'antibodies' – in their narratives. These 'antibodies', however, would pose problems for later Muslim writers and thinkers, especially once they began being weaponised by anti-Muslim ideologues.

Unsympathetic heterosexual examples

The existence of these 'antibodies' in biographical material about Muhammad has resulted in the same source material being used to propagate negative views of Islam. Sex, intimacy and age have all been weaponised in this way, too. For example, pre-modern Orientalist sources decried Muhammad's so-called lust and debauchery because he engaged in plural marriages, in contrast to the sexually pure characterisation of Jesus Christ. Yet it is fairly recent that Muhammad's marriage to the six-year-old Aisha in his 50s has become a target of condemnation, especially in Islamophobic sources (Ali, 2014). At the same time, there is a backlash among Islamic revivalists in different political contexts who now *defend* child marriage as non-negotiable religious right.

Sympathetic queer examples

I introduced the possibility of positive queer examples involving references to older age by highlighting an example in primary Islamic sources of men admiring the Prophet Muhammad's beauty – even into his 50s. Such examples are not necessarily sexual or even erotic, but they are intimate and even sensual.

Such intimate and sensual odes by Muslim men to other men flourished in non-modern Islamic texts, but with a reversal in the age difference. It was older men who composed love poetry admiring the beauty of the beardless youths they were infatuated with. I have already mentioned the idea that these relationships shared the characteristics of a Hellenistic pederastic template which got diffused into Muslim cultures, especially in Sufism. Yet this is not the full picture – many Muslim poets who extolled the virtues of loving young men were also legal specialists whose formal judgments condemned *liwat*, or anal sex.

Unsympathetic queer examples

If we are to understand *liwat* as a restricted definition of a particular act – penetrative anal sex – then it makes sense that premodern Islamic legal scholars might condemn it while finding other expressions of same-sex intimacy unobjectionable or even favourable. Yet this was not the rationale of the Victorians who encountered this phenomenon in Muslim environments, which eventually led to the idea that Islam was too sexually permissive and perverse. Such European views were received with shame, for example, among Qajar elites in Iran, who sought to purge the love of *amrad*, or beardless youth, from their cultural memory.

The disappearance of the *amrad* was part of a path towards a more politicised, aggressive and fixed heterosexual binary in the modern Iranian context. Yet the disappearance of the *amrad* did not only signal the disappearance of more fluid notions of sex, gender and intimacy. It also swept the role of age under the carpet, because the social acceptability of adult male and *amrad* relationships relied upon age to legitimise certain forms of intimacy at certain points of an individual male's life.

The next and final section of this chapter takes this discussion forward by investigating references to older life in two premodern Muslim texts – one primarily addressing queer relationships and the other heteronormative relationships.

Two Islamic 'sex manuals'

Sometimes, a good way to challenge our present assumptions and stereotypes requires a fresh look at the past. The two texts chosen for analysis in this section are not the only kinds of premodern Muslim literature that discussed sex and intimacy. There were genres of 'love literature', for example, with further sub-branches, including some that were more philosophical and others classifiable as the 'literature of debauchery' (Dangler, 2015).

The first text, *The Delight of Hearts* by Ahmad al-Tifashi (1184–1253) (hereafter *Delight*) was composed at a time when different factions – the Almohads, Hafsids, Ayyubids and Mamluks – were vying for political power in Northern Africa (Dangler, 2015). Al-Tifashi was a jurist from the Sunni Maliki school which did not find favour with the ruling Almohads in Tunisia, and so he spent a good chunk of his life in Alexandria and Cairo. *Delight* contains 12 chapters of erotic guidance whose insights were derived from the author's conversations and observations in plazas, markets and literary salons, and conveyed through a combination of humorous verse and prose anecdotes. A substantial part of the book is devoted to stories of non-heterosexual relations – between men and between women.

The second text, *The Perfumed Garden of Sensual Delight* by Muhammad ibn Muhammad al-Nafzawi (hereafter *Perfumed Garden*) comes nearly two centuries later. Although the book is addressed to the author's sponsor, the chief minister to the Sultan of Tunis (1394–1434), it is written in a popular style for a lay audience. It contains 21 chapters of varying length which, like *Delight*, can be read separately according to the reader's interest. Unlike *Delight*, the focus is largely on heterosexual relations and some of the topics are clearly more technical and instructional – chapter titles include 'Sexual Technique' (Chapter 6), 'Names for the Penis' (Chapter 8), 'Names for the Vulva' (Chapter 9), 'Remarks on Female Sterility & Methods of

Treatment' (Chapter 14), and 'The Causes of Male Sterility' (Chapter 15) (al-Nafzawi, 1999).

Perfumed Garden was probably first translated into French in 1850, and an infamous English translation by the British imperial explorer Richard Burton appeared in 1876. According to the translator of the version I referred to, Jim Colville (al-Nafzawi, 1999), these European translations were 'bizarre' and 'exaggerated' distortions of the original. While the text does not pretend to be literary, neither is it pornographic.

Both texts contain a wealth of anecdotes and verses that are lewd and explicit, yet they are also framed by religious invocations and formulae. The authors adopt the tone of raconteurs and, even though they ultimately disapprove of sexual activity outside of lawful heterosexual marriage, there is a lot of poetic licence and sometimes sympathy for sexually 'immoral' characters.

The Delight of Hearts

The verses and anecdotes in *Delight* are meant to educate and entertain the reader about a wide range of topics. These include the different roles men and boys can assume during anal sex, the slang words used by 'queens' for different acts or interactions, and the witty responses by queer people towards political or legal censure. Many of these are slightly subversive or sympathetic, with the queer transgressor sometimes having the last laugh in an exchange with a judge or political leader. Some stories even highlight the hypocrisy of harsh judges who secretly engage in homosexual behaviour. Some include playful subversions of religious formulae or interpretations of Quranic verses.

The translation choices by Edward A. Lacey render many of these stories intelligible to people who might be familiar with tales of gay life in contemporary New York or London. These include vignettes about arrogant young hustlers trying to take advantage of older 'queens', and the exploits of predatory older 'homosexuals' cruising 'boys'. Often, however, there are reversals which seem designed to have a moral lesson, or at least to serve as a punchline; for example, when the older 'queen' gets to have the last laugh. Quite a few stories challenge the idea that older men are 'tops' and younger men are 'bottoms' for comic effect, sometimes with the older character as the main protagonist.

Occasionally, some vignettes evoke the intersections of class, sex, older age, intimacy and politics, while maintaining their focus on the humorous, for example, in one excerpt which now merits detailed attention.

Al-Tifashi introduces it as an incident recorded by the ninth-century Arab thinker Al-Jahiz in his treatise *Concerning Thieves*. The scene begins with a respected old sheikh (a title usually reserved for older men and/or people of higher social rank) who, we are told, was a high-ranking thief brought before a judge. The sheikh's crimes included 'serious cases of robbery, murder' and 'ambushes laid for travellers' (al-Tifashi, 1988).

The sheikh had already been incarcerated for many years, with the authorities having exhausted all attempts to extract a confession that would have justified a death sentence. Eventually, the old sheikh was joined in his cell by an ex-accomplice who had just been imprisoned for theft – 'a young man he loved' (al-Tifashi, 1988). The dramatic action now unfolds:

> One day they were both taken out together to be flogged in public along with various other prisoners. First the young man got one hundred strokes of the lash. He was a teenager who was not even grown to full adulthood, but he could already speak eloquently, and his physical appearance was supremely radiant and blooming. He didn't utter a single word of complaint through the whole whipping. The prison warden and all the spectators were astonished.
>
> 'I admire that boy's self-control,' the warden confided to one of the important officials who were watching. 'Look how unflinchingly he takes his punishment! Now look at that sheikh, there among the other prisoners. Well, if you can imagine it, he commits immoral acts every day with the young man you see there.'
>
> As he spoke, he pointed out to his companion a puny, gaunt little yellow-skinned old man – the sheikh we have just mentioned. At each stroke the young man received, the old fellow writhed with pain, groaned and seemed on the verge of fainting. The spectators thought this reaction was due to the fear and anguish he felt, knowing that he was about to undergo the same treatment. Various other prisoners were whipped, after the young man.
>
> 'Take the sheikh back to his cell,' came the order finally. 'In his state, he wouldn't be able to stand even five strokes.' (al-Tifashi, 1988)

This dismissal of the old sheikh is a key dramatic – or comic, depending on one's point of view – turning point. In other words, his frail reaction to his young paramour's whipping seems to belie his fearsome reputation. But now, we are told, the sheikh 'bridled like an angry camel' at the warden's order, and his 'eyes flashed red' (al-Tifashi, 1988). The sheikh replied:

> 'For your information, I can take five thousand strokes of the lash!' he cried out. 'Because I shall draw strength not from my body but from my heart, from my endurance, from my steadfastness of purpose.'
>
> 'Strip him!' ordered the warden.
>
> The jailers were going to shackle him, to keep him from moving around. He refused:

'I have no need of it. I won't move.'

He stood up. His torturers closed ranks around him. They flogged him on the back and then on his stomach. They counted up to five hundred strokes of the lash. Sometimes they ordered him to remain standing; sometimes they made him sit down, with his arms tied to his sides. Throughout the whole operation, his feet didn't move from their place, but stayed as steady as stakes driven in the ground. The high official whom the warden had previously spoken to then leaned over toward the latter.

'You criticised the young man for his relationship with that fellow. I swear by God, if that old chap had asked me for the same favour, I'd have let him go ahead.'

This remark made the warden laugh so hard that he literally fell back head over heels. (al-Tifashi, 1988)

This anecdote contains a mix of elements that are stereotypical *and* surprising. On one hand, the story is set up for listeners with preconceptions about masculinity and about criminals of a lower socio-economic class. By the middle of the anecdote, there is a twist – it appears as though the youth (the 'bottom') is the more manly character. The sheikh is, by everyone's estimation, a wimp. And yet, in another twist, the sheikh takes it like a (super) man when his honour is at stake. The high official's begrudging admiration for the sheikh – to the extent that he would have let the older man treat him like a younger lover – is the punchline.

Beyond this conventional joke structure, however, there are hints of real affection and intimacy between the sheikh and his younger lover – the sheikh cries out in pain because he cannot bear watching his young lover tortured.

Delight contains many more stories with this mixture of stereotype and surprise, making it difficult to impose a single analytical perspective upon its contents. For now, it is enough to observe that these intriguing stories were composed by an Islamic legal scholar in thirteenth-century North Africa. We have come a long way from the purported Islamic ethos of avoiding references to sex and sexuality.

The Perfumed Garden of Sensual Delight

The chapters in *Perfumed Garden* are much shorter and many adopt a much more instructional tone than those in *Delight*, but they also contain numerous anecdotes and folk tales intended to entertain their audience. While the content is generally much more heteronormative, there is still some mention of same-sex activity between men and between women, which the author does not dwell on unduly. These relationships are usually plot devices placed within a bigger, usually humorous, heteronormative narrative.

There is also far less variety in references to age. References to older men highlight their wisdom, wealth or the need to preserve their libido – one frequently mentioned precondition of good sex is youth. When older women are referred to, however, the tone shifts noticeably.

A few mentions of older women appear to be neutral. For example, an excerpt about dream interpretation conveys that a 'bonnet, headscarf and slippers' are 'associated with woman' and, furthermore, their condition indicates the woman's 'social status and circumstances'. For example, if a man has a dream in which he sees new slippers, he will marry a virgin; if he dreams of used slippers, he will marry a divorcee 'of an age in proportion to that of the slippers' (al-Nafzawi, 1999).

More recurrently, older women are referred to as 'hags' and are portrayed as pimps who have led young virgins astray. There are also explicitly negative references reserved for sexual relations with older women, for example, 'Sex with old women is a deadly sure poison' (al-Nafzawi, 1999).

A reference to older women also suddenly makes its appearance in the dénouement of a series of stanzas, attributed to 'Bayadiq, the Persian', encouraging men to eat, drink and have coitus in moderation. The concluding pieces of advice to have a 'bath every two days' and to avoid 'too much sex' is augmented by a final reminder that 'sex with old women's a poisonous perversion'.

One interesting collection of verses cited is attributed to Abu Nuwas, the ninth-century poet who was renowned for his libertine and bacchic works. He often appears in fictive anecdotes contained in many premodern Muslim texts as a trickster figure of sorts. He is a recurring character in the previously discussed *Delight*, where his erotic homosexual exploits are recounted from the days of his youth (when he was pursued by older suitors) to his older age (when he would pursue handsome youth). One section of *Delight* describes him as follows: 'Among famous adulterers, much mention is naturally made of Abu Nuwas, who, despite his reputation as a notorious homosexual, also had affairs with women' (al-Tifashi, 1988).

In *Perfumed Garden*, the verses attributed to Abu Nuwas that were reproduced are as follows, at the end of 'Names for the Vulva' (Chapter 9):

> Women are demons you never should trust,
> What they want most is to satisfy lust.
> Their purpose in love is hidden, unspoken,
> Deceivers, betrayers, who loves will be broken.
>
> If you show her a sharing and generous attitude
> Then one day, for sure, you will know her ingratitude.
> Daily she'll ask you to buy for her more
> But when hot, she will pick up the servants and whore.

And when nothing is left then you can expect
That everything else about you she'll reject.
There's only one time when a woman is gratified
And that's when her craving for cock has been satisfied.

God save me from women and their fiendish plots
And from old hags especially, the worst of the lot!
(al-Nafzawi, 1999)

> [Used with permission of Taylor & Francis Informa UK Ltd,
> from Perfumed Garden V7, Al-Nafzawi, 1999; permission
> conveyed through Copyright Clearance Center, Inc.]

The thrust of *Perfumed Garden* is about giving advice, largely from a male perspective, to heterosexual men and women on how to have good sex. These scattered references to older women reinforce the gendered and unequal nature of age in this equation – largely, it is acceptable for older men to be sexually active, but not older women. Furthermore, in the text's dispensation of pragmatic or medical advice, there are scarcely any mentions of some of the major markers of a woman's life cycle, including menstruation and menopause.

Concluding remarks

The two sex manuals referred to – *The Delight of Hearts* and *The Perfumed Garden of Sensual Delight* – give us pause when thinking about the intersections of sex, intimacy and older life in different Muslim contexts and historical periods. On one hand, *Delight* contains anecdotes that, while formally disapproving of non-heterosexual intimacies, could be read as tolerant – or at the least, non-condemnatory on a social and cultural level – towards queer men of different ages, including older men. If anything, legal disapproval was distributed equally between men engaged in illicit heterosexual and homosexual relations. The tolerance based on age, however, disappears in *Perfumed Garden* when it comes to the sexual life of older women.

On the one hand, these texts challenge Orientalist and modern Eurocentric stereotypes of Islam as being anti-queer or even anti-sex – an analytical insight that informs a growing corpus of research on Islam, gender and sexuality. On the other hand, these texts reproduce and reinforce a double standard – sex and intimacy in older age is permissible and even praiseworthy for straight (and even queer) men, but not for women. Furthermore, these texts show that this combination of ageism and misogyny predated the colonial encounter and the contemporary flourishing of the 'clash of civilisations' thesis. And yet, these ageist, gender-differentiated attitudes emerged despite a core component of Islam's foundational narrative – Muhammad's happy first marriage to Khadija, an *older* woman, until the day she died.

Note

[1] For the spelling of Arabic terms, I rely upon the conventions of the *International Journal of Middle East Studies*, but without diacritics.

References

Ali, K. (2014) *The Lives of Muhammad*, London: Harvard University Press.

Amini, E. and McCormack, M. (2021) 'Older Iranian Muslim Women's Experiences of Sex and Sexuality: A Biographical Approach', *British Journal of Sociology*, 72, 300–14. Available at: https://doi.org/10.1111/1468-4446.12805

Charrad, M.M. (2011) 'Gender in the Middle East: Islam, State, Agency', *Annual Review of Sociology*, 37, 417–37. Available at: https://doi.org/10.1146/annurev.soc.012809.102554

cooke, m. (2001) *Women Claim Islam*, New York: Routledge.

Dangler, J. (2015) 'Expanding Our Scope: Nonmodern Love and Sex in Ibn Ḥazm al-Andalusī's Ṭawq al-ḥamāma and Aḥmad ibn Yūsuf al-Tīfāshī's Nuzhat al-albāb fīmā lā yūjad fī kitāb', *Africa Today*, 61(4), 13–25.

El-Rouayheb, K. (2009) *Before Homosexuality in the Arab-Islamic World, 1500–1800*, Chicago: University of Chicago Press.

Khalidi, T. (2009) *Images of Muhammad*, New York: Doubleday Religion.

Lings, M. (1991) *Muhammad: His Life Based on the Earliest Sources*, Great Shelford: Islamic Texts Society.

Massad, J. (2007) *Desiring Arabs*, Chicago: University of Chicago Press.

Murray, S.O. (1997) 'The Will Not to Know: Islamic Accommodations of Male Homosexuality', in Murray, S.O. and Roscoe, W. (eds) *Islamic Homosexualities: Culture, History, and Literature*, New York: New York University Press, pp 14–44.

al-Nafzawi, M. ibn M. (1999) *The Perfumed Garden of Sensual Delight*, translated by J. Colville, London: Routledge (Routledge Arabia Library).

Najmabadi, A. (2005) *Women with Mustaches and Men without Beards: Gender and Sexual Anxieties of Iranian Modernity*, Berkeley: University of California Press.

Najmabadi, A. (2008) 'Types, Acts, or What? Regulation of Sexuality in Nineteenth-Century Iran', in Babayan, K. and Najmabadi, A. (eds) *Islamicate Sexualities: Translations across Temporal Geographies of Desire*, Cambridge, MA: Center for Middle Eastern Studies of Harvard University, pp 275–96.

Najmabadi, A. (2011) 'Verdicts of Science, Rulings of Faith: Transgender/Sexuality in Contemporary Iran', *Social Research*, 78(2), 533–56.

Omar, S. (2012) 'From Semantics to Normative Law: Perceptions of Liwat (Sodomy) and Sihaq (Tribadism) in Islamic Jurisprudence (8th–15th Century CE)', *Islamic Law and Society*, 19, 222–56.

Peletz, M.G. (2011) 'Gender Pluralism: Muslim Southeast Asia Since Early Modern Times', *Social Research*, 78(2), 656–86.

Rahemtulla, S. and Ababneh, S. (2021) 'Reclaiming Khadija's and Muhammad's Marriage as an Islamic Paradigm: Toward a New History of the Muslim Present', *Journal of Feminist Studies in Religion*, 37(2), 83–102.

Roscoe, W. (1997) 'Precursors of Islamic Male Homosexualities', in Murray, S.O. and Roscoe, W. (eds) *Islamic Homosexualities: Culture, History, and Literature*, New York: New York University Press, pp 55–86.

Roscoe, W. and Murray, S.O. (1997) 'Introduction', in Murray, S.O. and Roscoe, W. (eds) *Islamic Homosexualities: Culture, History, and Literature*, New York: New York University Press, pp 3–13.

al-Tifashi, A. (1988) *The Delight of Hearts: Or What You Will Not Find in Any Book*, translated by E.A. Lacey, San Francisco: Gay Sunshine Press.

Ze'evi, D. (2006) *Producing Desire: Changing Sexual Discourses in the Ottoman Middle East, 1500–1900*, Los Angeles, CA: University of California Press.

11

Reflections: themes and issues emerging from the volume

Debra A. Harley, Krystal Nandini Ghisyawan, Shanon Shah and Paul Simpson

Introduction

An enormous amount of attention has been dedicated to Western views of sexuality and ageing and subsequently, has occluded the majority world. Thus, this volume has focused on the intersections of age, sex, sexuality and intimacy of individuals within the latter. Older adults' sexuality has been relegated to a position of silence, and/or abnormality, as if they are not sexual beings with desires, but rather with dysfunction. For LGBTQ adults, their sexuality has been marginalised and silenced or paraded as abnormality throughout their lives. Older adults' sexuality and intimacy have been gendered and, especially for older women, considered taboo for discussion or participation. Themes and issues emerging from contributors against the backdrop of geographical and cultural rigidity in this volume are identified and their implications discussed.

How ageing and getting older are defined is multifaceted and involves a numerical/chronological existence that is measured in time, culturally and perceptually. Ageing is further contextualised depending on identity, for example, older trans sex workers in India are perceived to have reached old age between 35 and 40 years old because their beauty is seen as beginning to fade. Older age is by far the largest period along the developmental continuum plagued by misconceptions and stereotypes (Dudek et al, 2022).

Intimacy, sexuality and sexual identities are commonly understood as natural (or naturalised) human expressions that are present across the life span and contribute to a meaningful personal life. In fact, expressions of intimacy and sexuality constitute one of our basic human needs and rights (Gewirtz-Meydan et al, 2018). Unfortunately, we have seen in this volume how stereotypes persist (part-imposed, part home-grown in some instances) regarding sexuality, intimacy and ageing, and especially for individuals who are constructed or identify as sexual minorities. These biases are culturally centred and influenced by political ideology and by religion and its importance in people's lives. The sexuality of older women is observed and commonly normalised through a patriarchal perspective and medical or biological function and dysfunction. Women from different cultural groups have different attitudes, different comfort levels about getting older, and concerning whether it is normal for a woman to continue to value sex as she gets older (Thomas, 2015). Exploring older women (aged 52 to 90) who were remarried after age 50, Clarke (2010) found a shift from emphasis on the importance of sexual intercourse and passion to greater valuing of companionship, cuddling, affection and intimacy. In addition, these women tend to have later life sexual experiences more positive than were their earlier sexual experiences.

For many countries in Africa, the Indian sub-continent and the Caribbean, homophobia is a by-product of colonisation and patriarchy, which contribute to the myriad national identities that define the social and moral fabric of the region's cultures (Givens, 2022). According to Buckle (nd), there is a direct correlation between countries which belong to the Commonwealth, and therefore have previously been under British rule, and countries that still have homophobic, biphobic and/or transphobic beliefs and practices towards LGBTQ people. In a survey of countries, acceptance of homosexuality differs by age (younger people being more inclined towards acceptance), education (higher educational attainment correlating with acceptance), income (wealthier people being more accepting) and, in some instances, gender (women being more accepting). People in less wealthy and developed countries, such as Nigeria and Kenya, are less accepting of homosexuality (Poushter and Kent, 2020). In 2013, public opinion on acceptance of homosexuality and gender identity variance in society remains sharply divided by country, region, and economic development. Countries in the Middle East and sub-Saharan Africa are less accepting of homosexuality than those in Western Europe and the Americas, and the publics in the Asia-Pacific region generally are split on this issue (Poushter and Kent, 2020; see also the survey-based study of Han and O'Mahoney, 2018). Implicit in such attitudes is an anticolonial and anti-Western sentiment. In the past two decades, acceptance of homosexuality in many countries has seen a double-digit increase. For example, South Africa and South Korea have seen a 21-point increase since 2002, India saw a 22-point increase since 2014, Mexico and Japan went from just over half being accepting in 2002 to seven-in-ten in 2019, and Kenya only went from 1-in-100 who said homosexuality should be accepted in 2002 to 14 per cent who said this in 2019 (Poushter and Kent, 2020).

Work by Bettinsoil, Suppes and Napier (2019) has tested how beliefs about gender norms and people's attitudes towards gay men and women compare across the globe, covering 23 countries representing both Western and non-Western societies. Overall, findings indicated: (1) gay men were disliked more than lesbian-identified women; (2) after adjusting for endorsement of traditional gender norms, the relationship between participant gender and sexual prejudice is inconsistent across Western countries, but heterosexual men in non-Western countries consistently report more negative attitudes than heterosexual women towards gay men; and (3) a significant association between gender norm endorsement and sexual prejudice across countries, but it was absent or reversed in China, India and South Korea. Collectively, this study suggests that gender and sexuality may be more liberally associated and have less strict interpretation in some non-Western contexts (Bettinsoil et al, 2019). Recent data indicate that, in many countries, especially among college-age people, those socialised as female are embracing sexual fluidity at much higher rates than they have in the past, and more significantly than men overall (Massey et al, 2021). Nevertheless, while some countries show friendlier attitudes towards lesbian and gay people, even in the more tolerant places, discriminatory attitudes persist.

Themes

Having provided a global sketch of toleration of sexual and gender diversity, we turn to re-examine key themes addressed in this volume. Themes represent accounts characterising perceptions, experiences, feelings, values and emotions of respondents in/or subjects of a research inquiry (Mishra and Dey, 2022). These are key to advancing understanding of sexuality and intimacy in later life in cultures and countries beyond the global North and West.

Invisibility = silence and secrecy/facades of respectability

'Coming out' is a Western concept for which there is no cultural equivalent in many other contexts. Many people of the majority world intentionally evoke non-disclosure and silence as a protective measure. However, for older LGBTQ adults, invisibility is perhaps the greatest ill associated with ageism (Espinoza, 2016). For gay and bisexual men in Hong Kong, for example, silence and secrecy are valued because it allows them to maintain respectability and avoid bringing disgrace to their family. Familial relationships are highly valued among gay and bisexual men; therefore, they will do nothing to reveal their sexual desires to the public and to expose their family to embarrassment. While heterosexual marriage was regarded as a duty, homosexual sex or romance were subjected to particular restrictions during a period of intense and widespread intolerance; paying homage to tradition and family values is an obligation not to be taken lightly.

For gay and bisexual men, invisibility is the act of keeping their social (public) and sexual (queerness) worlds compartmentalised, making sure the two shall never meet. To maintain respectability while participating in such a dichotomy requires knowledge and skills of navigation; that is, knowing the right places to go and how to express oneself. To engage in, if not embrace, bisexual or bi-curious aspects of one's life, segregation and privacy of a double life is essential. Use of the term 'bi-curious' is a means to maintain secrecy, as if exploring one's sexuality, rather than a term to describe one's sexual practices. Krystal Nandini Ghisyawan and Marcus Kissoon (see Chapter 2) have explained that, while one of their study participants chose not to name his sexual practices or claim his identity and give himself the privilege of perceiving 'curiosity' as non-commitment, another participant gave himself freedom to both explore his interests and seek pleasure, and to walk away because he has not owned this impermanent aspect of himself. Culturally, the naming of bisexuality or bi-curious is not commonplace in the Caribbean as with Western queer liberal politics. Choosing not to name one's sexual practices or claim a sexual identity, one can evade confirming either as part of one's self-concept; thus, 'curiosity' allows freedom to explore one's interest and seek pleasure (to have your cake and eat it too). In such instances, denial constitutes a safe place. Naming of sexual praxis, for example, is not commonplace in the Caribbean; it is a Western phenomenon. Even with the existence of homosexuality in ancient times and with some evolution in societal attitudes towards homo/bisexuality, 'the heterosexual act has remained the singularly socially acceptable sexual practice and the prevailing interaction among genders in community' and homosexuality has never secured social validation in society (Das and Rao, 2019, p 24).

Older women also participate in invisibility about sexuality and intimacy through not talking about it or not expressing sexual desires to avoid violation of expectation of age-appropriate behaviour. This theme was evident in Chapter 5, addressing intergenerational accounts of older migrant Indian women (to Malaysia) and their daughters. For these women, sexual invisibility is considered an obligation and a respectable role. Womanhood is a cultural role, not an individual identity. Conversely, boundaries of sexuality of older men have evolved more quickly over time, allowing them greater freedom of expression and practice.

The theme of respectability politics emerges repeatedly – in every chapter – and shapes personhood by constraining what forms of sexual performance are deemed acceptable, which are celebrated, and which are punished – which 'body-selves' are allowed to possess or mobilise sexuality and eroticism. Though we can see in Chapter 9 on Indigenous North American 'elders' how culture can propitiate agency concerning later life sexuality. Respectability politics simultaneously imposes the views of the majority and subjugates the struggles of those with minority group membership through the lens of 'normalisation'. In essence, the sexual expression of homosexuality as well as later life sexual expression is muted – another cross-cutting motif – and can reinforce continued marginalisation.

Gender role expectation

Gender role expectation is predicated upon prescribed behaviours and responsibilities of a gender binary affiliation (male and female). Oppositional behaviour is implicit in the binary role expectations, and the conceptualisation of a crossover or shared space violates these expectations. For example, girls and women are supposed to be feminine, polite and nurturing, and boys and men to be masculine, strong and bold. Gender roles are hierarchical and patriarchal. The role of men is expressed through being dependable, respectful and as an adviser in the family and community, whereas the role of women is honoured through domesticity and purity. Binary gender classification includes pressure to conform to traditional notions of masculinity and femininity.

Race and culture further define gender role expectations and behaviour. For example, society projects roles concerning Black male sexuality – what is not only expected but acceptable to fit social expectations. There is a parallel between Afrocentric males thought to embody hegemonic masculinity's sexual prowess and dominance more than other men, for example, Asian and South-Asian-Caribbean men who are desexualised and feminised in public discourse. Public image is important (you are known by the company you keep). If a gay man is dating, being seen with a masculine man rather than a feminine man, or a bisexual person, would legitimise his masculinity (normality). Furthermore, gender role expectations of males are highlighted by Kissoon (2019), whereby a man's masculinity is to be protected and he is discouraged from revealing experience of sexual abuse by a man in childhood because it would disrupt perceptions of his suitability for marriage, being a provider, protector, husband and father (and anything considered non-normative). In Chapter 9, Krystal Nandini Ghisyawan and Marcus Kissoon reveal the potency of expectations of marriage and 'normal' life of Indo-Caribbean male survivors of child sexual abuse that compels them to maintain silence and to promote behaviours of an idealised domestic life. The concept of monogamy developed from the dominant marriage-type practices of a heteronormative environment. The implication is that these types of gender binary relationships have more trust and morality, whereas non-normative relationships are portrayed as flawed, if not pathological. Heteronormative monogamy continues to thrive as the norm because it yields greater reproductive output for survival of the species. Yet, 'romantic love is not heteronormative; instead, it occurs irrespective of sexual orientation or gender' (Bakshi, 2020, p 1). Both religious and cultural values have been used as a measure to disregard the rights and freedoms of people in non-normative sexual relationships in non-Western countries (Amoah et al, 2016).

Honour and responsibility centre on family for men and women. Binary gender role expectations assert motherhood for women and, in India for example, religious and caste endogamy is the practice. Caste endogamy exercises control of female sexuality through normalisation of a discourse that attaches honour and pride of the group to the bodies of its women. The relationship between modernity and tradition of caste endogamy reveals an ongoing patriarchal framework which requires the oppression of women (Ingole, 2021). Sexuality and family are, of course, deeply intertwined, whereas love and marriage are separate entities for most Indian people. Love is emotional but has no validation, and marriage is a serious institution which is fundamental to the hierarchical superstructure of family (Biswal, 2020). In India, marriage can serve as a tool to build and exchange wealth through dowry rituals and to act as an institution to strengthen the caste system (Bakshi, 2020).

Role models

A role model is someone who, by example, demonstrates behaviour and occupies a social role to which others aspire, and assists others in developing similar personal qualities and abilities. Typically, role models are older adults who have had lived experiences that can be used to guide and mentor others. Throughout this volume, a common theme across populations and intergenerationally, is the valuing of role models and elders and mentors. Many people featured in this volume spoke of hiding their queerness because of a lack of role models (elders) to help them prepare and/or envision later life as queer subjects. Participants in interviews with Ghisyawan and Kissoon (see Chapter 2) reflected on the absence of role models of what a queer life could be in the context of traditional ideals of filial piety and expectations from their children. Study participants featuring in Anushkaa Arora's chapter (see Chapter 3) emphasised the need and desire to have elders, who have lived experiences, to guide them through and around treachery encountered early in life that can create difficulties later in life. For example, understanding that faded beauty and being perceived as old greatly reduces capacity to earn a living later in life as a *kinnar* is worth knowing when much younger. Further, older female subjects have stressed the important role of mothers as role models to assist them in their development of womanhood and motherhood. Many subjects appearing in this volume have recognised that role models can offer them valuable lessons. Role models can have direct interaction in an individual's life, or the presence of role models observationally can have a positive impact. In Chapter 10 by Shanon Shah, a textual role model (Khadiji) who was foundational to the story of a faith tradition (Islam) has subsequently been sanitised and/or marginalised.

Another crucial point about role models concerns desires to build community. A community broadly refers to a collection of individuals with common interests that is distinct in some respect from the larger society living. Community was a key theme that emerged from LGBTQ subjects and from two perspectives. One perspective included Black and ethnically diverse LGBTQ individuals who spoke of feeling unwanted in shared spaces (queer spaces) because of racial and ethnic identity. The other perspective centred on reliance on friendship families. Other ways community shows up in the text is in Indigenous communities, elders, *kinnars*, activism, role models and womanhood.

Ageing and being older

It is clear in this volume that ageing is a complex social and cultural process and with profound political ramifications. Avoiding reification of age and ageing, in Chapter 9 Madeline Burns describes ageing as a process in which experiences, and an accumulation of knowledge over the life course, contribute to how sexuality is lived in later life. Similarly, in Chapter 10, Shanon Shah refers to age in Muslim religious sources as an indicator of piety, wisdom, maturity and robust sexuality attributed to elders like the Prophet to suggest ageing as a process of spiritual trial and maturation. Becoming a sexual being differs for men and women, and women can find themselves more desexualised than men as they age because their sexual agency is limited even in youth and middle age. (This point is elaborated later in the theme of sex and sexuality.) LGBTQ people experience developmental crises as they get older (moving from their 20s to their 30s) in trying to find their identity (sense of self and self-actualisation). For many, age 30 counts as old age and their value and worth begin to diminish. Society often conflates beauty [and sexuality] with youth, and self-worth with appearance, which leaves many older LGBTQ people feeling unattractive, insecure and isolated as they age. In general, older adults are challenged by ageist attitudes and perceptions that hinder their sexual expression. Moreover, social constructs of beauty and ageist attitudes towards sexuality in later life are internalised, and many older adults become less sexually active (Gewirtz-Meydan et al, 2018). For older LGBTQ people, such standards contribute to heightened public perceptions of immorality and perversion.

Multiply marginalised people experience intersectional discrimination and devaluation over the life course. If LGBTQ-based discrimination and stigma have colluded with racial, economic and gender inequality to form a labyrinth of challenge for LGBTQ people over the life course, then ageism creates one more maze for older adults (Espinoza, 2016). Variance of devaluation and value of sexuality, gender and age are culturally determined. For example, Indigenous women, two-spirit, femme, and gender and/or sexually diverse people are significant and valued within and across many Indigenous communities. Women are highly respected across many Indigenous communities, as women have frequently held and continue to hold valuable positions and responsibilities. Trans women are fundamentally included from the outset in Indigenous communities because of the value of *all* women. Elders hold a position of respect and authority in the community, which includes normalisation of their sexual citizenship and belonging within the collective sexual imaginary. Again, we gain insight into how such cultures challenge the Western ageist panorama.

Sex and sexuality

Sex is discussed overwhelmingly in biological characteristics of maleness or femaleness and physiological processes related to procreation. Sexuality is commonly identified in terms of identity and attraction, behaviour, pleasures and intimacies. LGBTQ people who conceal sexual orientation and identity are forced to perform asexuality and exist in a desexualised way with family. As discussed earlier, family locality and commitment take precedence over individual desires and sexuality, especially when outside the parameters of 'normalcy'. Numerous participants across several studies in Chapter 2 conducted by Krystal Nandini Ghisyawan and Marcus Kissoon, and that by Barry Lee and Travis S.K. Kong in Chapter 4, expressed loyalty for and respect of family as more important than revealing (coming out about) their sexual orientation. In addition, some participants saw naming their sexual practices as a personal preference. They gave themselves the privilege of being seen in traditional roles in their family and unseen in their alternative identity.

Sexuality and intimacy in older women introduce life transitions that can create opportunities to redefine what sexuality and intimacy mean to them. Changes in the body, health conditions, stress and mental health, and physical problems as one ages can sometimes interfere with the desire and ability to enjoy sex. Concerns about body image and attractiveness also signify. Female sexuality is commonly observed in terms of sexual and reproductive health, with more focus on reproduction rather than intimacy and sexual expression. Often, women's sexuality is confined between giving birth and menopause, with menopause bookmarking the end of female reproduction and, subsequently, sexuality and intimacy. Then, women's sexuality becomes the focus of symptomology of menopause and deficit and dysfunctionality on arousal and orgasm, and by extension, frequency of and satisfaction with sexual activity. In essence, women's sexuality is constructed as pathological and dysfunctional. This recalls Simone de Beauvoir's work (1949), which observed that woman represents the 'other', the not-man, that needs explanation since man represents the default of humanity. Her thinking also acknowledged that, while women are in an oppressed group, they do not have a shared history of means of organising into a cohesive group (Library of Congress, nd). However, the female subjects featuring in the chapter by Shereen El-Feki and Selma Hajri offer a wider purview and insights, from indicating sexist and 'traditional' concerns about perceived loss of attractiveness (and thus value) to greater opportunities for more liberated lovemaking. Nevertheless, class and educational attainment significantly influence women's response to menopause and sexuality over the life course and less educated women report significantly elevated symptoms and signs of depression. More highly educated women were more able to talk positively about menopause. Such factors are significant because, in the Middle East, women are living longer and are likely to spend more than a third of their life in post-menopause.

As observed in Chapter 6 on older women in the Middle East and North Africa (MENA), menopause can be framed by women as a benefit: an excuse to finally evade sexual intercourse with husbands whom they did not like and did not choose. Some women found menopause to be a useful pretext to finally refuse sex with their husbands, particularly in cases of unhappy arranged marriages or histories of intimate partner violence (Hashemiparast et al, 2022). Yet other older women could leverage sex as a tool of empowerment and agency to keep husbands in line. Moreover, menopause did not reflect the end of femininity. Indeed, older women in MENA were looking for communication, companionship and romance and support from husbands during menopause. Desire, however, was not the sole determinant of sexual activity; many women also saw a need to conform to sexual scripts that frame women's fulfilment of their husbands' sexual needs as a religious duty and therefore continued sexual relations irrespective of their own waning desire. Older women with older children thought it unseemly to continue sexual relations when they had children old enough to have sexual needs of their own, and preferred to define themselves in asexual terms as mothers, rather than as sexual beings. We saw in Chapter 5 on Indian migrant women to Malaysia, in transitioning into later life, older women shared with their daughters marriage talk that consists of bridegroom worthiness and finding a husband to adhere to cultural propriety, rather than conversation about sexual intimacy when preparing for marriage. In these conversations, daughters in Sally Anne Param's study in the same chapter spoke of how they, not their parents, broached the topic of sex: even aunts and mothers-in-law were purveyors of information rather than their own mothers.

Further, older women can be marginalised because of multi-layered exclusion, for example, gendered ageism can deny them recognisable social space to talk about sex and intimacy even when they were younger. The intergenerational cycle for women of the complex, reciprocal relationship between being female and subscribing to cultural norms –- the process of nurturing children to grow up, get married and have children – can desexualise women's identity while promoting an existence based on procreation and sustaining family. Sex and sexual intimacy seem to be the means to have children, period. Apart from mothers, the younger women had important relationships with other female members within the extended family who supported the younger women's growth as individuals. These supportive relations celebrate the importance of kin within the community and clearly evidence how intergenerational kin-based female empowerment can challenge and even overcome private patriarchy. Again, the importance of family resonates as a constant theme: as constraint and as resource for autonomy.

Considering knowledge gaps concerning ageing sexuality and intimacy in diverse global South and East cultures, there are small but important shifts in intergenerational dynamics. While we have highlighted capitalism as a force for marginalisation and constraint, there are aspects of it that have enabled women's empowerment in terms of exercising agency to subvert certain patriarchal practices in their own culture. In Chapter 5, Sally Anne Param discusses the attitudes of older migrant Indian women in Malaysia as a rebuttal to gendered discrimination within the capitalist workforce in India, especially as women are part of the narrative of economic planning and workforce development. She concludes that while social location shapes the lives of women in ways distinct from men's lives, the connective strength of the mother–daughter dyads helps to subvert patriarchy. The relationships with other women members within the extended family such as grandmothers, mothers-in-law, sisters, aunts, and other kin help provide a support network that could be used to counter the hegemony of patriarchy. This source of female power encouraged the resilience and agency required to challenge household-based patriarchy. A few of the older women shared (only) marginal accounts of intimacy, such as hugging openly or holding hands with their husbands. The daughters, however, shared accounts of liberties their mothers did not encounter.

Another key theme concerns the distinction between same-sex admiration and attraction. For example, the admiration of the appearance of the Prophet Muhammad in his older years by younger men is not necessarily sexual or even erotic, but they are intimate (personal) and even sensual (sensory). There is room for intimacy between persons of the same sex without sexual activity or even interaction. In Chapter 10, Shanon Shah has explained how Bara, one of Muhammad's followers, commenting on the beauty of Muhammad's body, is not necessarily erotic or sexual, but at least is an example of homosocial bonding that was sensual and intimate. The same writer also highlights the double standard in texts concerning older Muslim men's and older Muslim women's sexuality, where older men are given the permission to live as active sexual beings and older women are denied this freedom. Indeed, older women's life cycle (menstruation to menopause) is barely mentioned in one key text covered in this chapter, and tolerance of the sexuality of older women is non-existent.

Furthermore, in Chapter 4, analysing gay coupled relationships in Hong Kong, attention was centred on monogamy (gay couple relationships) plus polygamy (gay secondary relationships). Such relationships allowed for one partner to engage in an intimate and sexual relationship with another while maintaining integrity of the primary relationship. As a couple aged and their sexual interests began to differ, the intimate relationship remained intact. Thus, monogamy plus polygamy presented a way to preserve a valued relationship. In Hong Kong's gay culture, sexual agreement appears commonplace and there are different forms of agreement in which all parties involved can give consent to engage in romantic, intimate and/or sexual relationships with multiple partners. In this context, participation in a partner 'plus' relationship does not have to be sexual; it can function to help men socialise. Although there is some openness within the gay community in Hong Kong, gay men may find it difficult to be open with their family because of stigmatisation and lack of protective legislation. Yet, in Chapter 4, participants in Barry Lee's and Travis S.K. Kong's study, while affected by heteronormative sexual norms, demonstrate how older Chinese gay men can manipulate and manage their lives between the oppression of heteronormativity and youth-oriented homonormative culture.

Issues emerging from the volume

Issues in this volume are an extension of themes that further provide elaboration on topics of concern. Although the issues that evolved may not offer resolutions, contributing authors offer many opportunities for introspection and reflection. Some of these issues highlighted are population-specific but all of them suggest a fruitful agenda and avenues for further and more specific research.

First, we observe that commonly older women are perceived mainly in their role as procreators and mothers, and not as sexual beings with desires. As women age, their identity as sexual beings is further marginalised and, as a corollary, their sexuality in later life is viewed as dysfunctional. Menopause and decline in mental health are highly correlated in women exhibiting signs of depression. Medicalisation of the menopause and sexuality, with its emphasis on sexual function (or rather, dysfunction) and performance is ill-suited to the more nuanced approach that is needed to illuminate both the fine details and the broad strokes of intimacy in later life. Chapter 6 by Shereen El-Feki and Selma Hajri demonstrates that it is not surprising that symptomology of and attitudes towards menopause are 'intimately' entwined. Moreover, in traditional societies, much value is placed on childbearing and rearing. Older women viewed mothering techniques and practices above and beyond any other self-expression, sexual or not. Their success has been raising good daughters as members of society with their own families in tow. The same chapter concludes, therefore, that what is needed is more social and less medical science to help convert a putative 'age of despair' into a time of fulfilment and self-reclamation for older women across the MENA.

A clear issue repeated through this volume is that women still cannot enjoy the freedom of expression in relation to open discussions on sex and intimacy. In Chapters 5 and 7, Sally Anne Param and Nafhesa Ali, respectively, found that older women choose partially to remain mute about their private intimate encounters. Their lived reality lies within the safe confines of heterosexual monogamous marriages. In Nafhesa Ali's study, older women's experience of desexualisation ramified intergenerationally, whereby moving into the revered elder position, they can impose sexual and sociocultural recommendations on others. Here, older women transmit and transfer their own gendered expectations onto younger generations that are rooted in the same foundations of their own socialisation of honour, gender and sexuality and are frequently framed within heteronormative practices. For older women, now in later life, early marriage (child marriage) was common, leading to premature sexualisation of women and girls through marriage. Among participants, both contributors found that for older, diasporan Indian women, sex and intimacy registered as superficial concerns that were difficult to address even in private conversations.

Under the current climate influenced by heteronormativity and ageism, older gay men's intimate lives have for the most part remained closeted, resulting in constraints on their basic rights imposed by society. In their respective chapters, Krystal Nandini Ghisyawan and Marcus Kissoon (Chapter 2), and Barry Lee and Travis S.K. Kong (Chapter 4), found that religious opposition, micro-aggressions and acts of violence still occur against gay men, despite decriminalisation of sexual practices of consenting adults both in Trinidad and Tobago and in Hong Kong.

As explored by Cuauhtémoc Sanchez Vega in Chapter 8, society and culture have a determining influence on the regulation of erotic life, of sexual practices and their manifestations, though this chapter also drew attention to older (Purépecha) women's sexual agency in the face of constraints. Such regulations do not work in the same way for men as for women; female oppression is evident in some backgrounds when women must assume obligatory reproduction, oversee domestic services without any remuneration, and show fidelity. It is assumed as a social and cultural mandate that pleasure is linked to reproduction, which is only valid within marriage: marriage and reproduction that women do not necessarily want or enjoy, but whose goal is to preserve family. It seems that the only event that can dissolve the mandate of imposed monogamy on women is the death of the spouse, which opens a small possibility of recuperating desire and erotic experience. Society and culture become so determining and quasi-totalising that even after the relationship ends due to the death of the spouse, for women social surveillance endures.

The discourse and practices of romantic love linked to monogamy specifically for women legitimise a system of oppression, of their relationships, bodies, desires and lives; since romantic love includes by definition monogamous fidelity, and this also introduces a series of demands such as: (a) exclusivity in its different manifestations (emotional, affective, sexual, relational); and (b) possession/property, which naturally brings with it the idea that this 'all of mine' concretely and symbolically represents possession of affections, of the body, desires and pleasures and even of the life of the partner. It should be made clear that all these factors invariably apply to women, though it works the same way for men, at least in a symbolic way.

In this volume, we have also seen how the state targets Indigenous women, girls, two-spirit, femmes, and sexually and/or gender diverse folks, whose existence, influence in Indigenous political orders, and value is directly oppositional to the state's character and foundational values, exposing its self-proclaimed sovereignty as invalid. In Chapter 9, Madeline Burns asserts that this targeted 'logic of elimination' results in a 'death drive' of the state, which is continually present and demonstrated by the horrifying rate of murdered and missing Indigenous girls, women, femmes, two-spirit and sexually and/or gender diverse peoples 'in' so-called 'Canada'.

In the majority world, many of the 'hard' attitudes concerning gender and sexuality (for example, patriarchal values, anti-queer attitudes, and so on) correlate with the relative 'new-ness' of independent post-colonial states (that is, attitudes towards gender and sexuality are influenced by an anticolonial or anti-Western factor). But, as the first and second generations of post-independent citizens mature/get older, have their attitudes changed? If yes, why? If no, why not? Further research could question how state polities can engender a shift in public attitudes. For example, the 'Women, Life, Freedom' protests in Iran clearly show the disjuncture between the Iranian and monumental societal shifts on a range of issues and where gender and sexuality are core to the struggle against fundamentalist, theocratic oppression.

The instances represented in this volume largely reflect countries/cultures unmarked by persistent instability. It may, then, be more urgent to examine ageing sexuality within countries with a more recent history of conflict (however caused), such as Afghanistan, Iraq, Liberia, Sierra Leone, Venezuela, Vietnam, and so on. Further, we might also consider investigating attitudinal shifts in ageing sexuality that could be affected by the turmoil of climate change, which is impacting more deleteriously on majority world populations. With the steady worsening of the climate crisis, it is the people who are most vulnerable to it (and who have done the least to cause it) who will suffer the most, such as those in the Caribbean, South America, sub-Saharan Africa, the Pacific, the Middle East, South and Southeast Asia, and so on. We might ask how would such an existential threat affect notions of sexual intimacy and later life in these populations, that is, in situations where older people are leaving behind a world in which younger people are very likely to lead very bleak and difficult lives?

Conclusion

Later life sex and intimacy in the majority world is an under-explored area and has been viewed and researched mostly from a Western orientation. We hope to have made an important start in highlighting key themes and political issues and, hopefully, inspiring further thought and research on later life sex and intimacy in cultures that are occluded by obsession with and hegemony of the global North and West and on its terms. Research on sexuality and ageing in the majority world issues a call to produce theories of homonormativity in and through a broader range of places in order to challenge global biases that have been reinforced by a narrow geographic range of places (that is, Western) that are repeatedly studied (Browne and McCartan, 2020). Moreover, sexualities of the majority world are being reimagined by their own cultures and decolonised, for example African sexualities (Livermon, 2018).

Contributors to this volume assert several perspectives. Erotic (hi)stories can represent older women and femmes as people with experience and knowledge, as well as assert them as sexual agents, people who are desirable and may bear desires themselves. Perceptions and interpretations of age and sexuality can be presented positively or negatively to best fit the situation. Moreover, there is not a dichotomy in which a single analytical perspective triumphs, but a mixture of both along a continuum wherein lies that which you seek. Gendered ageism in intimacy is prevalent, giving men across the sexual spectrum more freedom than women. Sexuality in older women is no longer to be viewed mostly from a pathological perspective, though women are generally more likely to be perceived as unsexual as they age. In addition, the term sex does not refer only to partnered sex and intercourse but various expressions of sexuality and sexual possibilities, including emotional and physical intimacy (Gore-Gorszewska, 2021). Although sexual changes in ageing are a normal part of the developmental process, understanding these changes behaviourally and culturally may help destigmatise their sexual expression.

In the future, as we continue to do research on and with the majority world, it is crucial that focus is given to several areas of sex in later life, including mental health; disability; sexuality, gender and intersectionality; and application of the Sexual Equity Framework (Fredriksen-Goldsen, 2023) adopted for application with the majority world. The concept of intersectionality (Crenshaw (1989) in research on sexuality and ageing is crucial to challenge a one-dimensional identity of sexuality and the systems of power and patriarchy that continue to dictate what and who is acceptable (Browne and McCartan, 2020). Curley and Johnson (2022) suggest that it is time for a new revolution in sexuality and ageing that is socially admirable and desirable. Thus, understanding sexual fluidity as adults age is also an important area yet to be studied. Finally, LGBTQ individuals are becoming an increasingly visible segment of the global population. However, due to cultural and structural stigma many still conceal their identities and sexual expression because it is unwise to reveal or positively claim them (Pachankis and Branstrom, 2019). For this reason, movement towards understanding identity, sexuality and culture is vitally important.

References

Amoah, P.A., Gyasi, R.M., and Halsall, J. (2016). Social Institutions and Same-sex Sexuality: Attitudes, Perceptions and Prospective Rights and Freedoms for Non-heterosexuals. *Cogent Social Sciences,* 2(1). https://doi.org/10.1080/23311886.2016.1198219

Bakshi, T. (2020). Challenging the Heteronormative Ideas of Love: A Commentary on Love and Marriage in the Popular Imagination with a Special Focus on India. *Feminism in India.* https://feminisminindia.com/2020/12/15/challenging-the-heteronormative-ideas-of-love

Bettinsoil, M.L., Suppes, A., and Napier, J. (2019). Predictors of Attitudes toward Gay Men and Lesbian Women in 23 Countries. *Social Psychological and Personality Science,* 11(5). https://doi.org/10.1177/1948550619887785

Biswal, B. (2020). *Indian Matchmaking and the Tradition of Caste Endogamy.* www.youthkiawaaz.com/2020/07/indian-matchmaking-and-the-tradition-of-caste-endogamy

Browne, K., and McCartan, A. (2020). Sexuality and Queer Geographies. In A. Kobayashi (ed), *International Encyclopaedia of Human Geography* (2nd edn), Amsterdam, Netherlands: Elsevier: pp 185–94.

Buckle, L. (nd). *African Sexuality and the Legacy of Imported Homophobia.* www.stonewall.org.uk/about-us/news/african-sexuality-and-legacy-imported-homophobia

Clarke, L.H. (2010). Older Women and Sexuality: Experiences in Marital Relationships across the Life Course. *Canadian Journal on Aging/La Revue Canadienne Du Vieillissement,* 25(2), 129–40. https://doi.org/10.1353/cja.2006.0034

Crenshaw, K. (1989). Demarginalising the Intersection of Race and Sex: A Black Feminist Critique of Antidiscrimination Doctrine, Feminist Theory and Antiracist Politics. *University of Chicago Legal Forum,* Issue 1, Article 8. https://chicagounbound.uchicago.edu/uclf/vol1989/iss1/8

Curley, C.M., and Johnson, B.T. (2022). Sexuality and Aging: Is it Time for a New Sexual Revolution? *Social Science & Medicine,* 301. https://doi.org/10.1016/j.socscimed.2022.114865

Das, K., and Rao, T.S.S. (2019). A Chronicle of Sexuality in the Indian Subcontinent. *Journal of Psychosexual Health,* 1(1), 20–5. https://doi.org/10.1177/2631831818822017

De Beauvoir, S. (1949). *The Second Sex,* New York: Alfred A. Knopf.

Dudek, D., Boyd, E.R., and Grobbelaar, M. (2022). 'I Want an Orgasm but Not Just Any Orgasm': How to Please a Woman Shifts the Way We Depict the Sexuality of Older Women. *The Conversation.* https://theconversation.com/i-want-an-orgasm-but-not-just-any-orgasm-how-to-please-a-woman-shifts-the-way-we-depict-the-sexuality-of-older-women-183129

Espinoza, R. (2016). *LGBT People: Let's Talk about Ageism.* https://lgbtagingcenter.org/resources/resource.cfm?r=447

Fredriksen-Goldsen, K. (2023). Blueprint for Future Research Advancing the Study of Sexuality, Gender and Equity in Later Life: Lessons Learned from Aging with Pride, the National Health, Aging, and Sexuality/Gender Study (NHAS). *Gerontologist,* 63(2), 373–81. https://doi.org/10.1093/geront/gnac146

Gewirtz-Meydan, A., Hafford-Letchfield, T., Benyamini, Y., Phelan, A., Jackson, J., and Ayalon, L. (2018). Ageism and Sexuality. In Ayalon, L., and Tesch-Romer, C. (eds), *Contemporary Perspectives on Ageism,* Switzerland: Springer International Publishing: pp 149–62.

Givens, M. (2022). *Queer and Caribbean: LGBTQ+ Culture and the Island Identity.* www.therainbowtimesmass.com/queer-and-caribbean-lgbtq-culture-the-island-identity/

Gore-Gorszewska, G. (2021). 'What do you mean Sex?' A Qualitative Analysis of Traditional Versus Evolved Meaning of Sexual Activity Among Older Women and Men. *Journal of Sex Research,* 58, 1035–49. https://doi.org:10.1080/00224499.2020.1798333

Han, E., and O'Mahoney, J. (2018). *British Colonialism and the Criminalization of Homosexuality: Queens, Crime and Empire,* London and New York: Routledge.

Hashemiparast, M., Naderi, B., Chattu, V.K., and Allahverdipour, H. (2022). Perceived Barriers of Expression of Sexual Desires among Older Adults: A Qualitative Study. *Sexual and Relationship Therapy,* 38, 1–14. https://doi.org/10.1080/14681994.2022.2056590

Ingole, A. (2021). Caste Endogamy. In *Caste Panchayats and Caste Politics in India,* Singapore: Palgrave Macmillan: pp 143–73.

Kissoon, M. (2019). *Processes of Disclosure and Gender Negotiations Amongst Indo-Caribbean Male Survivors of Child Sexual Abuse/Sexual Assault.* Master's Thesis. Institute for Gender and Development Studies, University of the West Indies, Trinidad.

Library of Congress. (nd). *Feminism & French Women in History: A Resource Guide.* https://guides.loc.gov/feminism-women-history/famous/simone-de-beauvoir

Livermon, X. (2018). Colonialism and African Sexualities. In Shanguhyia, M., and Falola, T. (eds) *The Palgrave Handbook of African Colonial and Postcolonial History*, New York: Palgrave Macmillan: pp 1175–91.

Massey, S.G., Chen, M.-H., and Young, S. (2021). Feminism's Legacy Sees College Women Embracing More Diverse Sexuality. *The Conversation.* https://theconversation.com/feminisms-legacy-sees-college-women-embracing-more-diverse-sexuality-159023

Mishra, S., and Dey, A.K. (2022). Understanding and Identifying Themes in Qualitative Case Study Research. *South Asian Journal of Business and Management Cases,* 11(3), 187–92. https://doi.org/10.1177/22779779221134659

Pachankis, J.E., and Branstrom, R. (2019). How Many Sexual Minorities Are Hidden? Projecting the Size of the Global Closet with Implications for Policy and Public Health. *PlosOne.* https://doi.org/10.1371/journal.pone.0218084

Poushter, J., and Kent, N.O. (2020). *The Global Divide on Homosexuality Persists.* www.pewresearch.org/global/2020/06/25/global-divide-on-homosexuality-persists/

Thomas, H. (2015). Correlates of Sexual Activity and Satisfaction in Midlife and Older Women. *Annals of Family Medicine,* 13(4), 336–42. https://doi.org/10.1370.afm.1820

Index

A

Abu Nuwas 188–189
adultery in Purépecha society 141–142
age-differentiated model of homosexuality 179, 180–181, 185–187
'age of despair' 93–94
'age of renewal' 94
ageing xvii, 2–3, 198–199
   and ageism, *kinnars* in COVID-19 pandemic 40–41, 42, 43–48, 50
   as contextualised 5
   contrasts between traditional and Western societies 3, 97
   decolonising and queering 165–166
   desexualisation and 123–127
   differing thresholds of 5, 192
   intersecting with sexuality and intimacy xviii–xix
   linear time and 162
   and older age referenced in Muslim sources 182–184
   queer men lacking models for 26–27
   and relationships for older gay men 33–34, 59–60
ageism
   and ageing, *kinnars* in COVID-19 pandemic 40–41, 42, 43–48, 50
   in gay community 56
   in Hong Kong 56, 61
   gendered 46, 51, 205
   in Malaysia 77
ageist erotophobia 46
Aisha 177–178, 182, 183
Ali, K. 176, 178, 182, 183
Ali, N. 116, 125, 129
amrad 180–181, 184
anal sex (*liwat*) 180, 183
Ardener, S. 10, 77, 78

B

'bad education' 151–152
badhai dena (blessing a new born baby) 41, 48
Bannerjee, D. 42, 43
Barkman, L.L.S. 77, 78, 79, 89
Beauvoir, S. de 199
Berger, J. 121, 129
Berlant, L. 55, 57, 161
Bettinsoil, M.L. 193, 194
Bhabha, H. 121, 127
Bhartrihari 40
'bi-curious' 28, 195
Binoojiinh Makes a Lovely Discovery' 166–167

bodies of women as sites of *izzat* 118, 120–123
Burns, M.M.L. 159, 166, 170

C

capitalism 3, 201
   links with colonialism 2, 7
   neocolonialist 15, 16
   patriarchal 15, 78
   positioning of home in 77–78, 82
   temporal structures and 162, 166
caste endogamy 197
Chattha, L. 116, 117, 118, 119, 122
child abuse 26, 175, 196
'child care' 85–86
child-marriages 122, 124–125
   Aisha 177–178, 182, 183
China, gay-friendly spaces in mainland 61
Chinese diaspora in Malaysia 76
Chinese gay men in Hong Kong 9–10, 54–71, 201–202
   being single 58–61, 66
      and preferring monogamy 58–60
      and preferring polyamory 60–61
   Confucianism 54, 55, 56–57, 63, 66
   homosexuality in Hong Kong 55–58, 67–68, 194
   Confucianism 56–57
   doing intimacy in a Chinese context 57–58, 66
   heteronormativity and homonormativity 55–56, 203
   long-term couple/committed relationships 61–66, 66–67
      1+1: negotiated monogamy 61–62
      2+ many: gay couple relationship plus anonymous sex 65–66
      2+ many: heterosexual marriage plus anonymous sex 64
      2+1: gay couple relationship plus gay secondary relationship 63–64
      2+1: heterosexual marriage plus homosexual romance 62–63
   methodology 58
   participants 58
Christianity 27, 55, 157, 178
Clarke, L.H. 193
climate change 204–205
closeted, gay men remaining 24, 57, 61, 62–63, 64, 68, 194–195
Colaizzi, P. 8, 39, 43–44, 50
colonialism
   capitalism and links with 2, 7

erasure of Indo-Trinidadian queer men 21–24
heteronormativity via Western religion and 55
homophobia a by-product of 193
perspectives on gender 22, 38, 161–162
and sexual repression in South Asia 117, 120–121
see also settler colonialism
'coming out'
  deciding against 24, 57, 61, 62–63, 64, 68, 194–195
  Western concept of 9, 24, 56–57
community building 31–34, 35, 57, 197–198
companionship 60, 66
compartmentalisation 24–30
Confucianism 54, 55, 56–57, 63, 66, 67
COVID-19 pandemic *see kinnars* in COVID-19 pandemic
cultural capital 86
culture
  'bad education' and questioning of 151–152
  and creativity 145
  influences on sex-erotic life of women in Purépecha society 147–149
  restrictions on sexual and erotic expression 144–145

D

Dávalos López, E. 140, 141, 142, 144
death of a spouse 148–149
decolonisation 162
  and queering of age and time 165–167
  and queering of relationalities 167–170, 170–171
The Delight of Hearts 184, 185–187, 188, 189
desexualisation
  and carrying honour (*izzat*) in later life 123–127, 128
  of gay men 26, 199
  of Indian masculinity 23
  of Indo-Trinidadian older women 33
  of older *kinnars* 47–48, 50
domestic violence 28–29
'don't-ask-don't-tell' strategies 65
'double life', leading a 27–30, 62–63
Douglass, M. 76, 82, 88
drag personas 25, 31–33
Driskill, Q. 2, 158, 159, 161

E

early marriage 122, 124–125
  of Aisha 177–178, 182, 183
eco-erotic (hi)stories 157, 163–165
  'Binoojiinh Makes a Lovely Discovery' 166–167
  decolonising and queering age and time 165–167

disrupting understandings of relationality 167–170, 170–171
knowledge sharing 163
'Why Ravens Smile to Little Old Ladies as They Walk by…' 163–164
'The Woman Who Married the Beaver' 164–165
education
  'bad' 151–152
  kinnars and differences of 46–47
  level and women's response to menopause 97, 98–99, 200
  prioritising of children's 83, 84, 85, 87
  sexual 104–105, 106
embodied knowledge 33
Esteban Galarza, M.L. 140, 147, 153

F

familial heteronormativity 9, 57
family honour and respectability 24–30, 34–35, 66, 67, 194–195
see also honour/respect (*izzat*)
El-Feki, S. 94, 95, 98, 106
female labour
  domestic 38, 76, 77–78, 85
  in workplace 77–78, 85, 88–89
feminist theory frameworks 77–79, 87, 89
femmes 158–159, 165, 166, 167, 170
  'Canadian' state targeting of 161–162
  see also Indigenous elders as sexual agents through storytelling
Ferrand, F. 98, 99
filial piety and duty
  Confucian beliefs in 55, 56–57, 63, 66
  Indo-Trinidadian queer men fulfilling expectations of 25–26
  in lives of gay Chinese men 62–63, 66, 67
France 99
Fredriksen-Goldsen, K. 43, 59, 68, 205
future research 204–205, 205–206

G

Gandhi, M.K. 122
gay saunas 61, 65
gender
  'Canadian' state targeting of Indigenous people on basis of 161–162
  changing attitudes in majority world to 204
  colonial perspectives on 22, 38, 161–162
  global attitudes to gender identity variance 193
  Indigenous understandings of sexuality and 158–159
  role expectation 196–197
  scripts, Indo-Caribbean women conforming to 23–24
  and sexuality in India 38–39
  legislation to liberalise non-normative expressions 39, 41, 48–50, 51

Index

'third gender' cultures in Muslim environments 179–180
gendered ageism 46, 51, 205
gendered power asymmetries 143–144
gendered violence during Partition 117, 118–119
Ghisyawan, K.N. 24, 25, 28
Giddens, A. 9, 57, 66
global North and West 39
  ageing sexualities 2–3, 97
  misunderstanding of sexual cultures of global South/East 3
  thresholds for ageing 5
global South and East 1–2
  North/West misunderstanding of sexual cultures of 3
  thresholds for ageing 5, 192

H

Hafford-Letchfield, T. xv, xix, 3
Hajri, S. 98, 99, 100
head coverings 21, 126
healthcare
  kinnars 47–48, 49, 51
  sexual 43, 51, 62
  sexual and reproductive health provision in MENA 95, 103–107
hegemonic masculinity 22–23, 29, 196
  fusing of homonormativity and 56
heteronormativity 55, 64, 161
  being gay and influenced by 59, 60
  and development of monogamy 196
  'familial' 9, 57
  and homonormativity 55–56
  overlapping with settler colonialism 161
  queer as disrupting 162
  resisting 61, 64, 66, 67
heterosexuality
  Islamic assertions of male-dominated 181
  positioned as the norm 55, 161, 195
Hockey, J.L. 3
'holiday sex' 62
homonormative masculinity 56
homonormativity 61, 62, 66, 67
  and heteronormativity 55–56
homophobia 63, 181, 193
homosexuality
  age-differentiated model of 179, 180–181, 185–187
  attitudes in Trinidad and Tobago to 24
  decriminalisation of 24, 35, 39, 55
  global attitudes to 193–194
  in Hong Kong 55–58, 67–68, 194
  Islamic homosexualities 179–181
  Islamic laws on 179
  Pentecostal church pastor on 27
  terminology in Arabic 93
  Western 'modern' homosexualities 179
homosociality 57–58, 178, 183, 201

Hong Kong *see* Chinese gay men in Hong Kong
honour/respect *(izzat)*
  desexualisation and carrying 123–127, 128
  women's bodies as sites of 118, 120–123
  see also family honour and respectability
Hosein, S. 23, 28

I

imaginative activity, restrictions on 145
India
  caste endogamy 197
  gender and sexuality in 38–39
  legal reforms 39, 41, 48–50, 51
  intersex individuals 49
  sexuality in older adults 43
  see also kinnars in COVID-19 pandemic; Partition of India, child survivors in later life
Indian masculinity 21, 23
Indian women in urban Malaysia, intimacy in lives of 10–11, 75–92
  child-bearing 86, 87
  female labour 76, 77–78, 85, 88–89
  feminist theory frameworks 77–79, 87, 89
  Marxist-feminist theory 77–78
  Muted Group Theory 77, 78–79, 89
  household management 76, 82, 89
  inter-ethnic diasporic past 75–77
  marriage 84–85, 86
  mothering role 82, 83, 84–85, 87, 89, 202
  participants 77, 79, 80
  patriarchy 77, 78, 79, 85
    female power subverting 86, 87–88, 201
    proximity to natal family 81–82, 86–87
  research design 79–81
  sexual silence of older 76, 77, 79, 83, 84, 87, 88, 89, 195
  shifts in intergenerational dynamics 77, 84, 88, 89
  shows of affection between parents 82
  'study hard' vs. romance and intimacy 83, 84–85, 87
Indigenous elders as sexual agents through storytelling 13–14, 157–173, 195, 198–199
  decolonising and queering age and time 165–167
  decolonising and queering relationalities 167–170, 170–171
  elders as eco-erotic storytellers and sexual beings 163–165
    Binoojiinh Makes a Lovely Discovery' 166–167
    'Why Ravens Smile to Little Old Ladies as They Walk by...' 163–164
    'The Woman Who Married the Beaver' 164–165

self-location 159–161
terminology 157–159
theoretical framework 161–162
understandings of sexuality and gender 158–159
Indo-Caribbean women
conforming to gender scripts 23–24
desexualising of older 33
domestic violence towards 28–29
orhni 21
queer 22, 24
Tanties 32, 33
Indo-Trinidadian masculinity 22, 23, 28–29, 196
Indo-Trinidadian queer men 7–8, 21–37, 195, 203
ageing and difficulties in meeting romantic partners 33–34
creating queer community 31–34, 35
Indo-Caribbean identity 21
lack of role models for building a 'queer life' 26–27, 35, 197
maintaining family honour and respectability 24–30, 34–35, 196
postcolonial erasure of 21–24
silencing sexuality with family 24–26
social media use 30, 34
infidelity in Purépecha society 141–142
intersectionality xviii–xix, 205–206
intersex individuals in India 49
intimacy xviii
creating queer community 31–34
decolonising and queering relationalities of 167–170
double standard for older men and women 189
emotional and sexual 60
gendered ageism in 205
intersecting with sexuality and ageing xviii–xix
menopause and 96–97, 99, 100, 102, 199
for older Chinese gay men in Hong Kong 54, 57–58, 66, 66–68
being single 58–61
long-term couple/committed relationships 61–66
older women encouraging appropriate behaviours 125–126
in Western sociology 57
see also Indian women in urban Malaysia, intimacy in lives of; Muslim contexts, sex, intimacy and older life in
in/visibility and ambivalence 7–10, 194–195
older migrant Indian women 76, 77, 79, 83, 84, 87, 88, 89, 195
see also Chinese gay men in Hong Kong; Indo-Trinidadian queer men; *kinnars* in COVID-19 pandemic

Iran
amrad 180–181, 184
homosexuality 180–181
menopause 102–103
educating men on 106
sexual and reproductive health provision 103
'Women, Life, Freedom' protests 204
issues 1–6, 15–16, 202–205
izzat (honour respect)
desexualisation and carrying 123–127, 128
women's bodies as sites of 118, 120–123
see also family honour and respectability

J
James, A. 3

K
Kent, N.O. 193
Khadija 176–177, 182
kinnars in COVID-19 pandemic 8–9, 38–53, 197, 198
ageing and ageism 40–41, 42, 43–48, 50
aged 23–35, fear of loss of youth and beauty 41, 44–45, 50
aged 38–45, distancing from 'older' category 42, 45–47, 50
aged 65 and 68, desexualisation 47–48, 50
badhai dena (blessing a new born baby) 41, 48
context 41–42
for older *kinnars* 42–43
education differences 46–47
legal reforms 39, 41, 48–50, 51
marriage 50
medical healthcare 47–48, 49, 51
methods and data collection 43–44, 50
need to address and resolve problems of older 50–51
numbers of older 41
sex work 41, 45, 48
victims of hate crimes and hostility 40–41
kinship
ethics 169–170
system and exchange of women 142–143
Kissoon, M. 26, 196
knowledge
embodied 33
sharing 163
Kong, T.S.K. 55, 56, 57, 58, 61, 64, 66

L
'La Relación' 139, 140, 141, 142–143, 144
labour, female
domestic 38, 76, 77–78, 85
in workplace 77–78, 85, 88–89
Lee, B. 63, 64
legal reforms, transgender 39, 41, 48–50, 51

Index

legal restrictions on sex 178–179
LGBTQ people
  ageing 198
  'coming out'
    deciding against 24, 57, 61, 62–63, 64, 68, 194
    Western concept of 9, 24, 56–57
  community building 31–34, 35, 57, 197–198
  global attitudes to 193–194
  invisibility 7–10, 194–195
  Muslim attitudes to 174, 179–181
  support networks 57
  see also Chinese gay men in Hong Kong; Indo-Trinidadian queer men; *kinnars* in COVID-19 pandemic; queer; transgender people
life expectancy 2, 97
liwat (anal sex) 180, 183
'logic of elimination' 161–162, 204
losing face 56, 63

M

Malaysia *see* Indian women in urban Malaysia, intimacy in lives of
marriage
  early 122, 124–125, 177–178, 182, 183
  filial piety and expectations of procreation and 25–26, 55
  gay men in heterosexual marriages 62–63, 64
  in India 197
  Indian women in urban Malaysia 84–85, 86
  kinnars 50
  for love as a modern invention 149
  Prophet Muhammad 176–178, 182, 183
  in Purépecha society 140–142, 148
  reproduction and 56, 148, 196, 203
  status in Tunisia 98
Marxist-feminist theory 77–78
masculinity
  Black 23, 196
  hegemonic 22–23, 29, 56, 196
  homonormative 56
  Indian 21, 23
  Indo-Trinidadian 22, 23, 28–29, 196
  role in same-sex behaviours 59
menopause 95–97, 200
  'age of despair' 93–94
  'age of renewal' 94
  and constructs of sexual dysfunction 95, 96, 99, 100–101, 102, 199, 202
  cross-cultural comparisons between France and Tunisia 99
  in MENA 97–103
    Iran 102–103
    Tunisia 98–100
    Turkey 100–101

  men's understanding and support for partners during 105–106
  need for improved health and social support systems in MENA 103–107
  numbers of women post- 97
  social status after 97, 99–100, 101
mental health 41, 68
  issues for trans people 41, 42, 43
  menopause and decline in 199, 202
Middle East and North Africa, women's sexuality in later life in 11–12, 93–114, 199, 200, 202–203
  Arabic literature on sex 94–95
  in Iran 102–103
  life expectancy for women 97
  menopause 95–97
  naming and reclaiming 93–95
  and relations with husbands 99, 100, 101, 102, 103, 104, 105–106
  sexual and reproductive health provision 95, 103–107
  sexual education 104–105, 106
  in Tunisia 98–99
    comparisons with France 99
  in Turkey 100–101
  women's rights groups 104–105
monogamy
  eco-erotic (hi)stories challenging ideas of 168
  gay single men preferring 59–60
  heteronormativity and development of 196
  'negotiated' and 'modified' 61–62, 66, 67
  obligatory 148, 149, 150, 153, 203
  romantic love and 149–150, 153, 204
more-than-human-beings 157–158, 168–169, 170
  eco-erotic (hi)stories 163–165, 167
mothering role 82, 83, 84–85, 87, 89, 202
Muhammad, Prophet 176–179, 182–183
multi-species relations 167–170, 170–171
Muslim contexts, sex, intimacy and older life in 14–15, 174–191, 197, 198, 201
  de-Orientalising 'older life' 174–176
  The Delight of Hearts 184, 185–187, 188, 189
  historical and cultural practices 179–182
  legality of sex 178–179
  Muslim sources 174–175, 179, 184–189
  The Perfumed Garden of Sensual Delight 184–185, 187–189
  Prophet Muhammad's sexual and intimate life 176–179, 182–183
  references to older age 182–184
  sympathetic heterosexual examples 182–183
  sympathetic queer examples 183
  unsympathetic heterosexual examples 183
  unsympathetic queer examples 183–184
Muted Group Theory 77–79, 78, 89

N

al-Nafzawi, M. ibn M. 184, 185–187, 188–189, 189
Nahuas societies 144
Najmabadi, A. 175, 180, 181
naming of sexual praxis 28, 195
Napier, J. 193
Nelson, M. 157, 158, 163, 164–165, 168, 169, 170

O

'Older South Asian migrant (SAm) women's experiences of old age and ageing in the United Kingdom (UK)' 116
orhni 21
Orientalism 3, 94
 challenging 174–176, 182, 183, 189

P

Param, S.A. 77, 82, 88
Partition of India, child survivors in later life 12, 115–135, 200–201
 controlling intergenerational sexuality and sexual behaviours 125–126, 128, 203
 desexualisation and carrying honour (*izzat*) in later life 123–127, 128
 diversity of experiences 128
 early marriage 122, 124–125
 experiences of Partition staying with older women 127
 gendered violence during Partition 117, 118–119
 participants 116, 129
 Partition event 117, 129n7
 purdah (covering/seclusion) 122, 123, 126
 Recovery Operation 118
 shame (*sharam*) 118, 124, 125, 126
 the veil 126
 women's bodies as sites of honour/respect (*izzat*) 118, 120–123
 women's embodied silences 119–120
 women's sexuality as a site for the nation 115, 116–120
patriarchy 15, 122, 161, 196–197
 in Indian community in urban Malaysia 77, 78, 79, 85
 female power subverting 86, 87–88, 201
 Indo-Caribbean 23
 and partition of India 116, 118, 122, 124
 in Purépecha society 151, 153
 in Tunisia 98
Pentecostal church 27
The Perfumed Garden of Sensual Delight 184–185, 187–189
 verses attributed to Abu Nuwas 188–189
Persadie, R. 21, 23, 32–33
Pessah, M. 140, 151
phenomenological approach 43–44, 50
polyamory 60–61, 62, 63–64, 66, 202
polygamy 141, 202
Poushter, J. 193
power-knowledge-pleasure triad 151
psychic life 145–146
Puar, J. 3, 31, 32
public toilets, cruising 64, 65
purdah (covering/seclusion) 122, 123, 126
Purépecha women *see* sexual fantasies and older Purépecha women

Q

Queen of Queens drag pageant 32
queer
 community 31–34, 35
 as a disrupting practice to heteronormativity 162
 references to older age
  sympathetic examples 183
  unsympathetic examples 183–184
 role models 26–27, 35, 197
 see also Indo-Trinidadian queer men
queering
 and decolonising age and time 165–167
 and decolonising of relationalities 167–170, 170–171

R

Rao, T.S.S. 42, 43, 195
Recovery Operation 118
Reddock, R. 23, 28
reflexivity, researcher 80–81
relationality, decolonising and queering 167–170, 170–171
Renukha Devi 49
reproduction
 end of 199
 marriage and 56, 148, 196, 203
 filial duty 25–26, 55
 sex and intimacy as a means to 86, 87
 women as instruments of 38
respectability and family honour 24–30, 34–35, 66, 67, 194–195
 see also honour/respect (*izzat*)
Reynolds, P. 165
role models (elders) 197–198
 queer 26–27, 35, 197
romantic love 149–150, 153, 196, 204
Rosso, N, 140, 148, 149
Rubin, G. 142, 143

S

Said, E. 3, 94
saunas 61, 65
Segato, R.L. 151
settler colonialism 159, 161–162
 intersections of 160

Index

knowledge sharing 163
'logic of elimination' 161–162, 204
temporal structures 162
  disrupting 166–167
sex
  Arabic literature on 94–95
  decolonising and queering relationalities 167–170
  engaging in anonymous 64, 65–66
  hidden away materials about 83
  Islamic 'manuals' 184–189
  legality of 35, 39, 98, 178–179
  out of a sense of duty 101, 102
  refusing 103
  and sexuality xvii–xviii, 199–202
  silence of older Indian women in Malaysia on 76, 77, 79, 83, 84, 87, 88, 89, 195
  work 41, 45, 48
sexual abuse 26, 48, 175, 196
sexual agency 12–15, 203
  see also Indigenous elders as sexual agents through storytelling; Muslim contexts, sex, intimacy and older life in; sexual fantasies and older Purépecha women
sexual agreements 60–61, 62, 64, 65, 202
Sexual Cultures of Justice Project 35
sexual desire
  in Islamic texts 95
  older women and 96, 99, 100, 101, 102, 165–166, 199, 200
  erotic (hi)stories disrupting negative narratives of 166
  Purépecha women's 144, 148–149, 152, 153
  seeking help for waning 104
sexual dysfunction
  erectile dysfunction 95, 100
  and impact on female partners 105–106
  menopause and 95, 96, 99, 100–101, 102, 199, 202
sexual education, MENA 104–105, 106
sexual fantasies and older Purépecha women 12–13, 139–156, 203–204
  accounts of romantic love 149–150, 153
  analysis from critical feminist perspective 147–149
  cultural influence on sex-erotic life of women 147–149
  restrictions on sexual and erotic expression 147–148
  key elements of experience 144–146, 152–153
  psychic life nourished by fantasy 145–146
  restrictions on imaginative activity 145
  restrictions on sexual and erotic expression 144–145
  personal agency regarding erotic life 150–152, 153

pre-Hispanic origins of practices associated with sexuality 140–144
  adultery, infidelity and morality in marriage 141–142
  gendered power asymmetries 143–144
  kinship system and exchange of women 142–143
  marriage, inbreeding and polygamy 140–141, 148
  sin of sexual transgression 144
  reference to a woman's desire 144
  research design 140, 146–147
sexual health
  of older adults 43, 51, 62
  and reproductive health provision 95, 103–107
sexual morality 21, 141–142, 151–152, 153
sexual violence 47, 98, 117, 118–119
sexuality 192–194
  changing attitudes in majority world to 204
  colonial rule and exclusion of non-normative forms of 38
  erotic (hi)stories disrupting narratives of older women's 165–166
  gendered assumptions xviii–xix
  Indigenous understandings of gender and 158–159
  intersecting with intimacy and ageing xviii–xix
  legislation to liberalise non-normative expressions of 39, 41, 48–50, 51
  of older Indian adults 43
  of older women 3, 165–166, 192–193, 199–201, 205
  sex and xvii–xviii, 199–202
  of women as a site for the nation 116–120
shame (*sharam*) 118, 124, 125, 126
Shankar, J. 125
Silverio, S.A. 94, 121, 124, 127
Simpson, A. 159, 161, 162
Simpson, L. 166
Simpson, P. xv, xvi, xix, 1, 5, 8, 12, 46, 56, 88, 123, 166
social media 30, 34, 35, 94
  TENA campaign on 93
stereotypes
  about Islam and Muslims 174, 175, 184, 189
  gender 22
  of global South/East 3
  of older age 123, 166, 192–193
  of South Asian women 120
storytelling *see* Indigenous elders as sexual agents through storytelling
Suppes, A. 193
'sworn brotherhood' 58, 64, 67

T

Tanties 32, 33
temporal structure of settler colonialism 162
   decolonising and queering 166–167
TENA 93–94
themes 1–6, 6–16, 194–202
al-Tifashi, A. 184, 188
transgender people 38, 49, 181
   contested status 39, 41–42
   'third gender' cultures 179–180
   see also kinnars in COVID-19 pandemic
Transgender Persons (Protection of Rights) Act 2019 39, 48–49
tricksters 157, 164, 168
Trinidad and Tobago (T&T)
   creating queer spaces in 31–32
   decriminalisation of same sex sexual contact 24, 35
   drag pageants 32
   Pride Parade 31
   Sexual Cultures of Justice Project 35
   see also Indo-Trinidadian queer men
Trouillot, M.-R. 120
Tunisia 98
   comparing with women's experiences in France 99
   research on menopause in 98–100
   sexual and reproductive health provision 103
Turkey 100–101
   sexual and reproductive health provision 103
two-spirit 158, 165, 170
   erotic (hi)stories disrupting negative narratives of 166
   state targeting of 161–162

V

Van Camp, R. 158, 163–164, 170
Vigotsky, L. 145

W

wahkohtowin 168–169
Walby, S. 77, 78, 85
Warner, M. 55, 161
'Why Ravens Smile to Little Old Ladies as They Walk by…' 163–164
Wilson, A. 121, 122, 123, 158, 159, 161, 162, 166
Wilson, S. 159, 160, 163, 169
Wolfe, P. 160, 161, 162
'The Woman Who Married the Beaver' 164–165
women 10–12, 202–203, 203–204
   attitude to sex in older Indian 43
   'Canadian' state's targeting of Indigenous 161–162
   gendered ageism 46, 51, 205
   in Indian society 38
   Indo-Caribbean
      conforming to gender scripts 23–24
      desexualising of older 33
      domestic violence towards 28–29
      orhni 21
      queer 22, 24
      Tanties 32, 33
   kinship system and exchange of 142–143
   portrayals in *The Perfumed Garden* 188–189
   sexual desire
      of older women 96, 99, 100, 101, 102, 165–166, 166, 199, 200
      of Purépecha women 144, 148–149, 152, 153
   sexual morality 151–152, 153
   sexuality of older 3, 165–166, 192–193, 199–201, 205
   socio-sexual status of older 3
   status of Indigenous 158, 198–199
   see also Indian women in urban Malaysia, intimacy in lives of; Middle East and North Africa, women's sexuality in later life in; Partition of India, child survivors in later life; sexual fantasies and older Purépecha women
women's rights groups 104–105
work identity 77–78, 85, 88–89
wu lun (five relations) 56

www.ingramcontent.com/pod-product-compliance
Lightning Source LLC
Chambersburg PA
CBHW051538020426
42333CB00016B/1980